EOTHEN

ALEXANDER WILLIAM KINGLAKE

EOTHEN

WITH AN INTRODUCTION BY
BARBARA KREIGER

THE MARLBORO PRESS

First published in 1844.

The present reprint of EOTHEN is based
upon the New York edition of 1900.

"Alexander Kinglake and the Making of *Eothen*"
Copyright, 1992, by Barbara Kreiger.

Publication of this volume is made possible
in part by a grant from the National
Endowment for the Arts.

Library of Congress Catalog Card Number 92-60852

ISBN 0-910395-82-9

The Marlboro Press
Marlboro, Vermont

CONTENTS

Alexander Kinglake and the Making
of Eothen

ENGLISHMEN were on the move in the first half of the 1800s; travel was by tacit definition a part of their education, and youthful tourists in abundance were to be found far from home. But in some respects it was a dangerous time; unlawfulness and disease ruled in certain far corners, and many cautious souls stayed close to home, satisfying themselves with trips to France and Italy. Others were undaunted; armed with enthusiasm and great hopes, they moved eastward and westward, travelling along ancient routes and roads uncharted, to the Near East and the Far East, to Africa and the Americas. And they wrote about it, in letters, journals, and books intended for a wide reading public that hungered for surrogate adventures. It is into this picture that the young Alexander William Kinglake fits.

Born on August 5, 1809 into a family of Scottish ancestry long settled near Taunton, Kinglake had that kind of conventional upbringing common to his generation and his sort. His father was a banker, his mother an affectionate and witty woman to whom he was deeply attached, and to whom he owed his love of riding and Homer. Childhood was apparently a happy time for him, marred only by those peculiar nightmares he described in *Eothen*. At age twelve the somewhat frail boy was sent to a grammar school run by the brother of the poet Coleridge. It was a bitter experience, and he later had poignant things to say about the crushing by his educators of a boy's love of literature. From there he went on to Eton, and from Eton to Cambridge, where he was a member of a star-filled class that included Tennyson.

Kinglake's hopes for a career in the Army were dashed on account of poor eyesight, so he studied the Law instead. But fate had other things in mind for the young Alec, a self-described "heathen" who chafed under the conventions of society and longed for release from them. In 1834 he met an old Eton friend, John Savile, who regaled him with stories of his recent trip to Russia, Persia, and India. Savile had bypassed the lands of the Ottoman Empire, and Kinglake was suddenly taken with the idea of visiting Turkey and the Levant. This projected journey was hardly the Grand Tour commonplace in those days, particularly as the plague was raging in Turkey and Egypt. But Kinglake, who would show himself to be a man of substantial physical courage, was bent on going, and he and Savile set out in the fall of that year. They travelled by way of Berlin, Prague, and Vienna to Semlin, and crossed the Save River to Belgrade, entering upon Ottoman territory. When at Smyrna Savile was called home, Kinglake went on by himself, with his guide and interpreter. This condition of solitary travel is our good fortune, for the trip became at that moment something other than it would have been, and *Eothen* its eventual result.

From Cyprus, Kinglake sailed to Beirut, where he obtained an audience with Lady Hester Stanhope, a childhood friend of his mother's who had earned a far-reaching reputation for her choice of a life among the Bedouin in the mountains of Lebanon. He went on to Nazareth, Tiberias, and Jerusalem, then to Cairo, and finally to Damascus. After more than a year away, the twenty-six-year-old Kinglake arrived home and resumed his law studies.

During the ensuing years he would work painstakingly on the composition of *Eothen*, but when it was finished he found that publishing the unusual book was not any easier than the writing had been. It was turned down by several publishers, including John Murray, who later regretted his decision, and was finally brought out anonymously in 1844 at Kinglake's own expense, ten years after his trip. The book was an immediate and major success.

Throughout his life Kinglake went on occasional travels, notably to Algeria, yet never attempted another travel book. He entered parliament in 1856, but was unseated twelve years later when his agents were accused of bribery. He was stunned, and later referred to himself as a "political corpse." He devoted the rest of his literary life to a history of the Crimean War, which he had begun years before, after following the campaign there in 1859. Kinglake, described as shy and quiet, slight and pale, had many friends, men and women, but never married. He died on New Year's Day, 1891.

These rather plain and straightforward facts of his life do not account—but then what can account?—for such an unlikely book as *Eothen*, a work, as his biographer Tuckwell pointed out in 1902, that violates every rule of the travel narrative. Kinglake's conversational style, sense of humor, his irony toward himself, his character portraits and invented conversation, his concentration on artifice and entertainment, make the book the paradigm for travel literature well into this century. Its influence may be discerned in comic travel writers who followed him by nearly one hundred years, from the erudite Robert Byron to the glib Peter Fleming. Kinglake threw wide open the doors of the genre, and travel literature has been enriched by his example ever since.

In his preface, Kinglake tells us that he made two unsuccessful attempts at starting a book about his travels to the East, and then realized that his failure resulted from his not knowing to whom he was addressing himself. "I was unable to speak out," he writes, and in an effort to find his voice he chose one person, his friend Eliot Warburton, and to him directed what he had to say. This artifice relieved him of constraints, and through years of meticulous composition he evidently never questioned the procedure. Kinglake's success owed itself to the decision to "speak" his book to one individual—to a friend—who could not possibly be addressed as if he were "a great and enlightened Community, or any other respectable Aggregate!" Indeed, we could say that that initial decision is the key to Kinglake's originality, for it insured an informal and conversational tone that corresponds perfectly to his intention.

And what was that intention? Kinglake promises that the book's title (which means "from the early dawn" or "from the East") is

the only "hard word" the reader will encounter, and he insists that
the book is superficial in character: "I have endeavoured to discard from it all valuable matter derived from the works of others."
His book is free of details of geography, history, science, politics,
religion, statistics, and of "good moral reflections." This may
sound like an anti-intellectual manifesto; it is actually a forthright
proclamation of unpretension and independence from received
wisdom. Only with such an attitude could he, for example, dismiss the pyramids as having been "piled up into the air for the
realization of some kingly crotchets about immortality," or describe the Holy Sepulcher at Easter as reminiscent of an English
fair—pieces of irreverence that did not win the hearts of all his
countrymen.

He lays no claims to scholarship or expertise, but invites the
reader on a different kind of literary journey altogether. "My
excuse for the book is its truth," he states, simply yet carefully
distinguishing the single, highly particular truth of his experience
from any other. The "truth" he wishes to convey is not a matter
of mere factualness, but a quality achieved through careful attention to sensations. His narrative "conveys, not those impressions
that *ought to have been* produced upon any 'well constituted
mind,' but those which were really and truly received at the time
of his rambles." Here is the key to his spontaneity and freshness of
style. The narrative works by an accumulation of impressions
which slowly takes shape and offers a version—his own—of travels in the East. As he put it, "You may listen to him for ever
without learning much in the way of Statistics; but, perhaps, if
you bear with him long enough, you may find yourself slowly and
faintly impressed with the realities of Eastern Travel."

Kinglake carefully prepares the reader to expect a narrative
more about himself and his own preferences than about the en-
vironment, in all its antique and religious import. His habit of
dwelling only on what interested him would not be acceptable in
"a regular book of travels." But because he was exploring a region
fully described by others, he felt at liberty to create, then recreate,
his own journey. "Now a traveller is a creature not always looking

at sights," he explains, "—he remembers (how often!) the happy lands of his birth . . . and if he gives to these feelings anything like the prominence which really belonged to them at the time of his travelling, he will not seem a very good teacher; . . . he will sing a sadly long strain about Self . . . and ruin the Ruins of Baalbec with eight or ten cold lines."

Kinglake left behind the binoculars that other travellers found indispensable and wrote only about what was close at hand, those things which registered on his own senses and could be verified by his own intelligence. "His very selfishness," he says of himself, "—his habit of referring the whole external world to his own sensations, compels him, as it were, in his writings, to observe the laws of perspective;—he tells you of objects, not as he knows them to be, but as they seemed to him. The people, and the things that most concern him personally, however mean and insignificant, take larger proportions in his picture, because they stand so near to him . . . but the proper wonders of the land—the cities—the mighty ruins and monuments of bygone ages, he throws back faintly in the distance."

This self-aware attitude is for us the very heart of travel writing, and it is what makes *Eothen* a truly modern travel book. What distinguishes travel literature from other records of encounters with foreign territory is the blend of, the merging, the clash at times between internal and external material. We expect periods of reverie; we anticipate self-reflection; we hope for insights into the states of being at home and away. The reader meets this challenge put forth by the writer with a special alertness; judgment must be both at hand and suspended, as we give ourselves over to the literary experience of seeing the world at one particular moment, through one particular pair of eyes, biased or fair, stale or fresh of vision.

An eastward journey in Kinglake's day was by definition an experience of other-worldiness. For one thing, it meant leaving Christendom and subjecting oneself to the cultural jurisdiction of the Ottoman Empire. The plague then raging in Turkish lands

EOTHEN

further heightened the acute feeling of departure from everything
one had always known. The towns on either side of the border
were only a stone's throw apart, but there is probably no equivalent today for the experience of getting into a small boat and
heading across the river, for return was impossible without spending weeks in quarantine. Travellers departed Europe with utmost
care; then, done with the civilized world as they knew it, they
went into the wardrobe, as it were, and entered the East.

But the awareness of risk was superseded for Kinglake by ex-
hilaration. How glad he was to be off, and what a wonderful sense
of leave-taking we get—the joy of moving, of being out there,
wherever that is, where life is not fixed:

"The first night of your first campaign . . . is a glorious time
in your life. It is so sweet to find onself free from the stale
civilization of Europe! Oh my dear ally, when first you spread
your carpet in the midst of these eastern scenes, do think for
a moment of those your fellow-creatures that dwell in
squares, and streets, andeven . . . in actual country houses;
think of the people that are 'presenting their compliments,'
and 'requesting the honour,' and 'much regretting,'—of those
that are pinioned at dinner tables, or stuck up in ball-rooms,
or cruelly planted in pews—ay, think of these, and so remem-
bering how many poor devils are living in a state of utter
respectability, and you will glory the more in your delightful
escape."

How aptly he summarized for so many travellers of succeeding
generations what it meant to leave Europe and the stultifying air
of a packaged life wrapped in strings of convention and manners,
a life handed to one like a carefully arranged dinner platter, from
which one takes a portion and passes it on. Who can say what it
meant to escape from the suffocating knowledge of what each day
would bring, into a life that was so utterly unknown, unexpected,
and impossible to foresee. And it was precisely that visceral sense
of uncertainty which rescued him from the boredom of familiarity
that a twenty-five-year-old can feel so acutely.

There comes a time, Kinglake reflects, when a man loathes the

[xii]

"wearisome ways of society" and embarks on a period of rebel-
lion—"a time, in short, for questioning, scoffing, railing—for
speaking lightly of the very opera, and of all our cherished institutions." Then it is one must fly from weariness of "that poor,
dear, middle-aged, deserving, accomplished, pedantic, and painstaking governess, Europe." Kinglake's appeal is a poignant one,
and his flight may be seen as a need to learn that others, deeply
unlike himself and his kind, roam this large world.

Kinglake had an abundant capacity for enjoying himself, and he
relished the newness of his surroundings and the freedom they
suggested. He never doubted his own superiority—as his hosts
were certain of theirs; yet he was capable of feeling fellowship
towards his servants as they sat around their campfire, and regarded them "as comrades, rather than as my servants, and took
delight in breaking bread with them, and merrily passing the cup."

As readers we feel his pleasure as it accumulates from small
things such as this, and it becomes our pleasure as well. That is the
paradox of a travel book: not intended for those who will follow
geographically, it is aimed at those who wish to live the journey
through the senses, aided by the imagination. An approximation
won't do; we want as finely detailed a representation of the journey as the writer can offer. Speaking of miles covered on a given
day, Kinglake reminds: "You look to the Sun, for he is your
taskmaster, and by him you know the measure of the work that
you have done." On drinking tea with mounds of scorched toast
and butter at the end of the day: "I feasted like a king,—like four
kings,—like a boy in the fourth form." About camel-riding, he
appreciated the height at which one sat, where the air was much
cooler than on the ground. When it was time to sleep, he was
proud of his "boundless bed-chamber." And on being totally
alone, it was with awe "that I swept with my sight the vacant
round of the horizon . . . but this very awe gave tone and zest to
the exultation with which I felt myself launched."

If we regard a true traveller as one not out to discover the
unknown, but to see what is there and assess how it meshes with
his or her own sensibility, then Kinglake may have been the first

modern traveller. He sounds like a contemporary of Freya Stark or Wilfred Thesiger, travellers for whom every moment of the journey is significant. Comparing European and eastern travel, he notes that in Europe the state of movement is so temporary that the traveller tends to be "unsettled so long as the wheels are going," and is focused on the end of the journey. In the East, however, the destination does not occupy this central place in the traveller's mind; for days on end one's foot is in the stirrup, and this becomes one's mode of life.

"If you are wise you will look upon the long period of time thus occupied in actual movement, not as the mere gulf dividing you from the end of your journey, but rather as one of those rare and plastic seasons of your life, from which, perhaps, in after times, you may love to date the moulding of your character—that is, your very identity."

This reflections suggests a definition of travel that would be articulated explicitly only in the next century by like-minded individuals, for whom "getting there" was equal in value to "being there." The traveller is one for whom self-definition is elastic; travel is the most challenging form of education, a confronting of one's own values and assumptions, which, undertaken when one is young, may establish a personal sense of being that will carry into later life.

In this way it can be said that *Eothen* is one of the very first real travel books, not written for those who will follow, but intended as a literary version of a journey, a recreation of the author's encounter with the unfamiliar, a testing of his sensibility. It is a wonderful narrative as a surface description of eastern travel, which is no small accomplishment. But no less so is it Kinglake's reflection on interior matters—his home, his youth, and, inevitably, his future. The inner conflict which slowly takes shape is about his abandonment and re-embracing of the West, a conflict to which the journey gives shape and urgency.

We may take nearly any chapter and find a finely constructed narrative, each with a small drama, with its measure of wit and irony, observation and portraiture. But behind it, sometimes distinct and sometimes less so, is a personal or lyrical gesture that reveals another level of the narrative. Thus, for example, when he meditates on his lifelong passion for Homer, we get a beautiful evocation of that moment in youth when the "untamed child" falls in love with a book, and a poignant recollection of how that love is threatened by "the dark ages of schoolboy life."

Or in Nazareth, the one place where he was truly moved by the material facts at hand, his passion and susceptibility to imaginative flights are once again revealed, this time in the adult. He describes his state of mind as feverish with "insane devotion" to Mary, and the chapter reaches an emotional climax as he kneels down to kiss the rock that she had touched. Half delirious with religious rapture, he bends until his lips meet the ground, when the fever lifts: "I rose from my knees. I felt hopelessly sane. The mere world reappeared."

The book as meditation assumes a pronounced shape in a chapter given to a mundane description of the routine of desert travel. Externally, it is an undramatic chapter; but the internal workings are notably otherwise. Kinglake describes the feeling of immensity in the empty desert around him, and the state of aloneness he sought by leaving their small encampment and wandering into the sands. Feeling pride as he stood alone "in the wideness of Asia," he was humble enough too to recognize that "wherever man wanders, he still remains tethered by the chain that links him to his kind," and he thus turned toward camp before dark. From the top of a hill he could see their fire below, where it seemed that "a very home . . . had sprung up for me in the midst of these solitudes." Packing up the next morning, he felt loath "to give back to the waste this little spot on the ground that had glowed for a while with the cheerfulness of a human dwelling."

This reflection, with its suggestion of fellowship with the Arabs, suggests a mind perhaps more open to the foreign than Kinglake's actually was. He possesses a hefty share of the conventional attitudes of his day, scorning the Jews whom he meets in nasty words, as well as disparaging the Arabs and Turks. Yet there are contradictions, too, and one feels that had he lived at a time when his nation's position in the world had been less supreme, he might have had the strength to break away from the magnetic field generated by the very name of England. On the one hand the prejudice in him is such that he cannot imagine that the *Arabian Nights* was written by a "mere Oriental, who, for creative purposes, is a thing dead and dry." On the other hand we have a sensitive explanation of the marketplace behavior of the Turkish merchant, whose initial demand of an excessive price for his goods disgusts many Europeans. This kind of fairness distinguishes Kinglake, and contrasts sharply with his casual expressions of denigration—expressions, one sometimes feels, that are arrived at more for the verbal effect than out of conviction. And if he is biased, at least it can be said that he is able also to see himself through their eyes: "Again and again you meet turbans, and faces of men, but they have nothing for you—no welcome—no wonder—no wrath—no scorn—they look upon you as we do upon a December's fall of snow—as a 'seasonable,' unaccountable, uncomfortable work of God that may have been sent for some good purpose, to be revealed hereafter."

The climax of his journey occurs as he crosses the mountains of Lebanon at the end of the book. Up and up he toiled through snow toward the summit, and suddenly there he was in "a nether heaven of fleecy clouds," and with a view of all Syria west of the range. But his gaze sought beyond, to the dim line of the sea which he could barely discern. He had grown used to the sights of Asia—"to tombs and ruins, to silent cities and deserted plains, to tranquil men, and women sadly veiled." Seeing before him the open sea permitted an imaginative leap to its far shore, to shrill Marseilles and the roar of London:

"My place upon this dividing barrier was as a man's puzzling station in eternity, between the birthless Past, and the Future that has no end. Behind me I left an old and decrepit World—Religions dead and dying—calm tyrannies expiring in silence—women hushed, and swathed, and turned into waxen dolls ... Before me there waited glad bustle and strife—Religion a Cause and a Controversy—men governed by rea-

sons and suasion of speech—wheels going—steam buzzing—a mortal race, and a slashing pace . . . I descended, and
went towards the West."

It is a skillfully articulated conclusion to the conflict which had
propelled Kinglake eastward, but it is not clear if he will return
home with a renewed appetite for the conventions that had first
sent him into exile. The drama is conveniently resolved, but the
individual, as he has been revealed to us, may be too complex for
easy resolution. Happily, we are under no pressure to answer this
speculation, and have only now to begin this marvelous book.

—BARBARA KREIGER

PREFACE

Addressed by the Author to One of His Friends

WHEN you first entertained the idea of traveling in the East, you asked me to send you an outline of the tour which I had made, in order that you might the better be able to choose a route for yourself. In answer to this request I gave you a large French map, on which the course of my journey had been carefully marked; but I did not conceal from myself that this was rather a dry mode for a man to adopt, when he wished to impart the results of his experience to a dear and intimate friend. Now, long before the period of your planning an Oriental tour, I had intended to write some account of my Eastern travels. I had, indeed, begun the task, and had failed; I had begun it a second time, and failing again, had abandoned my attempt with a sensation of utter distaste. I was unable to speak out, and chiefly, I think, for this reason—that I knew not to whom I was speaking. It might be to you, or, perhaps, our Lady of Bitterness, who would read my story; or it might be some member of the Royal Statistical Society, and how on earth was I to write in a way that would do for all three?

Well—your request for a sketch of my tour suggested to me the idea of complying with your wish by a revival of my twice-abandoned attempt. I tried; and the pleasure and confidence which I felt in speaking to you soon made my task so easy and even amusing that after a while (though not in time for your tour) I completed the scrawl from which this book was originally printed.

The very feeling, however, which enabled me to write thus freely prevented me from robing my thoughts in that grave and decorous style which I should have maintained if I had professed to lecture the public. Whilst I feigned to myself that you, and you only, were listening, I could not by possibility speak very solemnly. Heaven forbid that I should talk to my own genial friend as though he were a great and enlightened community, or any other respectable aggregate!

Yet I well understood that the mere fact of my professing to speak to you, rather than to the public generally, could not perfectly excuse me for printing a narrative too roughly worded, and accordingly, in revising the proof-sheets, I have struck out those phrases which seemed to be less fit for a published volume than for intimate conversation. It is hardly to be expected, however, that correction of this kind should be perfectly complete, or that the almost boisterous tone in which many parts of the book were originally written should be thoroughly subdued. I venture, therefore, to ask that the familiarity of language still possibly apparent in the work may be laid to the account of our delightful intimacy, rather than to any presumptuous motive. I feel, as you know, much too timidly, too distantly, and too respectfully toward the public to be capable of seeking to put myself on terms of easy fellowship with strange and casual readers.

It is right to forewarn people (and I have tried to do this as well as I can by my studiously unpromising title-page*) that the book is quite superficial in its character. I have endeavored to discard from it all valuable matter derived from the works of others, and it appears to me that my efforts in this direction have been attended with great success; I believe that I may truly acknowledge that from all details of geographical discovery or antiquarian research, from all display of "sound learning and religious knowledge," from all historical and scientific illustrations, from all useful statistics, from all political disquisitions, and from all good moral reflections, the volume is thoroughly free.

My excuse for the book is its truth: you and I know a man fond of hazarding elaborate jokes, who, whenever a story of his happens not to go down as wit, will evade the awkwardness of the

---

* "Eōthen is, I hope, almost the only hard word to be found in the book; it is written in Greek ἠωθεν (Atticè, with an early aspirated ε instead of the η), and signifies "from the early dawn," "from the East" (Donn. Lex., 4th edition).

failure by bravely maintaining that all he has said is pure fact. I can honestly take this decent, though humble, mode of escape. My narrative is not merely righteous in matters of fact (where fact is in question), but it is true in this larger sense: it conveys, not those impressions which *ought to have been* produced upon any "well constituted mind," but those which were really and truly received at the time of his rambles by a headstrong and not very amiable traveler, whose prejudices in favor of other people's notions were then exceedingly slight. As I have felt, so I have written; and the result is that there will often be found in my narrative a jarring discord between the associations properly belonging to interesting sites, and the tone in which I speak of them. This seemingly perverse mode of treating the subject is forced upon me by my plan of adhering to sentimental truth, and really does not result from any impertinent wish to tease or trifle with readers. I ought, for instance, to have felt as strongly in Judea as in Galilee, but it was not so in fact. The religious sentiment—born in solitude—which had heated my brain in the Sanctuary of Nazareth was rudely chilled at the foot of Zion by disenchanting scenes, and this change is accordingly disclosed by the perfectly worldly tone in which I speak of Jerusalem and Bethlehem.

My notion of dwelling precisely upon those matters which happened to interest me, and upon none other, would, of course, be intolerable in a regular book of travels. If I had been passing through countries not previously explored, it would have been sadly perverse to withhold careful descriptions of admirable objects merely because my own feelings of interest in them may have happened to flag; but where the countries which one visits have been thoroughly and ably described, and even artistically illustrated, by others, one is fully at liberty to say as little—though not quite so much—as one chooses. Now, a traveler is a creature not always looking at sights. He remembers (how often!) the happy land of his birth; he has, too, his moments of humble enthusiasm about fire and food, about shade and drink; and if he gives to these feelings anything like the prominence which really belonged to them at the time of his traveling, he will not seem a very good teacher. Once having determined to write the sheer truth concerning the things which chiefly have interested him, he must, and he will, sing a sadly long strain about Self; he will talk for whole pages together about his bivouac fire, and ruin the ruins of Baalbec with eight or ten cold lines.

But it seems to me that this egotism of a traveler, however incessant, however shameless and obtrusive, must still convey some true ideas of the country through which he has passed. His very selfishness—his habit of referring the whole external world to his own sensations—compels him, as it were, in his writings to observe the laws of perspective; he tells you of objects not as he knows them to be, but as they seemed to him. The people and the things that most concern him personally, however mean and insignificant, take large proportions in his picture, because they stand so near to him. He shows you his dragoman and the gaunt features of his Arabs, his tent, his kneeling camels, his baggage strewed upon the sand; but the proper wonders of the land—the cities, the mighty ruins, and monuments of bygone ages—he throws back faintly in the distance. It is thus that he felt, and thus he strives to repeat, the scenes of the Elder World. You may listen to him forever without learning much in the way of statistics, but perhaps if you bear with him long enough you may find yourself slowly and faintly impressed with the realities of Eastern travel.

My scheme of refusing to dwell upon matters which failed to interest my own feelings has been departed from in one instance—namely, in my detail of the late Lady Hester Stanhope's conversation on supernatural topics. The truth is that I have been much questioned on this subject, and I thought that my best plan would be to write down at once all that I could ever have to say concerning the personage whose career has excited so much curiosity amongst Englishwomen. The result is that my account of the lady goes to a length which is not justified either by the importance of the subject or by the extent to which it interested the narrator.

You will see that I constantly speak of "my people," "my party," "my Arabs," and so on, using terms which might possibly seem to imply that I moved about with a pompous retinue. This, of course, was not the case. I traveled with the simplicity proper to my station, as one of the industrious class, who was not flying from his country because of ennui, but was strengthening his will and tempering the metal of his nature for that life of toil and conflict in which he is now engaged. But an Englishman journeying in the East must necessarily have with him dragomen capable of interpreting the Oriental languages; the absence of wheeled carriages obliges him to use several beasts of burden for his baggage, as well as for himself and his attendants; the owners of the horses and camels, with *their* slaves or servants, fall in as part of his train; and altogether the cavalcade becomes rather numerous, without, however, occasioning any proportionate increase of expense. When a traveler speaks of all these followers in mass, he calls them his "people," or his "troop," or his "party," without intending to make you believe that he is therefore a sovereign prince.

You will see that I sometimes follow the custom of the Scots in describing my fellow-countrymen by the names of their paternal homes.

Of course all these explanations are meant for casual readers. To you, without one syllable of excuse or deprecation, and in all the confidence of a friendship that never yet was clouded, I give the long-promised volume, and add but this one "Good-by," for I dare not stand greeting you here.

EOTHEN

CHAPTER
I

Over the border.

A T Semlin I still was encompassed by the scenes and the sounds of familiar life; the din of a busy world still vexed and cheered me; the unveiled faces of women still shone in the light of day. Yet, whenever I chose to look southward, I saw the Ottoman's fortress,—austere, and darkly impending high over the vale of the Danube,—historic Belgrade. I had come, as it were, to the end of this wheel-going Europe, and now my eyes would see the splendor and havoc of the East.

The two frontier towns are less than a gunshot apart, yet their people hold no communion. The Hungarian, on the north, and the Turk and Servian, on the southern side of the Save, are as much asunder as though there were fifty broad provinces that lay in the path between them. Of the men that bustled around me in the street of Semlin, there was not, perhaps, one who had ever gone down to look upon the stranger race dwelling under the walls of that opposite castle. It is the plague, and the dread of the plague, that divide the one people from the other. All coming and going stands forbidden by the terrors of the yellow flag. If you dare to break the laws of the quarantine, you will be tried with military haste; the court will scream out your sentence to you from a tribunal some fifty yards off; the priest, instead of gently whispering to you the sweet hopes of religion, will console you at dueling distance, and after that you will find yourself carefully shot, and carelessly buried in the ground of the lazaretto.

When all was in order for our departure, we walked down to the precincts of the quarantine establishment, and here awaited us the "compromised"* officer of the Austrian government, whose

* A "compromised" person is one who has been in contact with people or things

duty it is to superintend the passage of the frontier, and who for that purpose lives in a state of perpetual excommunication. The boats, with their "compromised" rowers, were also in readiness.

After coming in contact with any creature or thing belonging to the Ottoman Empire, it would be impossible for us to return to the Austrian territory without undergoing an imprisonment of fourteen days in the lazaretto. We felt, therefore, that before we committed ourselves it was important to take care that none of the arrangements necessary for the journey had been forgotten, and in our anxiety to avoid such a misfortune we managed the work of departure from Semlin with nearly as much solemnity as if we had been departing this life. Some obliging persons from whom we had received civilities during our short stay in the place came down to say their farewell at the river's side; and now, as we stood with them at the distance of three or four yards from the "compromised" officer, they asked if we were perfectly certain that we had wound up all our affairs in Christendom, and whether we had no parting requests to make. We repeated the caution to our servants, and took anxious thought lest by any possibility we might be cut off from some cherished object of affection:—were they quite sure that nothing had been forgotten—that there was no fragrant dressing-case with its gold-compelling letters of credit, from which we might be parting forever? No; every one of our treasures lay safely stowed in the boat, and we—we were ready to follow. Now, therefore, we shook hands with our Semlin friends, and they immediately retreated for three or four paces, so as to leave us in the center of a space between them and the "compromised" officer. The latter then advanced, and asking once more if we had done with the civilized world, held forth his hand. I met it with mine, and there was an end to Christendom for many a day to come.

We soon neared the southern bank of the river, but no sounds

---

supposed to be capable of conveying infection. As a general rule, the whole Ottoman Empire lies constantly under this terrible ban. The "yellow flag" is the ensign of the quarantine establishment.

came down from the blank walls above, and there was no living thing that we could yet see, except one great hovering bird of the vulture race, flying low and intent, and wheeling round and round over the pest-accused city.

But presently there issued from the postern a group of human beings—beings with immortal souls, and possibly some reasoning faculties, but to me the grand point was this, that they had real, substantial, and incontrovertible turbans. They made for the point towards which we were steering, and when, at last, I sprang upon the shore, I heard and saw myself now first surrounded by men of Asiatic blood. I have since ridden through the land of the Osman-lis, from the Servian border to the Golden Horn, from the Gulf of Sataliah to the tomb of Achilles, but never have I seen such hyper-Turk looking fellows as those who received me on the banks of the Save. They were men in the humblest order of life, having come to meet our boat in the hope of earning something by carrying our luggage up to the city; but, poor though they were, it was plain that they were Turks of the proud old school, and had not yet forgotten the fierce, careless bearing of their once victorious race.

Though the province of Servia generally has obtained a kind of independence, yet Belgrade, as being a place of strength on the frontier, is still garrisoned by Turkish troops, under the command of a Pasha. Whether the fellows who now surrounded us were soldiers or peaceful inhabitants I did not understand. They wore the old Turkish costume—vests and jackets of many and brilliant colors, divided from the loose petticoat-trousers by heavy volumes of shawl, so thickly folded around their waists as to give the meager wearers something of the dignity of true corpulence. This cincture inclosed a whole bundle of weapons; no man bore less than one brace of immensely long pistols, and a yataghan (or cutlass), with a dagger or two, of various shapes and sizes. Most of these arms were inlaid with silver highly burnished, and they shone all the more lustrously for being worn along with garments decayed and even tattered (this carefulness of his arms is a point of honor with the Osmanli; he never allows his bright yataghan to suffer from his own adversity): the the long, drooping mustachios, and the ample folds of the once white turbans, that lowered over the piercing eyes and the haggard features of the men, gave them an air of gloomy pride, and that appearance of trying to be disdainful under difficulties, which one almost always sees in those of the Ottoman people who live and remember old times. They looked as if they would have thought themselves more usefully, more honorably, and more piously employed in cutting our throats than in carrying our portmanteaus. The faithful Steel (Methley's Yorkshire servant) stood aghast for a moment at the sight of his master's luggage upon the shoulders of these warlike porters, and when at last we began to move he could scarcely avoid turning round to cast one affectionate look towards Chris-'endom, but quickly again he marched on with the steps of a man not frightened exactly, but sternly prepared for death, or the Koran, or even for plural wives.

The Moslem quarter of a city is lonely and desolate; you go up and down, and on over shelving and hillocky paths through the narrow lanes walled in by blank, windowless dwellings; you come out upon an open space strewed with the black ruins that some late fire has left; you pass by a mountain of castaway things, the rubbish of centuries, and on it you see numbers of big, wolf-like dogs lying torpid under the sun, with limbs outstretched to the full, as if they were dead; storks or cranes, sitting fearless upon the low roofs, look gravely down upon you; the still air that you breathe is loaded with the scent of citron and pomegranate rinds scorched by the sun, or, as you approach the bazaar, with the dry, dead perfume of strange spices. You long for some signs of life, and tread the ground more heavily, as though you would wake the sleepers with the heel of your boot; but the foot falls noiseless upon the crumbling soil of an Eastern city, and silence follows you still. Again and again you meet turbans and faces of men, but they have nothing for you—no welcome, no wonder, no wrath, no scorn; they look upon you as we do upon a December's fall of snow—as a "seasonable," unaccountable, uncomfortable work of God, that may have been sent for some good purpose, to be revealed hereafter.

Some people had come down to meet us with an invitation from the Pasha, and we wound our way up to the castle. At the gates there were groups of soldiers, some smoking, and some lying flat like corpses upon the cool stones. We went through courts, ascended steps, passed along a corridor, and walked into an airy, whitewashed room, with an European clock at one end of it and Moostapha Pasha at the other. The fine old bearded potentate looked very like Jove—like Jove, too, in the midst of his clouds, for the silvery fumes of the narghile* hung lightly circling round him.

The Pasha received us with the smooth, kind, gentle manner that belongs to well-bred Osmanlis. Then he lightly clapped his hands, and instantly the sound filled all the lower end of the room with slaves; a syllable dropped from his lips, it bowed all heads and conjured away the attendants like ghosts. (Their coming and their going was thus swift and quiet because their feet were bare, and they passed through no door, but only by the yielding folds of a purdah.) Soon the coffee-bearers appeared, every man carrying separately his tiny cup in a small metal stand, and presently to each of us there came a pipe-bearer, a grave and solemn functionary, who first rested the bowl of the chibouk at a measured distance on the floor, and then, on this axis, wheeled round the long cherry tube, and gracefully presented it on half-bended knee. Already the fire (well kindled beforehand) was glowing secure in the bowl, and so, when I pressed the amber lip to mine, there was no coyness to conquer; the willing fume came up and answered my slightest sigh, and followed softly every breath inspired, till it touched me with some faint sense and understanding of Asiatic contentment.

Asiatic contentment! Yet hardly, perhaps, one hour before, I had been wanting my bill, and ringing for waiters in a shrill and busy hotel.

---

* The narghile is a water-pipe upon the plan of the hooka, but more gracefully fashioned; the smoke is drawn by a very long, flexible tube that winds its snake-like way from the vase to the lips of the beatified smoker.

In the Ottoman dominions there is scarcely any hereditary influence except that belonging to the family of the Sultan, and wealth, too, is a highly volatile blessing, not easily transmitted to the descendants of the owner. From these causes it results that the people standing in the place of nobles and gentry are official personages, and though many—indeed, the greater number—of these potentates are humbly born and bred, you will seldom, I think, find them wanting in that polished smoothness of manner and those well-undulating tones which belong to the best Osmanlis. The truth is that most of the men in authority have risen from their humble station by the arts of the courtier, and they keep in their high estate those gentle powers of fascination to which they owe their success. Yet, unless you can contrive to learn a little of the language, you will be rather bored by your visits of ceremony. The intervention of the dragoman is fatal to the spirit of conversation. I think I should mislead you if I were to attempt to give the substance of any particular conversation with Orientals. A traveler may write and say that "Pasha of So-and-so was particularly interested in the vast progress which has been made in the application of steam, and appeared to understand the structure of our machinery; that he remarked upon the gigantic results of our manufacturing industry; showed that he possessed considerable knowledge of our Indian affairs and of the constitution of the Company, and expressed a lively admiration of the many sterling qualities for which the people of England are distinguished." But the heap of commonplaces thus quietly attributed to the Pasha will have been founded perhaps on some such talking as this:

PASHA. The Englishman is welcome; most blessed among hours is this, the hour of his coming.

DRAGOMAN (to the Traveler). The Pasha pays you his compliments.

TRAVELER. Give him my best compliments in return, and say I'm delighted to have the honor of seeing him.

DRAGOMAN (to the Pasha). His Lordship, this Englishman, Lord of London, Scorner of Ireland, Suppressor of France, has quitted his governments, and left his enemies to breathe for a moment, and has crossed the broad waters in strict disguise, with a small but eternally faithful retinue of followers, in order that he might look upon the bright countenance of the Pasha among Pashas— the Pasha of the everlasting Pashalic of Karagholookoldour.

TRAVELER (*to his Dragoman*). What on earth have you been saying about London? The Pasha will be taking me for a mere cockney. Have not I told you *always* to say that I am from a branch of the family of Mudcombe Park, and that I am to be a magistrate for the county of Bedfordshire, only I've not qualified, and that I should have been a Deputy Lieutenant if it had not been for the extraordinary conduct of Lord Mountpromise, and that I was a candidate for Boughton-Soldborough at the last election, and that I should have won easy if my committee had not been bribed? I wish to heaven that if you *do* say anything about me, you'd tell the simple truth.

DRAGOMAN (*growing sulky and literal*). This friendly Englishman, this branch of Mudcombe, this head purveyor of Boughton-Soldborough, this possible policeman of Bedfordshire, is recounting his achievements and the number of his titles.

PASHA. The end of his honors is more distant than the ends of the earth, and the catalogue of his glorious deeds is brighter than the firmament of heaven!

DRAGOMAN (*to the Traveler*). The Pasha congratulates your Excellency.

TRAVELER. About Boughton-Soldborough? The deuce he does! But I want to get at his views in relation to the present state of the Ottoman Empire. Tell him the Houses of Parliament have met, and that there has been a speech from the Throne pledging England to maintain the integrity of the Sultan's dominions.

DRAGOMAN (*to the Pasha*). This branch of Mudcombe, this possible policeman of Bedfordshire, informs your Highness that in England the talking houses have met, and the integrity of the Sultan's dominions has been assured for ever and ever by a speech from the velvet chair.

PASHA. Wonderful chair! wonderful houses!—whir! whir! all by wheels!—whizz! whizz! all by steam!—wonderful chair! wonderful houses! wonderful people!—whir! whir! all by wheels!—whizz! whizz! all by steam!

TRAVELER (*to the Dragoman*). What does the Pasha mean by that whizzing? He does not mean to say, does he, that our Government will ever abandon their pledges to the Sultan?

DRAGOMAN. No, your Excellency, but he says the English talk by wheels and by steam.

TRAVELER. That's an exaggeration; but say that the English really have carried machinery to great perfection. Tell the Pasha— he'll be struck with that—that whenever we have any disturbances to put down, even at two or three hundred miles from London, we can send troops by the thousand to the scene of action in a few hours.

DRAGOMAN (*recovering his temper and freedom of speech*). His Excellency, this Lord of Mudcombe, observes to your Highness that whenever the Irish or the French or the Indians rebel against the English, whole armies of soldiers and brigades of artillery are dropped into a mighty chasm called Euston Square, and in the biting of a cartridge they rise up again in Manchester or Dublin or Paris or Delhi, and utterly exterminate the enemies of England from the face of the earth.

PASHA. I know it—I know all; the particulars have been faithfully related to me, and my mind comprehends locomotives. The armies of the English ride upon the vapors of boiling caldrons, and their horses are flaming coals!—whir! whir! all by wheels!—whizz! whizz! all by steam!

TRAVELER (*to his Dragoman*). I wish to have the opinion of an unprejudiced Ottoman gentleman as to the prospects of our English commerce and manufactures. Just ask the Pasha to give me his views on the subject.

PASHA (*after having received the communication of the Dragoman*). The ships of the English swarm like flies; their printed calicoes cover the whole earth; and by the side of their swords the blades of Damascus are blades of grass. All India is but an item in the ledger-books of the merchants, whose lumber-rooms are filled

with ancient thrones!—whir! whir! all by wheels!—whizz! whizz!
all by steam!

DRAGOMAN. The Pasha compliments the cutlery of England,
and also the East India Company.

TRAVELER. The Pasha's right about the cutlery. (I tried my sim-
itar with the common officers' sword belonging to our fellows at
Malta, and they cut it like the leaf of a novel.) Well (*to the
Dragoman*), tell the Pasha I am exceedingly gratified to find that
he entertains such a high opinion of our manufacturing energy,
but I should like him to know, though, that we have got something in England besides that. These foreigners are always fancy-
ing that we have nothing but ships and railways and East India
Companies. Do just tell the Pasha that our rural districts deserve
his attention, and that even within the last two hundred years
there has been an evident improvement in the culture of the tur-
nip, and if he does not take any interest about that, at all events,
you can explain that we have our virtues in the country—that we
are a truth-telling people, and, like the Osmanlis, are faithful in
the performance of our promises. Oh, and by the by, whilst you
are about it, you may as well just say, at the end, that the British
yeoman is still, thank God! the British yeoman.

PASHA (*after hearing the Dragoman*). It is true, it is true.
Through all Feringhistan the English are foremost and best; for
the Russians are drilled swine, and the Germans are sleeping
babes, and the Italians are the servants of songs, and the French
are the sons of newspapers, and the Greeks are the weavers of lies.
But the English and the Osmanlis are brothers together in righ-
teousness, for the Osmanlis believe in one only God, and cleave to
the Koran, and destroy idols; so do the English worship one God,
and abominate graven images, and tell the truth, and believe in a
book, and though they drink the juice of the grape, yet to say that
they worship their prophet as God, or to say that they are eaters
of pork, these are lies—lies born of Greeks and nursed by Jews!

DRAGOMAN. The Pasha compliments the English.

TRAVELER (*rising*). Well, I've had enough of this. Tell the Pasha
I am greatly obliged to him for his hospitality, and still more for

his kindness in furnishing me with horses, and say that now I must be off.

PASHA (*after hearing the Dragoman, and standing up on his divan*).* Proud are the sires and blessed are the dams of the horses that shall carry his Excellency to the end of his prosperous journey. May the saddle beneath him glide down to the gates of the happy city like a boat swimming on the third river of Paradise. May he sleep the sleep of a child, when his friends are around him, and the while that his enemies are abroad, may his eyes flame red through the darkness—more red than the eyes of ten tigers! Farewell!

DRAGOMAN. The Pasha wishes your Excellency a pleasant journey.

So ends the visit.

---

* That is, if he stands up at all. Oriental etiquette would not warrant his rising, unless his visitor were supposed to be at least his equal in point of rank and station.

CHAPTER
II

Turkish traveling.

IN two or three hours our party was ready. The servants, the Tatar, the mounted Suridgees, and the baggage-horses all together made up a strong cavalcade. The accomplished Mysseri, of whom you have heard me speak so often, and who served me so faithfully throughout my Oriental journeys, acted as our interpreter, and was, in fact, the brain of our corps. The Tatar, you know, is a government courier properly employed in carrying despatches, but also sent with travelers to speed them on their way, and answer with his head for their safety. The man whose head was thus pledged for our precious lives was a glorious-looking fellow, with that regular and handsome cast of countenance which is now characteristic of the Ottoman race.* His features displayed a good deal of serene pride, self-respect, fortitude, a kind of ingenuous sensuality, and something of instinctive wisdom without any sharpness of intellect. He had been a Janizary,—as I afterwards found,— and he still kept up the old pretorian strut which used to affright the Christians in former times—a strut so comically pompous that any close imitation of it, even in the broadest farce, would be looked upon as a very rough overacting of the character. It is occasioned, in part, by dress and accoutrements. The weighty bundle of weapons carried upon the chest throws back the body so as to give it a wonderful portliness, and moreover, the immense masses of clothes that swathe his limbs force the wearer in walking to swing himself heavily round from left to right, and from right to left. In truth, this great edifice of woolen and cotton and silk and silver and brass and steel is not at all fitted for moving on foot. It cannot even walk with-

---

* The continual marriages of these people with the chosen beauties of Georgia and Circassia have overpowered the original ugliness of their Tatar ancestors.

out frightfully discomposing its fair proportions, and as to running—our Tatar ran *once* (it was in order to pick up a partridge that Methley had winged with a pistol-shot), and the attempt was one of the funniest misdirections of human energy that wondering man ever saw. But put him in his stirrups, and then is the Tatar himself again. There he lives at his pleasure, reposing in the tranquillity of that true home (the home of his ancestors) which the saddle seems to afford him, and drawing from his pipe the calm pleasures of his "own fireside," or else dashing sudden over the earth, as though for a moment he felt the mouth of a Turkoman steed, and saw his own Scythian plains lying boundless and open before him.

It was not till his subordinates had nearly completed their preparations for the march that our Tatar, "commanding the forces," arrived. He came sleek and fresh from the bath (for so is the custom of the Ottomans when they start upon a journey), and was carefully accoutred at every point. From his thigh to his throat he was laden with arms and other implements of a campaigning life. These is no scarcity of water along the whole road from Belgrade to Stamboul, but the habits of our Tatar were formed by his ancestors, and not by himself, so he took good care to see that his leathern water-flask was amply charged and properly strapped to the saddle along with his blessed chibouk. And now at last he has cursed the Suridgees, in all proper figures of speech, and is ready for a ride of a thousand miles; but before he comforts his soul in the marble baths of Stamboul he will be another and a lesser man: his sense of responsibility, his too strict abstemiousness, and his restless energy, disdainful of sleep, will have worn him down to a fraction of the sleek Moostapha who now leads out our party from the gates of Belgrade.

The Suridgees are the men employed to lead the baggage-horses. They are most of them Gipsies. Their lot is a sad one. They are the last of the human race, and all the sins of their superiors—including the horses—can safely be visited on them. But the wretched look often more picturesque than their betters, and though all the world despise these poor Suridgees, their tawny skins and their grisly beards will gain them honorable standing in the foreground of a

EOTHEN

landscape. We had a couple of these fellows with us, each leading a baggage-horse, to the tail of which last another baggage-horse was attached. There was a world of trouble in persuading the stiff, angular portmanteaus of Europe to adapt themselves to their new condition, and sit quietly on pack-saddles; but all was right at last, and it gladdened my eyes to see our little troop file off through the winding lanes of the city, and show down brightly in the plain beneath. The one of our party most out of keeping with the rest of the scene was Methley's Yorkshire servant, who always rode doggedly on in his pantry jacket, looking out for "gentlemen's seats."

Methley and I had English saddles, but I think we should have done just as well (I should certainly have seen more of the country) if we had adopted saddles like that of our Tatar, who towered so loftily over the scraggy little beast that carried him. In taking thought for the East whilst in England, I had made one capital hit which you must not forget. I had brought with me a pair of common spurs; these were a great comfort to me throughout my horseback travels by keeping up the cheerfulness of the many unhappy nags that I had to bestride. The angle of that Oriental stirrup is a very poor substitute for spurs.

The Ottoman horseman, raised by his saddle to a great height above the humble level of the back that he bestrides, and using a very sharp bit, is able to lift the crest of his nag, and force him into a strangely fast shuffling walk, the orthodox pace for the journey. My comrade and I, using English saddles, could not easily keep our beasts up to this peculiar amble: besides, we thought it a bore to be *followed* by our attendants for a thousand miles, and we generally, therefore, did duty as the rear-guard of our "grand army." We used to walk our horses till the party in front had got into the distance, and then retrieve the lost ground by a gallop.

We had ridden on for some two or three hours, the stir and bustle of our commencing journey had ceased, the liveliness of our little troop had worn off with the declining day, and the night closed in as we entered the great Servian forest. Through this our road was to last for more than a hundred miles. Endless and endless now on either side the tall oaks closed in their ranks, and

[13]

stood gloomily lowering over us, as grim as an army of giants with a thousand years' pay in arrear. One strived with listening ear to catch some tidings of that forest world within,—some stirring of beasts, some night-bird's scream,—but all was quite hushed, except for the voice of the cicalas that peopled every bough, and filled the depths of the forest through and through with one same hum everlasting—more stilling than very silence.

At first our way was in darkness, but after a while the moon got up and touched the glittering arms and tawny faces of our men with light so pale and mystic that the watchful Tatar felt bound to look out for demons, and take proper means for keeping them off. Forthwith he determined that the duty of frightening away our ghostly enemies (like every other troublesome work) should fall upon the poor Suridgees: they, accordingly, lifted up their voices, and burst upon the dreaded stillness of the forest with shrieks and dismal howls. These precautions were kept up incessantly, and were followed by the most complete success, for not one demon came near us.

Long before midnight we reached the hamlet in which we were to rest for the night. It was made up of about a dozen clay huts standing upon a small tract of ground hardly won from the forest. The peasants living there spoke a Slavonic dialect, and Mysseri's knowledge of the Russian tongue enabled him to talk with them freely. We took up our quarters in a square room with white walls and an earthen floor, quite bare of furniture, and utterly void of women. They told us, however, that these Servian villagers lived in happy abundance, but that they were careful to conceal their riches, as well as their wives.

The burdens unstrapped from the pack-saddles very quickly furnished our den. A couple of quilts spread upon the floor, with a carpet-bag at the head of each, became capital sofas. Portmanteaus and hat-boxes and writing-cases and books and maps and gleaming arms soon lay strewed around us in pleasant confusion. Mysseri's canteen, too, began to yield up its treasures; but we relied upon finding some provisions in the village. At first the natives declared that their hens were mere old maids, and all their cows unmarried; but our Tatar swore such a grand, sonorous oath, and fingered the hilt of his yataghan with such persuasive touch, that the land soon flowed with milk, and mountains of eggs arose.

And soon there was tea before us, with all its welcome fragrance; and as we reclined on the floor, we found that a portmanteau was just the right height for a table. The duty of candlesticks was ably performed by a couple of intelligent natives. The rest of the villagers stood by the open doorway at the lower end of the room, and watched our banquet with grave and devout attention.

The first night of your first campaign (though you be but a mere peaceful campaigner) is a glorious time in your life. It is so sweet to find one's self free from the stale civilization of Europe! Oh, my dear ally, when first you spread your carpet in the midst of these Eastern scenes, do think for a moment of those your fellow-creatures that dwell in squares and streets, and even (for such is the fate of many!) in actual country houses; think of the people that are "presenting their compliments," and "requesting the honor," and "much regretting," of those that are pinioned at dinner-tables, or stuck up in ball-rooms, or cruelly planted in pews; aye, think of these, and so remembering how many poor devils are living in a state of utter respectability, you will glory the more in your own delightful escape.

But, with all its charms, a mud floor (like a mercenary match) does certainly promote early rising. Long before daybreak we were up and had breakfasted. Afterwards there was nearly a whole tedious hour to endure, whilst the horses were laden by torch-light; but this had an end, and then our day's journey began. Cloaked and somber, at first we made our sullen way through the darkness with scarcely one barter of words; but soon the genial morn burst down from heaven, and stirred the blood so gladly through our veins that the very Suridgees, with all their troubles, could now look up for an instant, and almost seem to believe in the temporary goodness of God.

The actual movement from one place to another, in Europeanized countries, is a process so temporary—it occupies, I mean, so

EOTHEN

small a proportion of the traveler's entire time—that his mind remains unsettled so long as the wheels are going. He may be alive enough to external objects of interest and to the crowding ideas which are often invited by the excitement of a changing scene, but he is still conscious of being in a provisional state, and his mind is forever recurring to the expected end of his journey. His ordinary ways of thought have been interrupted, and before any new mental habits can be formed he is quietly fixed in his hotel. It will be otherwise with you when you journey in the East. Day after day, perhaps week after week and month after month, your foot is in the stirrup. To taste the cold breath of the earliest morn, and to lead or follow your bright cavalcade till sunset through forests and mountain passes, through valleys and desolate plains—all this becomes your MODE OF LIFE, and you ride, eat, drink, and curse the mosquitos, as systematically as your friends in England eat, drink, and sleep. If you are wise, you will not look upon the long period of time thus occupied in actual movement as the mere gulf dividing you from the end of your journey, but rather as one of those rare and plastic seasons of your life from which, perhaps, in after times, you may love to date the molding of your character—that is, your very identity. Once feel this, and you will soon grow happy and contented in your saddle home. As for me and my comrade, however, in this part of our journey we often forgot Stamboul, forgot all the Ottoman Empire, and only remembered old times. We went back, loitering on the banks of the Thames—not grim old Thames of "after life," that washes the Parliament Houses, and drowns despairing girls, but Thames, the "old Eton fellow" that wrestled with us in our boyhood till he taught us to be stronger than he. We bullied Keate, and scoffed at Larrey Miller and Okes; we rode along loudly laughing, and talked to the grave Servian forest as though it were the "Brocas clump."

Our pace was commonly very slow, for the baggage-horses served us for a drag, and kept us to a rate of little more that five miles in the hour; but now and then, and chiefly at night, a spirit of movement would suddenly animate the whole party. The baggage-horses would be teased into a gallop, and when once this was done, there would be such a banging of portmanteaus, and such convulsions of carpet-bags upon their panting sides, and the Suridgees would follow them up with such a hurricane of blows and screams and curses, that stopping or relaxing was scarcely possible. Then the rest of us would put our horses into a gallop, and so all shouting cheerily would hunt and drive the sumpter-beasts like a flock of goats, up hill and down dale, right on to the end of their journey.

The distances between our relays of horses varied greatly. Some were not more than fifteen or twenty miles, but twice, I think, we performed a whole day's journey of more than sixty miles with the same beasts.

When at last we came out from the forest, our road lay through scenes like those of an English park. The greensward, unfenced and left to the free pasture of cattle, was dotted with groups of stately trees, and here and there darkened over with larger masses of wood, that seemed gathered together for bounding the domain, and shutting out some infernal fellow-creature in the shape of a newly made squire. In one or two spots the hanging copses looked down upon a lawn below with such sheltering mien that, seeing the like in England, you would have been tempted almost to ask the name of the spendthrift or the madman who had dared to pull down the old hall.

There are few countries less infested by "lions" than the provinces on this part of your route. You are not called upon to "drop a tear" over the tomb of "the once brilliant" anybody, or to pay your "tribute of respect" to anything dead or alive; there are no Servian or Bulgarian littérateurs with whom it would be positively disgraceful not to form an acquaintance; you have no staring, no praising to get through. The only public building of any interest that lies on the road is of modern date, but is said to be a good specimen of Oriental architecture. It is of a pyramidical shape, and is made up of thirty thousand skulls contributed by the rebellious Servians in the early part (I believe) of this century. I am not at all sure of my date, but I fancy it was in the year 1806 that the first skull was laid. I am ashamed to say that in the darkness of the early morning we unknowingly went by the neighborhood of this triumph of art, and so basely got off from admiring "the simple grandeur of the architect's conception," and "the exquisite beauty of the fretwork."

There being no "lions," we ought at least to have met with a few perils, but the only robbers we saw anything of had been long since dead and gone. The poor fellows had been impaled upon high poles, and so propped up by the transverse spokes beneath them that their skeletons, clothed with some white, wax-like remains of flesh, still sat up lolling in the sunshine, and listlessly stared without eyes.

One day it seemed to me that our path was a little more rugged than usual, and I found that I was deserving for myself the title of Sabalkansky, or "Transcender of the Balkan." The truth is that, as a military barrier, the Balkan is a fabulous mountain. Such seems to be the view of Major Keppell, who looked on it towards the east with the eye of a soldier, and certainly, in the Sofia Pass, there is no narrow defile and no ascent sufficiently difficult to stop, or delay for a long time, a train of siege artillery.

Before we reached Adrianople, Methley had been seized with we knew not what ailment, and when we had taken up our quarters in the city, he was cast to the very earth by sickness. Adrianople enjoyed an English consul, and I felt sure that, in Eastern phrase, his house would cease to be his house, and would become the house of my sick comrade. I should have judged rightly under ordinary circumstances, but the leveling plague was abroad, and the dread of it had dominion over the consular mind. So now (whether dying or not, one could hardly tell), upon a quilt stretched out along the floor, there lay the best hope of an ancient line, without the material aids to comfort of even the humblest sort, and (sad to say) without the consolation of a friend or even a comrade worth having. I have a notion that tenderness and pity are affections occasioned, in some measure, by living within doors. Certainly, at the time I speak of, the open-air life which I had been leading, or the wayfaring hardships of the journey, had so strangely blunted me that I felt intolerant of illness, and looked down upon my companion as if the poor fellow, in falling ill, had betrayed a want of spirit! I entertained, too, a most absurd idea—an idea that his illness was partly affected. You see that I have made a confession. This I hope—that I may hereafter look charitably upon the hard, savage acts of peasants and the cruelties of a "brutal" soldiery. God knows that I strived to melt myself into common charity, and to put on a gentleness which I could not feel; but this attempt did not cheat the keenness of the sufferer. He could not have felt the less deserted because that I was with him.

We called to aid a solemn Armenian (I think he was), half soothsayer, half hakim, or doctor, who, all the while counting his beads, fixed his eyes steadily upon the patient, and then suddenly dealt him a violent blow on the chest. Methley bravely dissembled his pain, for he fancied that the blow was meant to try whether or not the plague were on him.

Here was really a sad embarrassment—no bed, nothing to offer the invalid, in the shape of food, save a piece of thin, tough, flexible drab-colored cloth made of flour and mill-stones in equal proportions, and called by the name of "bread." The patient, of course, had no "confidence in his medical man," and, on the whole, the best chance of saving my comrade seemed to lie in taking him out of the reach of his doctor, and bearing him away to the neighborhood of some more genial consul. But how was this to be done? Methley was much too ill to be kept in his saddle, and wheel-carriages, as means of traveling, were unknown. There is, however, such a thing as an "araba," a vehicle drawn by oxen, in which the wives of a rich man are sometimes dragged four or five miles over grass by way of recreation. The carriage is rudely framed, but you recognize in the simple grandeur of its design a likeness to things majestic. In short, if your carpenter's son were to make a "Lord Mayor's coach" for little Amy, he would build a carriage very much in the style of a Turkish araba. No one had ever heard of horses being used for drawing a carriage in this part of the world, but necessity is the mother of innovation as well as of invention. I was fully justified, I think, in arguing that there were numerous instances of horses being used for that purpose in our own country; that the laws of nature are uniform in their operation over all the world (except Ireland); that that which was true in Piccadilly must be true in Adrianople; that the matter could not fairly be treated as an ecclesiastical question, for that the circumstance of Methley's going on to Stamboul in an araba drawn by horses, when calmly and dispassionately considered, would appear to be perfectly consistent with the maintenance of the Mohammedan religion, as by law established. Thus poor, dear, patient Reason would have fought her slow battle against Asiatic prejudice, and I am convinced that she would have established the possibility (and, perhaps, even the propriety) of harnessing horses in a hundred and fifty years; but, in the meantime, Mysseri, well seconded by our Tatar, contrived to bring the controversy to a premature end by having the horses put to.

It was a sore thing for me to see my poor comrade brought to this, for, young though he was, he was a veteran in travel. When scarcely yet of age, he had invaded India from the frontiers of Russia, and that so swiftly that, measuring by the time of his flight, the broad dominions of the king of kings were shriveled up to a dukedom; and now, poor fellow, he was to be poked into an araba, like a Georgian girl! He suffered greatly, for there were no springs for the carriage, and no road for the wheels, and so the concern jolted on over the open country, with such twists and jerks and jumps as might almost dislocate the supple tongue of Satan.

All day the patient kept himself shut up within the latticework of the araba, and I could hardly know how he was faring until the end of the day's journey, when I found that he was not worse, and was buoyed up with the hope of some day reaching Constantinople.

I was always conning over my maps, and fancied that I knew pretty well my line, but after Adrianople I had made more southing than I knew for, and it was with unbelieving wonder and delight that I came suddenly upon the shore of the sea. A little while, and its gentle billows were flowing beneath the hoofs of my beast. But the hearing of the ripple was not enough communion, and the seeing of the blue Propontis was not to know and possess it—I must needs plunge into its depth, and quench my longing love in the palpable waves; and so when old Moostapha (defender against demons) looked round for his charge, he saw with horror and dismay that he for whose life his own life stood pledged, was possessed of some devil who had driven him down into the sea— that the rider and the steed had vanished from earth, and that out among the waves was the gasping crest of a post-horse and the ghostly head of the Englishman moving upon the face of the waters.

We started very early indeed on the last day of our journey, and from the moment of being off until we gained the shelter of the imperial walls, we were struggling face to face with an icy storm that swept right down from the steppes of Tartary, keen, fierce, and steady as a northern conqueror. Methley's servant, who was the greatest sufferer, kept his saddle until we reached Stamboul, but was then found to be quite benumbed in limbs, and his brain was so much affected that when he was lifted from his horse, he fell away in a state of unconsciousness, the first stage of a dangerous fever.

Our Tatar, worn down by care and toil, and carrying seven heavens full of water in his manifold jackets and shawls, was a mere weak and vapid dilution of the sleek Moostapha who scarce more than one fortnight before came out like a bridegroom from his chamber to take the command of our party.

Mysseri seemed somewhat over-wearied, but he had lost none of his strangely quiet energy. He wore a grave look, however, for he now had learnt that the plague was prevailing at Constantinople, and he was fearing that our two sick men, and the miserable looks of our whole party, might make us unwelcome at Pera.

We crossed the Golden Horn in a caique. As soon as we had landed, some woebegone-looking fellows were got together and laden with our baggage. Then on we went, dripping and sloshing, and looking very like men that had been turned back by the Royal Humane Society for being incurably drowned. Supporting our sick, we climbed up shelving steps and threaded many windings, and at last came up into the main street of Pera, humbly hoping that we might not be judged guilty of the plague, and so be cast back with horror from the doors of the shuddering Christians.

Such was the condition of the little troop, which fifteen days before had filed away so gaily from the gates of Belgrade. A couple of fevers and a northeasterly storm had thoroughly spoiled our looks.

The interest of Mysseri with the house of Giuseppini was too powerful to be denied, and at once, though not without fear and trembling, we were admitted as guests.

CHAPTER
III

Constantinople.

E VEN if we don't take a part in the chant about "Mosques and Minarets," we can still yield praises to Stamboul. We can chant about the harbor. We can say and sing that nowhere else does the sea come so home to a city. There are no pebbly shores, no sand-bars, no slimy river-beds, no black canals, no locks, nor docks to divide the very heart of the place from the deep waters. If, being in the noisiest mart of Stamboul, you would stroll to the quiet side of the way amidst those cypresses opposite, you will cross the fathomless Bosporus; if you would go from your hotel to the bazaars, you must pass by the bright blue pathway of the Golden Horn, that can carry a thousand sail of the line. You are accustomed to the gondolas that glide among the palaces of St. Mark, but here at Stamboul it is a hundred-and-twenty-gun ship that meets you in the street. Venice strains out from the steadfast land, and in old times would send forth the Chief of the State to woo and wed the reluctant sea; but the stormy bride of the Doge is the bowing slave of the Sultan; she comes to his feet with the treasures of the world; she bears him from palace to palace; by some unfailing witchcraft, she entices the breezes to follow her,* and fan the pale cheek of her lord; she lifts his armed navies to the very gates of his garden; she watches the walls of his serail; she stifles the intrigues of his ministers; she quiets the scandals of his court; she extinguishes his rivals, and hushes his naughty wives all one by one. So vast are the wonders of the deep!

All the while that I stayed at Constantinople the plague was prevailing, but not with any violence; its presence, however, lent

---

* There is almost always a breeze, either from the Marmora or from the Black Sea, that passes along the course of the Bosporus.

a mysterious and exciting though not very pleasant interest to my first knowledge of a great Oriental city; it gave tone and color to all I saw and all I felt—a tone and a color somber enough, but true, and well befitting the dreary monuments of past power and splendor. With all that is most truly Oriental in its character the plague is associated; it dwells with the faithful in the holiest quarters of their city. The coats and the hats of Pera are held to be nearly as innocent of infection as they are ugly in shape and fashion; but the rich furs and the costly shawls, the broidered slippers and the gold-laden saddle-cloths, the fragrance of burning aloes and the rich aroma of patchouli—these are the signs that mark the familiar home of plague. You go out from your queenly London, the center of the greatest and strongest amongst all earthly dominions—you go out thence and travel on to the capital of an Eastern prince; you find but a waning power and a faded splendor that inclines you to laugh and mock; but let the infernal angel of plague be at hand, and he, more mighty than armies, more terrible than Suleyman in his glory, can restore such pomp and majesty to the weakness of the imperial city that if, *when He is there,* you must still go prying amongst the shades of this dead empire, at least you will tread the path with seemly reverence and awe.

It is the firm faith of almost all the Europeans living in the East that plague is conveyed by the touch of infected substances, and that the deadly atoms especially lurk in all kinds of clothes and furs. It is held safer to breathe the same air with a man sick of the plague, and even to come in contact with his skin, than to be touched by the smallest particle of woolen or of thread which may have been within the reach of possible infection. If this be a right notion, the spread of the malady must be materially aided by the observance of a custom prevailing amongst the people of Stamboul. It is this: when an Osmanli dies, one of his dresses is cut up, and a small piece of it is sent to each of his friends as a memorial of the departed—a fatal present, according to the opinion of the Franks, for it too often forces the living not merely to remember the dead man, but to follow and bear him company.

The Europeans, during the prevalence of the plague, if they are forced to venture into the streets, will carefully avoid the touch of every human being whom they pass; their conduct in this respect shows them strongly in contrast with the "true believers"; the Moslem stalks on serenely, as though he were under the eye of his God, and were "equal to either fate"; the Franks go crouching and slinking from death, and some (those chiefly of French extraction) will fondly strive to fence out destiny with shining capes of oilskin.

For some time you many manage by great care to thread your way through the streets of Stamboul without incurring contact, for the Turks, though scornful of the terrors felt by the Franks, are generally very courteous in yielding to that which they hold to be a useless and impious precaution, and will let you pass safe if they can. It is impossible, however, that your immunity can last for any length of time if you move about much through the narrow streets and lanes of a crowded city.

As for me, I soon got "compromised." After one day of rest, the prayers of my hostess began to lose their power of keeping me from the pestilent side of the Golden Horn. Faithfully promising to shun the touch of all imaginable substances, however enticing, I set off very cautiously, and held my way uncompromised till I reached the water's edge; but before my caique was quite ready some rueful-looking fellows came rapidly shambling down the steps with a plague-stricken corpse, which they were going to bury amongst the faithful on the other side of the water. I contrived to be so much in the way of this brisk funeral that I was not only touched by the men bearing the body, but also, I believe, by the foot of the dead man, as it hung lolling out of the bier. This accident gave me such a strong interest in denying the soundness of the contagion theory that I did in fact deny and repudiate it altogether; and from that time, acting upon my own convenient view of the matter, I went wherever I chose, without taking any serious pains to avoid a touch. It seems to me now very likely that the Europeans are right, and that the plague may be really con-veyed by contagion; but during the whole time of my remaining in the East my views on this subject more nearly approached to those

EOTHEN

of the fatalists; and so, when afterwards the plague of Egypt came
dealing his blows around me, I was able to live amongst the dying
without that alarm and anxiety which would inevitably have
pressed upon my mind if I had allowed myself to believe that every
passing touch was really a probable death-stroke.

And perhaps, as you make your difficult way through a steep
and narrow alley shut in between blank walls, and little frequented
by passers, you meet one of those coffin-shaped bundles of white
linen that implies an Ottoman lady. Painfully struggling against
the obstacles to progression interposed by the many folds of her
clumsy drapery, by her big mud-boots, and especially her two
pairs of slippers, she works her way on full awkwardly enough;
but yet there is something of womanly consciousness in the very
labor and effort with which she tugs and lifts the burden of her
charms; she is closely followed by her women slaves. Of her very
self you see nothing except the dark, luminous eyes that stare
against your face, and the tips of the painted fingers depending
like rose-buds from out of the blank bastions of the fortress. She
turns, and turns again, and carefully glances around her on all
sides to see that she is safe from the eyes of Mussulmans, and then
suddenly withdrawing the yashmak,* she shines upon your heart
and soul with all the pomp and might of her beauty. And this, it
is not the light, changeful grace that leaves you to doubt whether
you have fallen in love with a body or only a soul; it is the beauty
that dwells secure in the perfectness of hard, downright outlines,
and in the glow of generous color. There is fire, though, too—high
courage and fire enough in the untamed mind, or spirit, or whatever it is, which drives the breath of pride through those scarcely
parted lips.

You smile at pretty women; you turn pale before the beauty
that is great enough to have dominion over you. She sees, and
exults in your giddiness; she sees, and smiles; then presently, with

* The yashmak, you know, is not a mere semi-transparent veil, but rather a good
substantial petticoat applied to the face; it thoroughly conceals all the features
except the eyes; the way of withdrawing it is by pulling it down.

[26]

a sudden movement, she lays her blushing fingers upon your arm, and cries out: "Yumourdjak!" ("Plague!" meaning, "There is a present of the plague for you!") This is her notion of a witticism. It is a very old piece of fun, no doubt—quite an Oriental Joe Miller; but the Turks are fondly attached, not only to the institutions, but also to the jokes of their ancestors; so the lady's silvery laugh rings joyously in your ears, and the mirth of her women is boisterous and fresh, as though the bright idea of giving the plague to a Christian had newly lit upon the earth.

Methley began to rally very soon after we had reached Constantinople, but there seemed at first to be no chance of his regaining strength enough for traveling during the winter, and I determined to stay with my comrade until he had quite recovered; so I bought me a horse, and a pipe of tranquillity,* and took a Turkish phrase-master. I troubled myself a great deal with the Turkish tongue, and gained at last some knowledge of its structure. It is enriched, perhaps overladen, with Persian and Arabic words imported into the language chiefly for the purpose of representing sentiments and religious dogmas, and terms of art and luxury, entirely unknown to the Tatar ancestors of the present Osmanlis; but the body and the spirit of the old tongue are yet alive, and the smooth words of the shopkeeper at Constantinople can still carry understanding to the ears of the untamed millions who rove over the plains of northern Asia. The structure of the language, especially in its more lengthy sentences, is very like to the Latin; the subject-matters are slowly and patiently enumerated, without disclosing the purpose of the speaker until he reaches the end of his sentence, and then at last there comes the clenching word which gives a meaning and connection to all that has gone before. If you listen at all to speaking of this kind, your attention, rather than be suffered to flag, must grow more and more lively as the phrase marches on.

---

* The "pipe of tranquillity" is a chibouk too long to be conveniently carried on a journey; the possession of it therefore implies that its owner is stationary, or at all events that he is enjoying a long repose from travel.

The Osmanlis speak well. In countries civilized according to the European plan, the work of trying to persuade tribunals is almost all performed by a set of men who seldom do anything else; but in Turkey this division of labor has never taken place, and every man is his own advocate. The importance of the rhetorical art is immense, for a bad speech may endanger the property of the speaker, as well as the soles of his feet and the free enjoyment of his throat. So it results that most of the Turks whom one sees have a lawyer-like habit of speaking connectedly and at length. Even the treaties continually going on at the bazaar for the buying and selling of the merest trifles are carried on by speechifying rather than by mere colloquies, and the eternal uncertainty as to the market value of things in constant sale gives room enough for discussion. The seller is forever demanding a price immensely beyond that for which he sells at last, and so occasions unspeakable disgust in many Englishmen, who cannot see why an honest dealer should ask more for his goods than he will really take. The truth is, however, that an ordinary tradesman of Constantinople has no other way of finding out the fair market value of his property. His difficulty is easily shown by comparing the mechanism of the commercial system in Turkey with that of our own people. In England, or in any other great mercantile country, the bulk of the things bought and sold goes through the hands of a wholesale dealer, and it is he who higgles and bargains with an entire nation of purchasers, by entering into treaty with retail sellers. The labor of making a few large contracts is sufficient to give a clue for finding the fair market value of the goods sold throughout the country. But in Turkey, from the primitive habits of the people, and partly from the absences of great capital and great credit, the importing merchant, the warehouseman, the wholesale dealer, the retail dealer, and the shopman, are all one person. Old Moost-apha, or Abdallah, or Hadgi Mohammed waddles up from the water's edge with a small packet of merchandise, which he has bought out of a Greek brigantine, and when at last he has reached his nook in the bazaar, he puts his goods *before* the counter, and himself *upon* it; then laying fire to his chibouk, he "sits in permanence," and patiently waits to obtain "the best price that can be got in an open market." This is his fair right as a seller, but he has no means of finding out what that best price is, except by actual experiment. He cannot know the intensity of the demand, or the abundance of the supply, otherwise than by the offers which may be made for his little bundle of goods; so he begins by asking a perfectly hopeless price, and then descends the ladder until he meets a purchaser, forever

"striving to attain
By shadowing out the unattainable."

This is the struggle which creates the continual occasion for debate. The vender, perceiving that the unfolded merchandise has caught the eye of a possible purchaser, commences his opening speech. He covers his bristling broadcloths and his meager silks with the golden broidery of Oriental praises, and as he talks, along with the slow and graceful waving of his arms, he lifts his undulating periods, upholds and poises them well till they have gathered their weight and their strength, and then hurls them bodily forward, with grave, momentous swing. The possible purchaser listens to the whole speech with deep and serious attention; but when it is over, *his* turn arrives. He elaborately endeavors to show why he ought not to buy the things at a price twenty times larger than their value. Bystanders, attracted to the debate, take a part in it as independent members; the vender is heard in reply, and, coming down with his price, furnishes the materials for a new debate. Sometimes, however, the dealer, if he is a very pious Mussulman and sufficiently rich to hold back his ware, will take a more dignified part, maintaining a kind of judicial gravity, and receiving the applicants who come to his stall as if they were rather suitors than customers. He will quietly hear to the end some long speech that concludes with an offer, and will answer it all with that bold monosyllable "Yok," which means distinctly "No."

I caught one glimpse of the old heathen world. My habits of studying military subjects had been hardening my heart against poetry. Forever staring at the flames of battle, I had blinded myself to the lesser and finer lights that are shed from the imaginations of men. In my reading at this time, I delighted to follow from out of Arabian sands the feet of the armed believers, and to stand in the broad, manifest storm-tract of Tatar devastation; and thus, though surrounded at Constantinople by scenes of much interest to the "classical scholar," I had cast aside their associations like an old Greek grammar, and turned my face to the "shining Orient," forgetful of old Greece and all the pure wealth she left to this matter-of-fact-ridden world. But it happened to me one day to mount the high grounds overhanging the streets of Pera. I sated my eyes with the pomps of the city, and its crowded waters, and then I looked over where Scutari lay, half veiled in her mournful cypresses; I looked yet farther and higher, and saw in the heavens a silvery cloud that stood fast and still against the breeze; it was pure and dazzling white as might be the veil of Cytherea, yet touched with such fire as though, from beneath, the loving eyes of an immortal were shining through and through. I knew the bearing, but had enormously misjudged its distance and underrated its height, and so it was as a sign and a testimony—almost as a call from the neglected gods—that now I saw and acknowledged the snowy crown of the Mysian Olympus.

CHAPTER
IV

The Troad.

M ETHLEY recovered almost suddenly, and we determined to go through the Troad together.

My comrade was a capital Grecian; it is true that his singular mind so ordered and disposed his classic lore as to impress it with something of an original and barbarous character—with an almost Gothic quaintness more properly belonging to a rich native ballad than to the poetry of Hellas. There was a certain impropriety in his knowing so much Greek—an unfitness in the idea of marble fauns and satyrs, and even Olympian gods, lugged in under the oaken roof and the painted light of an odd old Norman hall. But Methley, abounding in Homer, really loved him (as I believe) in all truth, without whim or fancy; moreover, he had a good deal of the practical sagacity "of a Yorkshireman hippodamoio," and this enabled him to apply his knowledge with much more tact than is usually shown by people so learned as he.

I, too, loved Homer, but not with a scholar's love. The most humble and pious among women was yet so proud a mother that she could teach her first-born son, no Watts's hymns, no collects for the day: she could teach him in earliest childhood no less than this—to find a home in his saddle, and to love old Homer and all that Homer sung. True it is that the Greek was ingeniously rendered into English,—the English of Pope,—but not even a mesh like that can screen an earnest child from the fire of Homer's battles.

I pored over the Odyssey as over a story-book, hoping and fearing for the hero whom yet I partly scorned. But the Iliad—line by line I clasped it to my brain with reverence as well as with love. As an old woman deeply trustful sits reading her Bible because of the world to come, so, as though it would fit me for the coming strife of this temporal world, I read and read the Iliad. Even outwardly it was not like other books; it was throned in towering folios. There was a preface or dissertation printed in type still more majestic than the rest of the book; this I read, but not till my enthusiasm for the Iliad had already run high. The writer, compiling the opinions of many men, and chiefly of the ancients, set forth, I know not how quaintly, that the Iliad was all in all to the human race—that it was history, poetry, revelation; that the works of men's hands were folly and vanity, and would pass away like the dreams of a child, but that the kingdom of Homer would endure for ever and ever.

I assented with all my soul. I read, and still read; I came to know Homer. A learned commentator knows something of the Greeks in the same sense as an oil-and-color man may be said to know something of painting; but take an untamed child and leave him alone for twelve months with any translation of Homer, and he will be nearer by twenty centuries to the spirit of old Greece; *he* does not stop in the ninth year of the siege to admire this or that group of words; *he* has no books in his tent: but he shares in vital counsels with the "King of men," and knows the inmost souls of the impending gods. How profanely he exults over the powers divine when they are taught to dread the prowess of mortals! and most of all, how he rejoices when the God of War flies howling from the spear of Diomed, and mounts into heaven for safety! Then, the beautiful episode of the sixth book! The way to feel this is not to go casting about and learning from pastors and masters how best to admire it. The impatient child is not grubbing for beauties, but pushing the siege; the women vex him with their delays and their talking; the mention of the nurse is personal, and little sympathy has he for the child that is young enough to be frightened at the nodding plume of a helmet: but all the while that he thus chafes at the pausing of the action, the strong vertical light of Homer's poetry is blazing so full upon the people and things of the Iliad that soon, to the eyes of the child, they grow familiar as his mother's shawl; yet of this great gain he is unconscious, and on he goes, vengefully thirsting for the best blood of Troy, and never remitting his fierceness till almost suddenly it is changed for sorrow—the new and generous sorrow that he learns to feel when the noblest of all his foes lies sadly dying at the Scæan gate.

Heroic days are these, but the dark ages of school-boy life come closing over them. I suppose it's all right in the end, yet, at first sight it does seem a sad intellectual fall from your mother's dressing-room to a buzzing school. You feel so keenly the delights of early knowledge! You form strange, mystic friendships with the mere names of mountains and seas and continents and mighty rivers; you learn the ways of the planets, and transcend their narrow limits, and ask for the end of space; you vex the electric cylinder till it yields you, for your toy to play with, that subtle fire in which our earth was forged; you know of the nations that have towered high in the world, and the lives of the men who have saved whole empires from oblivion. What more will you ever learn? Yet the dismal change is ordained, and then, thin meager Latin (the same for everybody), with small shreds and patches of Greek, is thrown like a pauper's pall over all your early lore; instead of sweet knowledge, vile, monkish, doggerel grammars and graduses, dictionaries and lexicons, and horrible odds and ends of dead languages are given you for your portion, and down you fall from Roman story to a three-inch scrap of "Scriptores Romani," from Greek poetry, down, down to the cold rations of "Poetae Graeci," cut up by commentators and served out by schoolmasters!

It was not the recollection of school nor college learning, but the rapturous and earnest reading of my childhood, which made me bend forward so longingly to the plains of Troy.

Away from our people and our horses, Methley and I went loitering along by the willowy banks of a stream that crept in quietness through the low, even plain. There was not stir of weather overhead, no sound of rural labor, no sign of life in the land, but all the earth was dead and still, as though it had lain for thrice a thousand years under the leaden gloom of one unbroken Sabbath.

Softly and sadly the poor, dumb, patient stream went winding and winding along through its shifting pathway; in some places its waters were parted, and then again, lower down, they would meet once more. I could see that the stream from year to year was finding itself new channels, and flowed no longer in its ancient track; but I knew that the springs which fed it were high on Ida—the springs of Simois and Scamander!

It was coldly and thanklessly, and with vacant, unsatisfied eyes, that I watched the slow coming and the gliding away of the waters; I tell myself now, as a profane fact, that I did indeed stand by that river (Methley gathered some seeds from the bushes that grew there), but since that I am away from his banks, "divine Scamander" has recovered the proper mystery belonging to him as an unseen deity: a kind of indistinctness, like that which belongs to far antiquity, has spread itself over my memory of the winding stream that I saw with these very eyes. One's mind regains in absence that dominion over earthly things which has been shaken by their rude contact; you force yourself hardily into the material presence of a mountain or a river whose name belongs to poetry and ancient religion, rather than to the external world; your feelings, wound up and kept ready for some sort of half-expected rapture, are chilled and borne down for the time under all this load of real earth and water; but let these once pass out of sight, and then again the old fanciful notions are restored, and the mere realities which you have just been looking at are thrown back so far into distance that the very event of your intrusion upon such scenes begins to look dim and uncertain, as though it belonged to mythology.

It is not over the plain before Troy that the river now flows; its waters have edged away far towards the north since the day that "divine Scamander" (whom the gods call Xanthus) went down to do battle for Ilion, "with Mars, and Phœbus, and Latona, and Diana glorying in her arrows, and Venus, the lover of smiles."

And now, when I was vexed at the migration of Scamander, and the total loss or absorption of poor, dear Simois, how happily Methley reminded me that Homer himself had warned us of some such changes! The besiegers, in beginning their wall, had neglected the hecatombs due to the gods, and so, after the fall of Troy, Apollo turned the paths of the rivers that flow from Ida, and sent them flooding over the wall till all the beach was smooth and free from the unhallowed works of the Greeks. It is true I see now, on looking to the passage, that Neptune, when the work of destruction was done, turned back the rivers to their ancient ways:

> . . . ποταμους δ' ετρεψε νεεσθαι
> Καρ' ροον ἠπερ προσθεν ιεν χυλλιρροον ὕδωρ.

But their old channels passing through that light, pervious soil would have been lost in the nine days' flood, and perhaps the god, when he willed to bring back the rivers to their ancient beds, may have done his work but ill; it is easier, they say, to destroy than it is to restore.

We took to our horses again, and went southward towards the very plain between Troy and the tents of the Greeks, but we rode by a line at some distance from the shore. Whether it was that the lay of the ground hindered my view towards the sea, or that I was all intent upon Ida, or whether my mind was in vacancy, or whether, as is most like, I had strayed from the Dardan plains all back to gentle England, there is now no knowing nor caring, but it was—not quite suddenly, indeed, but rather, as it were, in the swelling and falling of a single wave, that the reality of that very sea view which had bounded the sight of the Greeks now visibly acceded to me and rolled full in upon my brain. Conceive how deeply that eternal coast-line, that fixed horizon, those island rocks, must have graven their images upon the minds of the Grecian warriors by the time that they had reached the ninth year of the siege! Conceive the strength and the fanciful beauty of the speeches with which a whole army of imagining men must have told their weariness, and how the sauntering chiefs must have whelmed that daily, daily scene with their deep Ionian curses!

And now it was that my eyes were greeted with a delightful surprise. Whilst we were at Constantinople, Methley and I had pored over the map together; we agreed that whatever may have been the exact site of Troy, the Grecian camp must have been nearly opposite to the space betwixt the islands of Imbros and Tenedos:

[35]

Μεσσηγὺς Τενέδοιο καὶ Ἰμβρου παιπαλοέσσης.

But Methley reminded me of a passage in the Iliad in which Neptune is represented as looking at the scene of action before Ilion from above the island of Samothrace. Now, Samothrace, according to the map, appeared to be not only out of all seeing distance from the Troad, but to be entirely shut out from it by the intervening Imbros, a larger island which stretches its length right athwart the line of sight from Samothrace to Troy. Piously allowing that the dread Commotor of our globe might have seen all mortal doings, even from the depths of his own cerulean kingdom, I still felt that if a station were to be chosen from which to see the fight, old Homer, so material in his ways of thought, so averse from all haziness and overreaching, would have *meant* to give the god for his station some spot within reach of men's eyes from the plains of Troy. I think that this testing of the poet's words by map and compass may have shaken a little of my faith in the completeness of his knowledge. Well, now I had come; there to the south was Tenedos, and here at my side was Imbros, all right and according to the map; but aloft over Imbros, aloft in a far-away heaven, was Samothrace, the watch-tower of Neptune!

So Homer had appointed it, and so it was; the map was correct enough, but could not, like Homer, convey the *whole truth*. Thus vain and false are the mere human surmises and doubts which clash with Homeric writ!

Nobody whose mind had not been reduced to the most deplorably logical condition could look upon this beautiful congruity betwixt the Iliad and the material world, and yet bear to suppose that the poet may have learned the features of the coast from mere hearsay; now, then, I believed; now I knew that Homer had *passed along here*—that this vision of Samothrace overtowering the nearer island was common to him and to me.

After a journey of some few days by the route of Adramiti and Pergamo, we reached Smyrna. The letters which Methley here received obliged him to return to England.

CHAPTER
V

Infidel Smyrna.

SMYRNA, or Giaour Izmir, "Infidel Smyrna" as the Mussulmans call it, is the main point of commercial contact betwixt
Europe and Asia; you are there surrounded by the people and
confused customs of many and various nations; you see the fussy
European adopting the East and calming his restlessness with the
long Turkish pipe of tranquillity; you see Jews offering services
and receiving blows;* on one side you have a fellow whose dress
and beard would give you a good idea of the true Oriental if it
were not for the *gobemouche* expression of countenance with
which he is swallowing an article in a French newspaper, and
there, just by, is a genuine Osmanli, smoking away with all the
majesty of a Sultan; but before you have time to admire sufficiently his tranquil dignity and his soft Asiatic repose, the poor old
fellow is ruthlessly "run down" by an English midshipman who
has set sail on a Smyrna hack. Such are the incongruities of the
"infidel city" at ordinary times; but when I was there our friend
Carrigaholt had imported himself and his oddities, as an accession
to the other and inferior wonders of Smyrna.

I was sitting alone in my room one day, at Constantinople,

---

* The Jews of Smyrna are poor, and having little merchandise of their own to
dispose of, they are sadly importunate in offering their services as intermediaries.
Their troublesome conduct has led to the custom of beating them in the open
streets. It is usual for Europeans to carry long sticks with them, for the express
purpose of keeping off the chosen people. I always felt ashamed to strike the poor
fellows myself, but I confess to the amusement with which I witnessed the observance of this custom by other people. The Jew seldom got hurt much, for he was
always expecting the blow, and was ready to recede from it the moment it came;
one could not help being rather gratified at seeing him bound away so nimbly, with
his long robes floating out in the air, and then again wheel around, and return with
fresh importunities.

when I heard Methley approaching my door with shouts of laughter and welcome, and presently I recognized that peculiar cry by which our friend Carrigaholt expresses his emotions. He soon explained to us the final causes by which the Fates had worked out their wonderful purpose of bringing him to Constantinople. He was always, you know, very fond of sailing; but he had got into such sad scrapes (including, I think, a lawsuit) on account of his last yacht that he took it into his head to have a cruise in a merchant vessel. So he went to Liverpool and looked through the craft lying ready to sail till he found a smart schooner that perfectly suited his taste. The destination of the vessel was the last thing he thought of, and when he was told that she was bound for Constantinople, he merely assented to that as a part of the arrangement to which he had no objection. As soon as the vessel had sailed, the hapless passenger discovered that his skipper carried on board an enormous wife with an inquiring mind and an irresistible tendency to impart her opinions. She looked upon her guest as upon a piece of waste intellect that ought to be carefully tilled. She tilled him accordingly. If the Dons at Oxford could have seen poor Carrigaholt thus absolutely "attending lectures" in the Bay of Biscay, they would surely have thought him sufficiently punished for all the wrongs he did them whilst he was preparing himself under their care for the other and more boisterous university. The voyage did not last more than six or eight weeks, and the philosophy inflicted on Carrigaholt was not entirely fatal to him. Certainly he was somewhat emaciated, and, for aught I know, he may have subscribed too largely to the "Feminine-right-of-reason Society"; but it did not appear that his health had been seriously affected. There was a scheme on foot, it would seem, for taking the passenger back to England in the same schooner—a scheme, in fact, for keeping him perpetually afloat, and perpetually saturated with arguments; but when Carrigaholt found himself ashore, and remembered that the skipperina (who had imprudently remained on board) was not there to enforce her suggestions, he was open to the hints of his servant (a very sharp fellow), who arranged a plan for escaping, and finally brought off his master to Giuseppini's hotel.

[38]

Our friend afterwards went by sea to Smyrna, and there he now was in his glory. He had a good or at all events a gentleman-like judgment in matters of taste, and as his great object was to surround himself with all that his fancy could dictate, he lived in a state of perpetual negotiation; he was forever on the point of purchasing, not only the material productions of the place, but all sorts of such fine ware as "intelligence," "fidelity," and so on. He was most curious, however, as the purchaser of the "affections." Sometimes he would imagine that he had a marital aptitude, and his fancy would sketch a graceful picture, in which he appeared reclining on a divan, with a beautiful Greek woman fondly couched at his feet, and soothing him with the witchery of her guitar. Having satisfied himself with the ideal picture thus created, he would pass into action: the guitar he would buy instantly, and would give such intimations of his wish to be wedded to a Greek as could not fail to produce great excitement in the families of the beautiful Smyrniotes. Then again—and just in time, perhaps, to save him from the yoke—his dream would pass away, and another would come in its stead. He would suddenly feel the yearnings of a father's love, and willing by force of gold to transcend all natural preliminaries, he would issue instructions for the purchase of some dutiful child that could be warranted to love him as a parent. Then at another time he would be convinced that the attachment of menials might satisfy the longings of his affectionate heart, and thereupon he would give orders to his slave-merchant for something in the way of eternal fidelity. You may well imagine that this anxiety of Carrigaholt to purchase, not only the scenery, but the many dramatis personæ belonging to his dreams, with all their goodness and graces complete, necessarily gave an immense stimulus to the trade and intrigue of Smyrna, and created a demand for human virtues which the moral resources of the place were totally inadequate to supply. Every day, after breakfast, this lover of the Good and the Beautiful held a levee. In his anteroom there would be not only the sellers of pipes and slippers and shawls, and such like Oriental merchandise, not only embroiderers and cunning workmen patiently striving to realize his visions of Albanian dresses, not only the servants offering for places, and the slave-dealer tendering his sable ware, but there would be the Greek master waiting to teach his pupil the grammar of the soft Ionian tongue in which he was to delight the wife of his imagination, and the music-master who was to teach him some sweet replies to the anticipated tones of the fancied guitar; and then, above all, and proudly eminent with undisputed preference of entrée, and fraught with the mysterious tidings on which the realization of the whole dream might depend, was the mysterious match-maker,* enticing and postponing the suitor, yet ever keeping alive in his soul the love of that pictured virtue whose beauty (unseen by eyes) was half revealed to the imagination.

You would have thought that this practical dreaming must have soon brought Carrigaholt to a bad end, but he was in much less danger than might be supposed: for besides that the new visions of happiness almost always came in time to counteract the fatal completion of the preceding scheme, his high breeding and his delicately sensitive taste almost always befriended him at times when he was left without any other protection, and the efficacy of these qualities in keeping a man out of harm's way is really immense. In all baseness and imposture there is a coarse, vulgar spirit which, however artfully concealed for a time, must sooner or later show itself in some little circumstance sufficiently plain to occasion an instant jar upon the minds of those whose taste is lively and true; to such men a shock of this kind, disclosing the *ugliness* of a cheat, is more effectively convincing than any mere proofs could be.

Thus guarded from isle to isle, and through Greece and through Albania, this practical Plato, with a purse in his hand, carried on his mad chase after the Good and the Beautiful, and yet returned in safety to his home. But now, poor fellow, the lowly grave that is the end of men's romantic hopes has closed over all his rich fancies and all his high aspirations. He is utterly married! No

---

* Marriages in the East are arranged by professed match-makers; many of these, I believe, are Jewesses.

more hope, no more change, for him; no more relays: he must go Vetturiniwise to the appointed end of his journey!

Smyrna, I think, may be called the chief town and capital of that Grecian race against which you will be cautioned so carefully as soon as you touch the Levant. You will say that I ought not to confound as one people the Greeks living under a constitutional government with the unfortunate Rayas who "groan under the Turkish yoke," but I can't see that political events have hitherto produced any strongly marked difference of character. If I could venture to rely (this I feel that I cannot at all do) upon my own observation, I should tell you that there were more heartiness and strength in the Greeks of the Ottoman Empire than in those of the new kingdom; the truth is that there is a greater field for commercial enterprise, and even for Greek ambition, under the Ottoman scepter than is to be found in the dominions of Otho. Indeed, the people, by their frequent migrations from the limits of the constitutional kingdom to the territories of the Porte, seem to show that, on the whole, they prefer "groaning under the Turkish yoke" to the honor of "being the only true source of legitimate power" in their own land.

For myself, I love the race; in spite of all their vices, and even in spite of all their meannesses, I remember the blood that is in them, and still love the Greeks. The Osmanlis are, of course, by nature, by religion, and by politics, the strong foes of the Hellenic people; and as the Greeks, poor fellows! happen to be a little deficient in some of the virtues which facilitate the transaction of commercial business (such as veracity, fidelity, etc.), it naturally follows that they are highly unpopular with the European merchants. Now, these are the persons through whom, either directly or indirectly, is derived the greater part of the information which you gather in the Levant, and therefore you must make up your mind to hear an almost universal and unbroken testimony against the character of the people whose ancestors invented virtue. And strange to say, the Greeks themselves do not attempt to disturb this general unanimity of opinion by any dissent on their part. Question a Greek on the subject, and he will tell you at once that the people are "traditori," and will then, perhaps, endeavor to shake off his fair share of the imputation by asserting that his father had been dragoman to some foreign embassy, and that he (the son), therefore, by the law of nations, had ceased to be Greek.

"E dunque no siete traditore?"

"Possibile, signor, ma almeno Io no sono Greco."

Not even the diplomatic representatives of the Hellenic kingdom are free from the habit of depreciating their brethren. I recollect that at one of the ports in Syria a Greek vessel was rather unfairly kept in quarantine by order of the Board of Health, a board which consisted entirely of Europeans. A consular agent from the kingdom of Greece had lately hoisted his flag in the town, and the captain of the vessel drew up a remonstrance, and requested his consul to lay it before the Board.

"Now, *is* this reasonable?" said the consul. "Is it reasonable that I should place myself in collision with all the principal European gentlemen of the place for the sake of you, a Greek?" The skipper was greatly vexed at the failure of his application, but he scarcely even questioned the justice of the ground which his consul had taken. Well, it happened some time afterwards that I found myself at the same port, having gone thither with the view of embarking for the port of Syra. I was anxious, of course, to elude as carefully as possible the quarantine detentions which threatened me on my arrival, and hearing that the Greek consul had a brother who was a man in authority at Syra, I got myself presented to the former, and took the liberty of asking him to give me such a letter of introduction to his relative at Syra as might possibly have the effect of shortening the term of quarantine. He acceded to this request with the utmost kindness and courtesy; but when he replied to my thanks by saying that "in serving an Englishman he was doing no more than his strict duty commanded," not even my gratitude could prevent me from calling to mind his treatment of the poor captain who had the misfortune of *not* being an alien in blood to his consul and appointed protector.

I think that the change which has taken place in the character of the Greeks has been occasioned, in great measure, by the doctrines and practice of their religion. The Greek Church has animated the Muscovite peasant, and inspired him with hopes and ideas which, however humble, are still better than none at all; but the faith and the forms and the strange ecclesiastical literature which act so advantageously upon the mere clay of the Russian serf seem to hang like lead upon the ethereal spirit of the Greek. Never, in any part of the world, have I seen religious performances so painful to witness as those of the Greeks. The horror, however, with which one shudders at their worship is attributable, in some measure, to the mere effect of costume. In all the Ottoman dominions, and very frequently, too, in the kingdom of Otho, the Greeks wear turbans or other head-dresses, and shave their heads, leaving only a rat's tail at the crown of the head. They, of course, keep themselves covered within doors, as well as abroad, and they never remove their head-gear merely on account of being in a church: but when the Greek stops to worship at his proper shrine, then, and then only, he always uncovers; and as you see him thus with shaven skull, and savage tail depending from his crown, kissing a thing of wood and glass, and cringing with base prostrations and apparent terror before a miserable picture, you see superstition in a shape which, outwardly at least, is sadly abject and repulsive.

The fasts, too, of the Greek Church produce an ill effect upon the character of the people, for they are not a mere farce, but are carried to such an extent as to bring about a real mortification of the flesh. The febrile irritation of the frame, operating in conjunction with depression of the spirits occasioned by abstinence, will so far answer the objects of the rite as to engender some religious excitement; but this is of a morbid and gloomy character, and it seems to be certain that, along with the increase of sanctity, there comes a fiercer desire for the perpetration of dark crimes. The number of murders committed during Lent is greater, I am told, than at any other time of the year. A man under the influence of a bean dietary—for this is the principal food of the Greeks during their fasts— will be in an apt humor for enriching the shrine of his saint and passing a knife through his next-door neighbor. The moneys deposited upon the shrines are appropriated by priests;

[43]

the priests are married men, and have families to provide for; they "take the good with the bad," and continue to recommend fasts.

Then, too, the Greek Church enjoins her followers to keep holy such a vast number of saints' days as practically to shorten the lives of the people very materially. I believe that one third out of the number of days in the year are "kept holy," or rather *kept stupid*, in honor of the saints. No great portion of the time thus set apart is spent in religious exercises, and the people don't betake themselves to any such animating pastimes as might serve to strengthen the frame, or invigorate the mind, or exalt the taste. On the contrary, the saints' days of the Greeks in Smyrna are passed in the same manner as the Sabbaths of well-behaved Protestant housemaids in London—that is to say, in a steady and serious contemplation of street scenery. The men perform this duty *at the doors* of their houses, the women *at the windows*. Windows, indeed, by the custom of Greek towns, are so decidedly appropriated to the gentle sex that a man would be looked upon as utterly effeminate if he ventured to choose such a position for the keeping of his saints' days. I was present one day at a treaty for the hire of some apartments at Smyrna, which was carried on between Carrigaholt and the Greek woman to whom the rooms belonged. Carrigaholt objected that the windows commanded no view of the street. Immediately the brow of the majestic matron was clouded, and with all the scorn of a Spartan mother she coolly asked Carrigaholt and said: "Art thou a tender damsel that thou wouldst sit and gaze from windows?" The man whom she addressed, however, had not gone to Greece with any intention of placing himself under the laws of Lycurgus, and was not to be diverted from his views by a Spartan rebuke, so he took care to find himself windows after his own heart, and there, I believe, for many a month he kept the saints' days, and all the days intervening, after the fashion of Grecian women.

Oh, let me be charitable to all who write, and to all who lecture, and to all who preach, since even I, a layman not forced to write at all, can hardly avoid chiming in with some tuneful cant! I have had the heart to talk about the pernicious effects of the Greek holidays; and yet to these I owe most gracious and beautiful visions! I will let the words stand, as a humbling proof that I am subject to that nearly immutable law which compels a man with a pen in his hand to be uttering every now and then some sentiment not his own. It seems as though the power of expressing regrets and desires by written symbols were coupled with a condition that the writer should from time to time express the regrets and desires of other people—as though, like a French peasant under the old régime, he were bound to perform a certain amount of work *upon the public highways*. I rebel as stoutly as I can against this horrible corvée; I try not to deceive you; I try to set down the thoughts which are fresh within me, and not to pretend any wishes or griefs which I do not really feel: but no sooner do I cease from watchfulness in this regard than my right hand is, as it were, seized by some false angel, and even now, you see, I have been forced to put down such words and sentences as I ought to have written if really and truly I had wished to disturb the saints' days of the beautiful Smyrniotes!

Disturb their saints' days? Oh, no! for as you move through the narrow streets of the city, at these times of festival, the transom-shaped windows suspended over your head on either side are filled with the beautiful descendants of the old Ionian race; all (even yonder empress throned at the window of that humblest mud cottage) are attired with seeming magnificence. Their classic heads are crowned with scarlet and laden with jewels or coins of gold— the whole wealth of the wearers;* their features are touched with a savage pencil, hardening the outline of eyes and eyebrows, and lending an unnatural fire to the stern, grave looks with which they pierce your brain. Endure their fiery eyes as best you may, and ride on slowly and reverently, for, facing you from the side of the transom that looks longwise through the street, you see the one glorious shape transcendent in its beauty; you see the massive

---

* A Greek woman wears her whole fortune upon her person, in the shape of jewels or gold coins. I believe that this mode of investment is adopted in great measure for safety's sake. It has the advantage of enabling a suitor to *reckon* as well as to admire the objects of his affection.

braid of hair as it catches a touch of light on its jetty surface, and the broad, calm, angry brow; the large eyes, deeply set and self-relying, as the eyes of a conqueror, with all their rich shadows of thought lying darkly around them; you see the thin, fiery nostril, and the bold line of the chin and throat, disclosing all the fierceness and all the pride, passion, and power that can live along with the rare womanly beauty of those sweetly turned lips. But then there is a terrible stillness in this breathing image; it seems like the stillness of a savage that sits intent and brooding day by day upon some one fearful scheme of vengeance; and yet more like it seems to the stillness of an immortal, whose will must be known and obeyed without sign or speech. Bow down! bow down and adore the young Persephone, transcendent Queen of Shades!

CHAPTER
VI

Greek mariners.

I SAILED from Smyrna in the *Amphitrite*, a Greek brigantine which was confidently said to be bound for the ocast of Syria; but I knew that this announcement was not to be relied upon with positive certainty, for the Greek mariners are practically free from the stringency of ship's papers, and where they will, there they go. However, I had the whole of the cabin for myself and my attendant Mysseri, subject only to the society of the captain at the hour of dinner; being at ease in this respect, being furnished, too, with plenty of books, and finding an unfailing source of interest in the thorough Greekness of my captain and my crew, I felt less anxious than most people would have been about the probable length of the cruise. I knew enough of Greek navigation to be sure that our vessel would cling to earth like a child to its mother's knee, and that I should touch at many an isle before I set foot upon the Syrian coast; but I had no invidious preference for Europe, Asia, or Africa (I was safe from all danger of America), and I felt that I could defy the winds to blow me upon a coast that was blank and void of interest. My patience was extremely useful to me, for the cruise altogether endured some forty days, and that in the midst of winter.

According to me, the most interesting of all the Greeks (male Greeks) are the mariners, because their pursuits and their social condition are so nearly the same as those of their famous ancestors. You will say that the occupation of commerce must have smoothed down the salience of their minds; and this would be so, perhaps, if their mercantile affairs were conducted according to the fixed, businesslike routine of Europeans: but the ventures of the Greeks are surrounded by such a multitude of imagined dangers and (from the absence of regular marts, in which the true

[47]

value of merchandise can be ascertained), are so entirely speculative, and besides are conducted in a manner so wholly determined upon by the wayward fancies and wishes of the crew, that they belong to enterprise rather than to industry, and are very far indeed from tending to deaden any freshness of character.

The vessels in which war and piracy were carried on during the years of the Greek Revolution became merchantmen at the end of the war; but the tactics of the Greeks as naval warriors were so exceedingly cautious, and their habits as commercial mariners are so wild, that the change has been more slight than you might imagine. The first care of Greeks (Greek Rayas), when they undertake a shipping enterprise, is to procure for their vessel the protection of some European power; this is easily managed by a little intriguing with the dragoman of one of the embassies at Constantinople, and the craft soon glories in the ensign of Russia, or the dazzling tricolor, or the Union Jack; thus, to the great delight of her crew, she enters upon the ocean world with a flaring lie at her peak. But the appearance of the vessel does no discredit to the borrowed flag; she is frail, indeed, but is gracefully built and smartly rigged; she always carries guns, and, in the short, gives good promise of mischief and speed.

The privileges attached to the vessel and her crew by virtue of the borrowed flag are so great as to imply a liberty wider even than that which is often enjoyed in our more strictly civilized countries, so that there is no good ground for saying that the development of the true character belonging to Greek mariners is prevented by the dominion of the Ottoman. These men are free, too, from the power of the great capitalist—a power more withering than despotism itself to the enterprises of humble venturers. The capital employed is supplied by those whose labor is to render it productive. The crew receive no wages, but have all a share in the venture, and in general, I believe, they are the owners of the whole freight: they choose a captain to whom they intrust just power enough to keep the vessel on her course in fine weather, but not quite enough for a gale of wind; they also elect a cook and a mate. The cook whom we had on board was particularly careful

about the ship's reckoning, and when, under the influence of the
keen sea-breezes, we grew fondly expectant of an instant dinner,
the great author of pilafs would be standing on deck with an
ancient quadrant in his hands calmly affecting to take an observation. But then, to make up for this, the captain would be exer-
cising a controlling influence over the soup, so that all in the end
went well. Our mate was a Hydriot, a native of that island rock
which grows nothing but mariners and mariners' wives. His character seemed to be exactly that which is generally attributed to the
Hydriot race: he was fierce and gloomy and lonely in his ways.
One of his principal duties seemed to be that of acting as counter-
captain, or leader of the opposition, denouncing the first symptoms of tyranny, and protecting even the cabin-boy from
oppression. Besides this, when things went smoothly he would
begin to prognosticate evil, in order that his more light-hearted
comrades might not be puffed up with the seeming good fortune
of the moment.

It seemed to me that the personal freedom of these sailors, who
own no superiors except those of their own choice, is as like as
may be to that of their seafaring ancestors. And even in their mode
of navigation they have admitted no such an entire change as you
would suppose probable; it is true that they have so far availed
themselves of modern discoveries as to look to the compass instead of the stars, and that they have superseded the immortal
gods of their forefathers by St. Nicholas in his glass case,* but they
are not yet so confident, either in their needle or their saint, as to
love an open sea, and they still hug their shores as fondly as the
Argonauts of old. Indeed, they have a most unsailor-like love for
the land, and I really believe that in a gale of wind they would
rather have a rock-bound coast on their lee than no coast at all.
According to the notions of an English seaman, this kind of navigation would soon bring the vessel on which it might be practised
to an evil end. The Greek, however, is unaccountably successful in

---

* St. Nicholas is the great patron of Greek sailors; a small picture of him inclosed
in a glass case is hung up like a barometer at one end of the cabin.

escaping the consequences of being "jammed in," as it is called, upon a lee shore.

These seamen, like their forefathers, rely upon no winds unless they are right astern or on the quarter; they rarely go *on* a wind if it blows at all fresh; and if the adverse breeze approaches to a gale, they at once fumigate St. Nicholas and put up the helm. The consequence, of course, is that under the ever-varying winds of the Ægean they are blown about in the most whimsical manner. I used to think that Ulysses, with his ten years' voyage, had taken his time in making Ithaca, but my experience in Greek navigation soon made me understand that he had had, in point of fact, a pretty good "average passage."

Such are now the mariners of the Ægean; free, equal amongst themselves, navigating the seas of their forefathers with the same heroic and yet childlike spirit of venture, the same half-trustful reliance upon heavenly aid, they are the liveliest images of true old Greeks that time and the new religion have spared to us.

With one exception, our crew were "a solemn company," and yet, sometimes, if all things went well, they would relax their austerity, and show a disposition to fun, or rather to quiet humor. When this happened, they invariably had recourse to one of their number who went by the name of "Admiral Nicolou." He was an amusing fellow, the poorest, I believe, and the least thoughtful of the crew, but full of rich humor. His oft-told story of the events by which he had gained the sobriquet of "Admiral" never failed to delight his hearers, and when he was desired to repeat it for my benefit, the rest of the crew crowded round with as much interest as if they were listening to the tale for the first time. The tale was this: A number of Greek brigs and brigantines were at anchor in the bay at Beirut; a festival of some kind, particularly attractive to the sailors, was going on in the town, and whether with or without leave I know not, the crews of all the craft, except that of Nicolou, had gone ashore; on board his vessel (she carried dollars) there was, it would seem, a more careful or more influential captain—a man who was able to enforce his determination that at least one of the crew should be left on board. Nicolou's good nature was with him so powerful an impulse that he could not resist the delight of volunteering to stay with the vessel whilst his comrades went ashore; his proposal was accepted, and the crew and captain soon left him alone on the deck of his vessel. The sailors, gathering together from their several ships, were amusing themselves in the town, when suddenly there came down from betwixt the mountains one of those sudden hurricanes which sometimes occur in southern climes. Nicolou's vessel, together with four of the craft which had been left unmanned, broke from her moorings, and all five of the vessels were carried out seaward. The town is on a salient point at the southern side of the bay, so that the "Admiral" was close under the eyes of the inhabitants and the shore-gone sailors when he gallantly drifted out at the head of his little fleet. If Nicolou could not entirely control the manœuvers of the squadron, there was at least no human power to divide his authority, and thus it was that he took rank as "Admiral." Nicolou cut his cable, and so, for the time, saved his vessel; the rest of the fleet under his command were quickly wrecked, whilst the "Admiral" got away clear to the open sea. The violence of the squall soon passed off, but Nicolou felt that his chance of one day resigning his high duties as an admiral for the enjoyments of private life on the steadfast shore mainly depended upon his success in working the brig with his own hands; so after calling on his namesake, the saint (not for the first time, I take it), he got up some canvas and took the helm; he became equal, he told us, to a score of Nicolous, and the vessel, as he said, was "manned with his terrors." For two days, it seems, he cruised at large; but at last, either by his seamanship or by the natural instinct of the Greek mariners for finding land, he brought his craft close to an unknown shore that promised well for his purpose of running in the vessel, and he was preparing to give her a good berth on the beach when he saw a gang of ferocious-looking fellows coming down to the point for which he was making. Poor Nicolou was a perfectly unlettered and untutored genius, and for that reason, perhaps, a keen listener to tales of terror; his mind had been impressed with some horrible legend of cannibalism, and he now did not doubt for a moment that the men awaiting him on the beach were the monsters at whom he had shuddered in the days of his childhood. The coast on which Nicolou was running his vessel was somewhere, I fancy at the foot of the Anzairie Mountains, and the fellows who were preparing to give him a reception were probably very rough specimens of humanity; it is likely enough that they might have given themselves the trouble of putting the "Admiral" to death, for the purpose of simplifying their claim to the vessel and preventing litigation, but the notion of their cannibalism was, of course, utterly unfounded. Nicolou's terror had, however, so graven the idea on his mind that he could never after dismiss it. Having once determined the character of his expectant hosts, the "Admiral" naturally thought that it would be better to keep their dinner waiting any length of time than to attend their feast in the character of a roasted Greek, so he put about his vessel and tempted the deep once more. After a farther cruise the lonely commander ran his vessel upon some rocks at another part of the coast; there she was lost with all her treasures, and Nicolou was but too glad to scramble ashore, though without one dollar in his girdle. These adventures seem flat enough as I repeat them, but the hero expressed his terrors by such odd terms of speech and such strangely humorous gestures that the story came from his lips with an unfailing zest, so that the crew who had heard the tale so often could still enjoy to their hearts the rich fright of the "Admiral," and still shuddered with unabated horror when he came to the loss of the dollars.

The power of listening to long stories (and for this, by the by, I am giving you large credit) is common, I fancy, to most sailors, and the Greeks have it to a high degree, for they can be perfectly patient under a narrative of two or three hours' duration. These long stories are mostly founded upon Oriental topics, and in one of them I recognized with some alteration an old friend of the "Arabian Nights." I inquired as to the source from which the story had been derived, and the crew all agreed that it had been handed down unwritten from Greek to Greek; their account of the matter does not, perhaps, go very far towards showing the real origin of the tale, but when I afterwards took up the "Arabian Nights," I became strongly impressed with a notion that they must have sprung from the brain of a Greek. It seems to me that these stories, whilst they disclose a complete and habitual *knowledge* of things Asiatic, have about them so much of freshness and life, so much of the stirring and volatile European character, that they cannot have owed their conception to a mere Oriental, who, for creative purposes, is a thing dead and dry—a mental mummy that may have been a live king just after the flood, but has since lain balmed in spice.

At the time of the Califate the Greek race was familiar enough to Bagdad; they were the merchants, the peddlers, the barbers, and intriguers-general, of southwestern Asia, and therefore the Oriental materials with which the Arabian tales were wrought must have been completely at the command of the inventive people to whom I would attribute their origin.

We were nearing the isle of Cyprus, when there arose half a gale of wind, with a heavy, chopping sea. My Greek seamen considered that the weather amounted not to a half but to an integral gale of wind at the very least; so they put up the helm, and scudded for twenty hours. When we neared the mainland of Anadoli, the gale ceased, and a favorable breeze springing up, soon brought us off Cyprus once more. Afterwards the wind changed again, but we were still able to lay our course by sailing close-hauled.

We were, at length, in such a position that by holding on our course for about half an hour we should get under the lee of the island and find ourselves in smooth water; but the wind had been gradually freshening; it now blew hard, and there was a heavy sea running.

As the grounds for alarm arose, the crew gathered together in one close group; they stood pale and grim under their hooded capotes, like monks awaiting a massacre, anxiously looking by turns along the pathway of the storm, and then upon the eye of the captain, who stood by the helmsman. Presently the Hydriot came aft, more moody than ever, the bearer of fierce remonstrance against the continuing of the struggle; he received a resolute answer, and still we held our course. Soon there came a heavy sea, that caught the bow of the brigantine as she lay jammed in betwixt the waves. She bowed her head low under the waters, and shuddered through all her timbers, then gallantly stood up again over the striving sea with bowsprit entire. But where were the crew? It was a crew no longer, but rather a gathering of Greek citizens; the shout of the seamen was changed for the murmuring of the people—the spirit of the old demos was alive. The men came aft in a body and loudly asked that the vessel should be put about, and that the storm be no longer tempted. Now, then, for speeches:— the captain, his eyes flashing fire, his frame all quivering with emotion, wielding his every limb like another and a louder voice, pours forth the eloquent torrent of this threats and his reasons, his commands and his prayers; he promises, he vows, he swears that there is safety in holding on—safety *if Greeks will be brave!* The men hear, and are moved; but the gale rouses itself once more, and again the raging sea comes trampling over the timbers that are the life of all. The fierce Hydriot advances one step nearer to the captain, and the angry growl of the people goes floating down the wind, but they listen; they waver once more, and once more resolve, then waver again, thus doubtfully hanging between the terrors of the storm and the persuasion of glorious speech, as though it were the Athenian that talked, and Philip of Macedon that thundered on the weather bow.

Brave thoughts winged on Grecian words gained their natural mastery over terror; the brigantine held on her course, and reached smooth water at last. I landed at Limesol, the westernmost port of Cyprus, leaving the brigantine to sail for Larnecca, and there await my arrival.

CHAPTER
VII

Cyprus.

THERE was a Greek at Limesol who hoisted his flag as an English vice-consul, and he insisted upon my accepting his hospitality; with some difficulty, and chiefly by assuring him that I could not delay my departure beyond an early hour in the afternoon, I induced him to allow my dining with his family instead of banqueting all alone with the representative of my sovereign, in consular state and dignity. The lady of the house, it seemed, had never sat at table with an European. She was very shy about the matter, and tried hard to get out of the scrape; but the husband, I fancy, reminded her that she was theoretically an Englishwoman by virtue of the flag that waved over her roof, and that she was bound to show her nationality by sitting at meat with me. Finding herself inexorably condemned to bear with the dreaded gaze of European eyes, she tried to save her innocent children from the hard fate awaiting herself; but I obtained that all of them (and I think there were four or five) should sit at the table. You will meet with abundance of stately receptions and of generous hospitality, too, in the East, but rarely, very rarely in those regions (or even, so far as I know, in any part of southern Europe), does one gain an opportunity of seeing the familiar and indoor life of the people.

This family party of the good consul's (or rather of mine, for I originated the idea, though he furnished the materials) went off very well. The mama was shy at first, but she veiled her awkwardness by affecting to scold the children; these had all immortal names—names, too, which they owed to tradition, and certainly not to any classical enthusiasm of their parents. Every instant I was delighted by some such phrases as these: "Themistocles, my love, don't fight." "Alcibiades, can't you sit still?" "Socrates, put down the cup." "Oh, fie! Aspasia, don't; oh, don't be naughty!"

It is true that the names were pronounced Socrāhtie, Aspāhsie—
that is, according to accent, and not according to quantity, but I
suppose it is scarcely now to be doubted that they were so sounded
in ancient times.

To me it seems that of all the lands I know (you will see in a
minute how I connect this piece of prose with the isle of Cyprus)
there is none in which mere wealth, mere unaided wealth, is held
half so cheaply—none in which a poor devil of a millionaire without birth or ability occupies so humble a place—as in England.
My Greek host was chatting with me, I think upon the roof of the
house (for that is the lounging-place in Eastern climes), when
suddenly he assumed a serious air, and intimated a wish to talk
over the British Constitution, a subject with which, as he assured
me, he was thoroughly acquainted. He presently, however, remarked that there was one anomalous circumstance attendant
upon the practical working of our political system which he had
never been able to hear explained in a manner satisfactory to
himself. From the fact of his having found a difficulty in his subject, I began to think that my host might really know rather more
of it than his announcement of a thorough knowledge had led me
to expect; I felt interested at being about to hear from the lips of
an intelligent Greek, quite remote from the influence of European
opinions, what might seem to him the most astonishing and in-
comprehensible of all those results which have followed from the
action of our political institutions. The anomaly—the only anomaly which had been detected by the vice-consular wisdom—consisted in the fact that Rothschild (the late money-monger) had
never been the Prime Minister of England! I gravely tried to throw
some light upon the mysterious causes that had kept the worthy
Israelite out of the Cabinet; but I think I could see that my explanation was not satisfactory. Go and argue with the flies of
summer that there is a Power divine yet greater than the sun in the
heavens, but never dare hope to convince the people of the South
that there is any other God than Gold.

My intended journey was to the site of the Paphian temple. I
take no antiquarian interest in ruins, and care little about them,

unless they are either striking in themselves, or else serve to mark some spot very dear to my fancy. I knew that the ruins of Paphos were scarcely, if at all, discernible; but there was a will and a longing more imperious than mere curiosity that drove me thither.

For this just then was my pagan soul's desire: that (not forfeiting my inheritance for the life to come) it had yet been given me to live through this world—to live a favored mortal under the old Olympian dispensation; to speak out my resolves to the listening Jove, and hear him answer with approving thunder; to be blessed with divine counsels from the lips of Pallas Athene; to believe, aye, only to believe—to believe for one rapturous moment that in the gloomy depths of the grove by the mountain's side there were some leafy pathway that crisped beneath the glowing sandal of Aphrodite—Aphrodite, not coldly disdainful of even a mortal's love! And this vain, heathenish longing of mine was father to the thought of visiting the scene of the ancient worship.

The isle is beautiful; from the edge of the rich, flowery fields on which I trod, to the midway sides of the snowy Olympus, the ground could only here and there show an abrupt crag, or a high, straggling ridge, that up-shouldered itself from out of the wilderness of myrtles, and of a thousand bright-leaved shrubs that twined their arms together in lovesome tangles. The air that came to my lips was warm and fragrant as the ambrosial breath of the goddess, infecting me, not, of course, with a faith in the old religion of the isle, but with a sense and apprehension of its mystic power—a power that was still to be obeyed—obeyed by *me*; for why otherwise did I toil on with sorry horses to "where, for HER, the hundred altars glowed with Arabian incense, and breathed with the fragrance of garlands ever fresh"?*

I passed a sadly disenchanting night in the cabin of a Greek priest—not a priest of the goddesss, but of the Greek Church. There was but one humble room, or rather shed, for man and priest and beast. The next morning I reached Baffa (Paphos), a

---

* ". . . ubi templum illi, centumque Sabaeo
Thure calent arae, sertisque recentibus halant."
                                        Æneid, i. 415.

[57]

village not far distant from the site of the temple; there was a
Greek husbandman there who (not for emolument, but for the
sake of the protection and dignity which it afforded) had got leave
from the man at Limesol to hoist his flag as a sort of deputy-
provisionary-sub-vice-pro-acting-consul of the British sovereign;
the poor fellow instantly changed his Greek head-gear for the cap
of consular dignity, and insisted upon accompanying me to the
ruins. I would not have stood this if I could have felt the faintest
gleam of my yesterday's pagan piety, but I had ceased to dream,
and had nothing to dread from any new disenchanters.

The ruins (the fragments of one or two prostrate pillars) lie
upon a promontory, bare, and unmystified by the gloom of surrounding groves. My Greek friend in his consular cap stood by,
respectfully waiting to see what turn my madness would take now
that I had come at last into the presence of the old stones. If you
have no taste for research, and can't affect to look for inscriptions,
there is some awkwardness in coming to the end of a merely
sentimental pilgrimage, when the feeling which impelled you has
gone. In such a strait you have nothing to do but to laugh the thing
off as well as you can, and, by the by, it is not a bad plan to turn
the conversation (or rather allow the natives to turn it) towards
the subject of hidden treasures; this is a topic on which they will
always speak with eagerness, and if they can fancy that you, too,
take an interest in such matters, they will not only begin to think
you perfectly sane, but will even, perhaps, give you credit for some
more than human powers of forcing dark earth to show you its
hoards of gold.

When we returned to Baffa, the vice-consul seized a club, with
the quietly determined air of a brave man resolved to do some
deed of note. He went into the yard adjoining his cottage, where
there were some thin, thoughtful, canting cocks, and serious, Low-
Church-looking hens, respectfully listening, and chickens of tender years so well brought up as scarcely to betray in their conduct
the careless levity of youth. The vice-consul stood for a moment
quite calm—collecting his strength; then suddenly he rushed into
the midst of the congregation, and began to deal death and de-

struction on all sides; he spared neither sex nor age. The dead and dying were immediately removed from the field of slaughter, and in less than an hour, I think, they were brought to the table, deeply buried in mounds of snowy rice.

My host was in all respects a fine, generous fellow; I could not bear the idea of impoverishing him by my visit, and my faithful Mysseri not only assured me that I might safely offer money to the vice-consul, but recommended that I should give no more to him than to "the others," meaning any other peasant. I felt, however, that there was something about the man, besides the flag and cap, which made me shrink from offering coin, and as I mounted my horse on departing, I gave him the only thing fit for a present that I happened to have with me, a rather handsome clasp-dagger, brought from Vienna. The poor fellow was ineffably grateful, and I had some difficulty in tearing myself from out of the reach of his thanks. At last I gave him what I supposed to be the last farewell, and rode on; but I had not gained more than about a hundred yards, when my host came bounding and shouting after me, with a goat's-milk cheese in his hand, and this (it was rather a burdensome gift) he fondly implored me to accept. In old times the shepherd of Theocritus, or (to speak less dishonestly) the shepherd of the "Poetae Graeci," sang his best song; I in this latter age presented my best dagger: and both of us received the same rustic reward.

It had been known that I should return to Limesol, and when I arrived there I found that a noble old Greek had been hospitably plotting to have me for his guest. I willingly accepted his offer. The day of my arrival happened to be my host's birthday, and during all the morning there was a constant influx of visitors who came to offer their congratulations. A few of these were men, but most of them were young, graceful girls. Almost all of them went through the ceremony with the utmost precision and formality: each in succession spoke her blessing, in the tone of a person repeating a set formula, then deferentially accepted the invitation to sit, partook of the proffered sweetmeats, and the cold glittering water, remained for a few minutes, either in silence or engaged in very thin conversation, then arose, delivered a second benediction, followed by an elaborate farewell, and departed.

The bewitching power attributed at this day to the women of Cyprus is curious in connection with the worship of the sweet goddess who called their isle her own; the Cypriote is not, I think, nearly so beautiful in face as the Ionian queens of Izmir, but she is tall, and slightly formed; there is a high-souled meaning and expression, a seeming consciousness of gentle empire, that speaks in the wavy lines of the shoulder, and winds itself like Cytherea's own cestus around the slender waist; then, the richly abounding hair (not enviously gathered together under the head-dress) descends the neck, and passes the waist in sumptuous braids. Of all other women with Grecian blood in their veins, the costume is graciously beautiful; but these, the maidens of Limesol—their robes are more gently, more sweetly imagined, and fall like Julia's cashmere in soft, luxurious folds. The common voice of the Levant allows that in face the women of Cyprus are less beautiful than their majestic sisters of Smyrna; and yet, says the Greek, he may trust himself to one and all of the bright cities of the Ægean, and may still weigh anchor with a heart entire, but that so surely as he ventures upon the enchanted isle of Cyprus, so surely will he know the rapture or the bitterness of love. The charm, they say, owes its power to that which the people call the astonishing "politics" (πολιτικη) of the women, meaning, I fancy, their tact and their witching ways. The word, however, plainly fails to express one half of that which the speakers would say. I have smiled to hear the Greek, with all his plenteousness of fancy, and all the wealth of his generous language, yet vainly struggling to describe the ineffable spell which the Parisians dispose of in their own smart way by a summary "Je ne sais quoi."

I went to Larnecca, the chief city of the isle, and over the water at last to Beirut.

CHAPTER
VIII

Lady Hester Stanhope.

B EIRUT on its land side is hemmed in by mountains. There
dwell the Druses.

Often enough I saw the ghostly images of the women, with their
exalted horns, stalking through the streets, and I saw, too, in
traveling, the affrighted groups of the mountaineers as they fled
before me, under the fear that my troop might be a company of
income-tax commissioners, or a press-gang enforcing the conscription for Mehemet Ali; but nearly all my knowledge of the
people, except in regard of their mere costume and outward appearance, is drawn from books and despatches;* to these last I
have the honor to refer you.

I received hospitable welcome at Beirut, from the Europeans as
well as from the Syrian Christians, and I soon discovered that in
all society the standing topic of interest was an Englishwoman,
Lady Hester Stanhope, who lived in an old convent on the Lebanon range, at the distance of about a day's journey from the town.
The lady's habit of refusing to see Europeans added the charm of
mystery to a character which, even without that aid, was sufficiently distinguished to command attention.

Many years of Lady Hester's early womanhood had been passed
with Lady Chatham at Burton Pynsent, and during that inglorious
period of the heroine's life, her commanding character, and (as
they would have called it in the language of those days) her "con-
descending kindness" towards my mother's family, had increased
in them those strong feelings of respect and attachment which her
rank and station alone would have easily won from people of the
middle class. You may suppose how deeply the quiet women in

* The papers laid before Parliament by the Foreign Office in 1840 and 1841.

Somersetshire must have been interested when they slowly learned by vague and uncertain tidings that the intrepid girl who had been used to break their vicious horses for them was reigning in sovereignty over the wandering tribes of western Asia! I know that her name was made almost as familiar to me in my childhood as the name of Robinson Crusoe; both were associated with the spirit of adventure, but whilst the imagined life of the castaway mariner never failed to seem glaringly real, the true story of the Englishwoman ruling over Arabs always sounded to me like a fable. I never had heard, nor indeed, I believe, had the rest of the world ever heard, anything like a certain account of the heroine's adventures. All I knew was that in one of the drawers, the delight of my childhood, along with the attar of roses and fragrant wonders from Hindustan, there were letters carefully treasured, and trifling presents which I was taught to think valuable because they had come from the Queen of the Desert—a Queen who dwelt in tents and reigned over wandering Arabs.

The subject, however, died away, and from the ending of my childhood up to the period of my arrival in the Levant, I had seldom even heard a mentioning of the Lady Hester Stanhope; but now wherever I went I was met by the name so familiar in sound, and yet so full of mystery from the vague, fairy-tale sort of idea which it brought to my mind. I heard it, too, connected with fresh wonders; for it was said that the woman was now acknowledged as an inspired being by the people of the mountains, and it was even hinted with horror that she claimed to be *more than a prophet*.

I felt at once that my mother would be sorry to hear that I had been within a day's ride of her early friend without offering to see her, and I therefore despatched a letter to the recluse, mentioning the maiden name of my mother (whose marriage was subsequent to Lady Hester's departure), and saying that if there existed on the part of her Ladyship any wish to hear of her old Somersetshire acquaintance, I should make a point of visiting her. My letter was sent by a foot messenger, who was to take an unlimited time for his journey, so that it was not, I think, until either the third or fourth day that the answer arrived. A couple of horsemen covered with mud suddenly dashed into the little court of the *locanda*, in which I was staying, bearing themselves as ostentatiously as though they were carrying a cartel from the Devil to the angel Michael. One of these (the other being his attendant) was an Italian by birth, (though now completely Orientalized), who lived in my lady's establishment as doctor nominally, but practically as an upper servant. He presented me a very kind and appropriate letter of invitation.

It happened that I was rather unwell at this time, so that I named a more distant day for my visit than I should otherwise have done, and after all, I did not start at the time fixed. Whilst still remaining at Beirut I received another letter from Lady Hester; this I will give you, for it shows that whatever the eccentricities of the writer may have been, she could at least be thoughtful and courteous:

SIR: I hope I shall be disappointed in seeing you on Wednesday, for the late rains have rendered the river Damoor, if not dangerous, at least very unpleasant to pass for a person who has been lately indisposed, for if the animal swims you would be immerged in the waters. The weather will probably change after the 21st of the moon, and after a couple of days the roads and the river will be passable; therefore I shall expect you either Saturday or Monday.

It will be a great satisfaction to me to have an opportunity of inquiring after your mother, who was a sweet, lovely girl when I knew her.

Believe me, sir,
Yours Sincerely,
HESTER LUCY STANHOPE.

Early one morning I started from Beirut. There are no established relays of horses in Syria, at least not in the line which I took, and therefore hire your cattle for the whole journey, or at all events for your journey to some large town. Under these circumstances you don't, of course, require a functionary empowered to compel the supply of horses, and you can therefore dispense with a Tatar. In other respects the mode of traveling through Syria differs very little from that which I have described as prevailing in Turkey. I hired my horses and mules for the whole of the journey from Beirut to Jerusalem. The owner of the beasts (he had a couple of fellows under him) was the most dignified member of my party; he was, indeed, a magnificent old man, and was called *shereef*, or "holy"—a title of honor, which, with the privilege of wearing the green turban, he well deserved, not only from the blood of the Prophet that glowed in his vains, but from the well-known sanctity of his life and the length of his blessed beard. Mysseri, of course, still traveled with me; but the Arabic was not one of the seven languages which he spoke so perfectly, and I was therefore obliged to hire another interpreter. I had no difficulty in finding a proper man for the purpose—one Demetrius, or, as he was always called, Dthemetri, a native of Zante, who had been tossed about by fortune in all directions. He spoke the Arabic well, and communicated with me in Italian. The man was a very zealous member of the Greek Church. He had been a tailor. He had a thoroughly Tatar countenance—a countenance so odd and ugly that it expressed all his griefs of body and mind in the most ludicrous manner imaginable; he embellished the natural carica-ture of his person by suspending about his neck and shoulders and waist quantities of little bundles and bags filled with treasures which he thought too valuable to be intrusted to the jerking of pack-saddles. The mule that fell to his lot on this journey every now and then forgetting that his rider was a saint, and remem-bering that he was a tailor, took a quiet roll upon the ground, and stretched his limbs calmly and lazily, like a good man awaiting a sermon. Dthemetri never got seriously hurt, but the subversion and dislocation of his bundles made him for the moment a sad spectacle of ruin, and when he regained his legs, his wrath with the mule was sure to be very amusing. He always addressed the beast in language implying that he, a Christian and saint, had been personally insulted and oppressed by a Mohammedan mule. Dthemetri, however, on the whole, proved to be a most able and capital servant; I suspected him of now and then leading me out of my way in order that he might have the opportunity of visiting the shrine of a saint, and on one occasion, as you will see by and by, he was induced, by religious motives, to commit a gross breach of duty; but putting these pious faults out of the question (and they were faults of the right side), he was always faithful and true to me.

I left Saide (the Sidon of ancient times) on my right, and about an hour, I think, before sunset, began to ascend one of the many low hills of Lebanon. On the summit before me was a broad, gray mass of irregular building, which from its position, as well as from the gloomy blankness of its walls, gave the idea of a neglected fortress; it had, in fact, been a convent of great size, and, like most of the religious houses in this part of the world, had been made strong enough for opposing an inert resistance to any mere casual band of assailants who might be unprovided with regular means of attack; this was the dwelling-place of Chatham's fiery grand-daughter.

The aspect of the first court I entered was such as to keep one in the idea of having to do with a fortress rather than a mere peaceable dwelling-place. A number of fierce-looking and ill-clad Albanian soldiers were hanging about the place inert, and striving as well as they could to bear the curse of tranquillity; two or three of them were smoking their chibouks, but the rest were lying torpidly upon the flat stones, like the bodies of departed brigands. I rode on to an inner part of the building, and at last, quitting my horses, was conducted through a doorway that led me at once from an open court into an apartment on the ground floor. As I entered, an Oriental figure in male costume approached me from the farther end of the room with many and profound bows, but the growing shades of evening prevented me from distinguishing the features of the personage who was receiving me with this solemn welcome. I had always, however, understood that Lady Hester Stanhope wore the male attire, and I began to utter in English the common civilities that seemed to be proper on the commencement of a visit by an uninspired mortal to a renowned prophetess; but the figure which I addressed only bowed so much

[65]

the more, prostrating itself almost to the ground, but speaking to me never a word. I feebly strived not to be outdone in gestures of respect, but presently my bowing opponent saw the error under which I was acting, and suddenly convinced me that, at all events, I was not *yet* in the presence of a superhuman being by declaring that he was far from being "Miladi," and was, in fact, nothing more or less godlike than the poor doctor who had brought his mistress's letters to Beirut.

Lady Hester, in the right spirit of hospitality, now sent and commanded me to repose for a while after the fatigues of my journey, and to dine.

The cuisine was of the Oriental kind, highly artifcial, and, as I thought, very good. I rejoiced, too, in the wine of the Lebanon.

After dinner the doctor arrived with Miladi's compliments, and an intimation that she would be happy to receive me if I were so disposed. It had now grown dark, and the rain was falling heavily, so that I got rather wet in following my guide through the open courts that I had to pass in order to reach the presence-chamber. At last I was ushered into a small chamber, protected from the drafts of air passing through the doorway by a folding-screen; passing this, I came alongside of a common European sofa; there sat the Lady Prophetess. She rose from her seat very formally, spoke to me a few words of welcome, pointed to a chair,—one already placed exactly opposite to her sofa, at a couple of yards' distance,—and remained standing up to the full of her majestic height, perfectly still and motionless, until I had taken my appointed place. She then resumed her seat, not packing herself up according to the mode of the Orientals, but allowing her feet to rest on the floor, or the footstool; at the moment of seating herself she covered her lap with a mass of loose white drapery. It occurred to me at the time that she did this in order to avoid the awkwardness of sitting in manifest trousers under the eye of an European, but I can hardly fancy now that, with her wilful nature, she would have brooked such a compromise as this.

The woman before me had exactly the person of a prophetess—not, indeed, of the divine sibyl imagined by Domenichino, so sweetly distracted betwixt love and mystery, but of a good, businesslike, practical prophetess, long used to the exercise of her sacred calling. I have been told by those who knew Lady Hester Stanhope in her youth that any notion of a resemblance betwixt her and the great Chatham must have been fanciful; but at the time of my seeing her, the large, commanding features of the gaunt woman, then sixty years old or more, certainly reminded me of the statesman that lay dying* in the House of Lords, according to Copley's picture. Her face was of the most astonishing whiteness;† she wore a large turban, made seemingly of pale cashmere shawls, and so disposed as to conceal the hair; her dress, from the chin down to the point at which it was concealed by the drapery on her lap, was a mass of white linen loosely folding—an ecclesiastical sort of affair, more like a surplice than any of those blessed creations which our souls love under the names of "dress," and "frock," and "bodice," and "collar," and "habit-shirt," and sweet "chemisette."

Such was the outward seeming of the personage that sat before me, and indeed she was almost bound by the fame of her actual achievements, as well as by her sublime pretensions, to look a little differently from the rest of womankind. There had been something of grandeur in her career. After the death of Lady Chatham, which happened in 1803, she lived under the roof of her uncle, the second Pitt, and when he resumed the government in 1804, she became the dispenser of much patronage, and sole Secretary of State, for the department of Treasury banquets. Not having seen the lady until late in her life, when she was fired with spiritual ambition, I can hardly fancy that she could have performed her political duties in the saloons of the minister with much of feminine sweetness and patience; I am told, however, that she managed matters very well indeed. Perhaps it was better for the lofty-minded leader of the House to have his reception-rooms guarded by this stately creature than by a merely clever and managing

---

* Historically *"fainting"*; the death did not occur until long afterwards.
† I am told that in youth she was exceedingly sallow.

woman; it was fitting that the wholesome awe with which he filled the minds of the country gentlemen should be aggravated by the presence of his majestic niece. But the end was approaching; the sun of Austerlitz showed the Czar madly sliding his splendid army, like a weaver's shuttle, from his right hand to his left, under the very eyes—the deep, gray, watchful eyes—of Napoleon. Before night came the coalition was a vain thing, meet for history, and the heart of its great author when the terrible tidings came to his ears was wrung with grief—fatal grief. In the bitterness of his despair, he cried out to his niece, and bid her, "ROLL UP THE MAP OF EUROPE!" There was a little more of suffering; and at last, with his swollen tongue (so they say) still muttering something for England, he died by the noblest of all sorrows.

Lady Hester, meeting the calamity in her own fierce way, seems to have scorned the poor island that had not enough of God's grace to keep the "heaven-sent" minister alive. I can hardly tell why it should be, but there is a longing for the East very commonly felt by proud people when goaded by sorrow. Lady Hester Stanhope obeyed this impulse. For some time, I believe, she was at Constantinople, and there her magnificence as well as her near alliance to the late minister gained her great influence. Afterwards she passed into Syria. The people of that country, excited by the achievements of Sir Sydney Smith, had begun to imagine the possibility of their land being occupied by the English, and many of them looked upon Lady Hester as a princess who came to prepare the way for the expected conquest. I don't know it from her own lips, or indeed from any certain authority, but I have been told that she began her connection with the Bedouins by making a large present of money (five hundred pounds, immense in piasters) to the sheik whose authority was recognized in the desert between Damascus and Palmyra. The prestige created by the rumors of her high and undefined rank, as well as of her wealth and corresponding magnificence, was well sustained by her imperious character and her dauntless bravery. Her influence increased. I never heard anything satisfactory as to the real extent or duration of her sway, but I understood that, for a time at least, she certainly exercised something like sovereignty amongst the wandering tribes.* And now that her earthly kingdom had passed away, she strove for spiritual power, and impiously dared, as it was said, to boast some mystic union with the very God of very God!

A couple of black slave girls came at a signal, and supplied their mistress, as well as myself, with lighted chibouks and coffee.

The custom of the East sanctions and almost commands some moments of silence whilst you are inhaling the first few breaths of the fragrant pipe. The pause was broken, I think, by my lady, who addressed to me some inquiries respecting my mother, and particularly as to her marriage; but before I had communicated any great amount of family facts the spirit of the prophetess kindled within her, and presently (though with all the skill of a woman of the world) she shuffled away the subject of poor, dear Somersetshire, and bounded onward into loftier spheres of thought.

My old acquaintance with some of "the twelve" enabled me to bear my part (of course a very humble one) in conversation relative to occult science. Milnes once spread a report that every gang of Gipsies was found, upon inquiry, to have come last from a place to the westward, and to be about to make the next move in an eastern direction; either, therefore, they were to be all gathered together towards the rising of the sun by the mysterious finger of Providence, or else they were to revolve round the globe for ever and ever. Both of these suppositions were highly gratifying, because they were both marvelous; and though the story on which they were founded plainly sprang from the inventive brain of a poet, no one had ever been so odiously statistical as to attempt a contradiciton of it. I now mentioned the story as a report to Lady Hester Stanhope, and asked her if it were true. I could not have touched upon any imaginable subject more deeply interesting

---

* This was my impression at the time of writing the above passage—an impression created by the popular and uncontradicted accounts of the matter, as well as by the tenor of Lady Hester's conversation. I have now some reason to think that I was deceived, and that her sway in the desert was much more limited than I had supposed. She seems to have had from the Bedouins a fair five hundred pounds' worth of respect, and not much more. [In third Edition.]

to my hearer—more closely akin to her habitual train of thinking. She immediately threw off all the restraint belonging to an interview with a stranger; and when she had received a few more similar proofs of my aptness for the marvelous, she went so far as to say that she would adopt me as her élève in occult science.

For hours and hours this wondrous white woman poured forth her speech, for the most part concerning sacred and profane mysteries; but every now and then she would stay her lofty flight and swoop down upon the world again. Whenever this happened I was interested in her conversation.

She adverted more than once to the period of her lost sway amongst the Arabs, and mentioned some of the circumstances that aided her in obtaining influence with the wandering tribes. The Bedouin, so often engaged in irregular warfare, strains his eyes to the horizon in search of a coming enemy just as habitually as the sailor keeps his "bright lookout" for a strange sail. In the absence of telescopes a far-reaching sight is highly valued, and Lady Hester had this power. She told me that on one occasion, when there was good reason to expect hostilities, a far-seeing Arab created great excitement in the camp by declaring that he could distinguish some moving objects upon the farthest point within the reach of his eyes. Lady Hester was consulted, and she instantly assured her comrades in arms that there were, indeed, a number of horses within sight, but that they were without riders. The assertion proved to be correct, and from that time forth her superiority over all others in respect of far sight remained undisputed.

Lady Hester related to me this other anecdote of her Arab life. It was when the heroic qualities of the Englishwoman were just beginning to be felt amongst the people of the desert that she was marching, one day, along with the forces of the tribe to which she had allied herself. She perceived that preparations for an engagement were going on, and upon her making inquiry as to the cause, the sheik at first affected mystery and concealment, but at last confessed that war had been declared against his tribe on account of his alliance with the English princess, and that they were now, unfortunately, about to be attacked by a very superior force. He made it appear that Lady Hester was the sole cause of hostility betwixt his tribe and the impending enemy, and that his sacred duty of protecting the Englishwoman whom he had admitted as his guest was the only obstacle which prevented an amicable settlement of the dispute. The sheik hinted that his tribe was likely to sustain an almost overwhelming blow, but, at the same time, declared that no fear of the consequences, however terrible to him and his whole people, should induce him to dream of abandoning his illustrious guest. The heroine instantly took her part; it was not for her to be a source of danger to her friends, but rather to her enemies, so she resolved to turn away from the people, and trust for help to none save only her haughty self. The sheiks affected to dissuade her from so rash a course, and fairly told her that although they (having been freed from her presence) would be able to make good terms for themselves, yet that there were no means of allaying the hostility felt towards her, and that the whole face of the desert would be swept by the horsemen of her enemies so carefully as to make her escape into other districts almost impossible. The brave woman was not to be moved by terrors of this kind, and bidding farewell to the tribe which had honored and protected her, she turned her horse's head and rode straight away, without friend or follower. Hours had elapsed, and for some time she had been alone in the center of the round horizon, when her quick eye perceived some horsemen in the distance. The party came nearer and nearer; soon it was plain that they were making towards her, and presently some hundreds of Bedouins, fully armed, galloped up to her, ferociously shouting, and apparently intending to take her life at the instant with their pointed spears. Her face at the time was covered with the yashmak, according to Eastern usage; but at the moment when the foremost of the horsemen had all but reached her with their spears, she stood up in her stirrups, withdrew the yashmak that veiled the terrors of her countenance, waved her arm slowly and disdainfully, and cried out with a loud voice, "Avaunt!"* The horsemen recoiled from her

---

* She spoke it, I dare say, in English; the words would not be the less effective for

glance, but not in terror. The threatening yells of assailants were suddenly changed for loud shouts of joy and admiration at the bravery of the stately Englishwoman, and festive gunshots were fired on all sides around her honored head. The truth was that the party belonged to the tribe with which she had allied herself, and that the threatened attack, as well as the pretended apprehension of an engagement, had been contrived for the mere purpose of testing her courage. The day ended in a great feast prepared to do honor to the heroine, and from that time her power over the minds of the people grew rapidly. Lady Hester related this story with great spirit, and I recollect that she put up her yashmak for a moment, in order to give me a better idea of the effect which she produced by suddenly revealing the awfulness of her countenance.

With respect to her then present mode of life, Lady Hester informed me that for her sin she had subjected herself during many years to severe penance, and that her self-denial had not been without its reward. "Vain and false," said she, "is all the pretended knowledge of the Europeans. Their doctors will tell you that the drinking of milk gives yellowness to the complexion; milk is my only food, and you see if my face is not white." Her abstinence from food intellectual was carried as far as her physical fasting; she never, she said, looked upon a book nor a newspaper, but trusted alone to the stars for her sublime knowledge; she usually passed the nights in communing with these heavenly teachers, and lay at rest during the daytime. She spoke with great contempt of the frivolity and benighted ignorance of the modern Europeans, and mentioned, in proof of this, that they were not only untaught in astrology, but were unacquainted with the common and every-day phenomena produced by magic art. She spoke as if she would make me understand that all sorcerous spells were completely at her command, but that the exercise of such powers would be derogatory to her high rank in the heavenly kingdom. She said that the spell by which the face of an absent person is

---

being spoken in an unknown tongue. Lady Hester, I believe, never learned to speak the Arabic with a perfect accent.

thrown upon a mirror was within the reach of the humblest and most contemptible magicians, but that the practice of such like arts was unholy as well as vulgar.

We spoke of the bending twig by which it is said precious metals may be discovered. In relation to this the prophetess told me a story rather against herself, and inconsistent with the notion of her being perfect in her science; but I think that she mentioned the facts as having happened before she attained to the great spiritual authority which she now arrogated. She told me that vast treasures were known to exit in a situation which she mentioned, if I rightly remember, as being near Suez; that Napoleon, profanely brave, thrust his arm into the cave containing the coveted gold and that instantly his flesh became palsied; but the youthful hero (for she said he was great in his generation) was not to be thus daunted. He fell back characteristically upon his brazen resources, and ordered up his artillery. Yet man could not strive with demons, and Napoleon was foiled. In latter years came Ibrahim Pasha, with heavy guns and wicked spells to boot; but the infernal guardians of the treasure were too strong for him. It was after this that Lady Hester passed by the spot, and she described, with animated gesture, the force and energy with which the divining-twig had suddenly leaped in her hands. She ordered excavations, and no demons opposed her enterprise; the vast chest in which the treasure had been deposited was at length discovered, but, lo and behold! it was full of pebbles! She said, however, that the times were approaching in which the hidden treasures of the earth would become available to those who had true knowledge.

Speaking of Ibrahim Pasha, Lady Hester said that he was a bold, bad man, and was possessed of some of those common and wicked magical arts upon which she looked down with so much contempt; she said, for instance, that Ibrahim's life was charmed against balls and steel, and that after a battle he loosened the folds of his shawl and shook out the bullets like dust.

It seems that the St. Simonians once made overtures to Lady Hester; she told me that the Père Enfantin (the chief of the sect) had sent her a service of plate, but that she had declined to receive

it; she delivered a prediction as to the probability of the St. Simonians finding the "mystic mother," and this she did in a way which
would amuse you; unfortunately I am not at liberty to mention
this part of the woman's prophecies; why, I cannot tell, but so it
is, that she bound me to eternal secrecy.

Lady Hester told me that since her residence at Djoun she had
been attacked by an illness so severe as to render her for a long
time perfectly helpless; all her attendants fled, and left her to
perish. Whilst she lay thus alone, and quite unable to rise, robbers
came, and carried away her property;* she told me that they
actually unroofed a great part of the building, and employed engines with pulleys for the purpose of hoisting out such of her
valuables as were too bulky to pass through doors. It would seem
that before this catastrophe Lady Hester had been rich in the
possession of Eastern luxuries, for she told me that when the
chiefs of the Ottoman force took refuge with her after the fall of
Acre, they brought their wives also in great numbers; to all of
these Lady Hester, as she said, presented magnificent dresses, but
her generosity occasioned strife only instead of gratitude, for every
woman who fancied her present less splendid than that of another
with equal or less pretension became absolutely furious; all these
audacious guests had now been got rid of, but the Albanian soldiers who had taken refuge with Lady Hester at the same time still
remained under her protection.

In truth, this half-ruined convent, guarded by the proud heart of
an English gentlewoman, was the only spot throughout all Syria

---

* The proceedings thus described to me by Lady Hester as having taken place
during her illness were afterwards re-enacted at the time of her death. Since I wrote
the words to which this note is appended, I received from Warburton an interesting
account of the heroine's death, or rather of the circumstances attending the discovery of the event; and I caused it to be printed in the former editions of this
work. I must now give up the borrowed ornament, and omit my extract from my
friend's letter, for the rightful owner has reprinted it in "The Crescent and the
Cross." I know what a sacrifice I am making, for in noticing the first edition of this
book, reviewers turned aside from the text to the note, and remarked upon the
interesting information which Warburton's letter contained, and the descriptive
force with which it was written.

and Palestine in which the will of Mehemet Ali and his fierce
lieutenant was not the law. More than once had the Pasha of
Egypt commanded that Ibrahim should have the Albanians delivered up to him, but this white woman of the mountain (grown
classical, not by books, but by very pride) answered only with a
disdainful invitation to "come and take them." Whether it was
that Ibrahim was acted upon by any superstitious dread of interfering with the prophetess (a notion not at all incompatible with
his character as an able Oriental commander), or that he feared
the ridicule of putting himself in collision with a gentlewoman, he
certainly never ventured to attack the sanctuary, and so long as
Chatham's granddaughter breathed a breath of life, there was
always this one hillock, and that, too, in the midst of a most
populous district, which stood out and kept its freedom. Mehemet
Ali used to say, I am told, that the Englishwoman had given him
more trouble than all the insurgent people of Syria and Palestine.

The prophetess announced to me that we were upon the eve of
a stupendous convulsion, which would destroy the then recognized value of all property upon earth, and declaring that those
only who should be in the East at the time of the great change
could hope for greatness in the new life that was then close at
hand, she advised me, whilst there was yet time, to dispose of my
property in poor, frail England, and gain a station in Asia; she told
me that, after leaving her, I should go into Egypt, but that in a
little while I should return into Syria. I secretly smiled at this last
prophecy as a "bad shot," because I had fully determined, after
visiting the Pyramids, to take ship from Alexandria for Greece.
But men struggle vainly in the meshes of their destiny; the unbe-
lieved Cassandra was right, after all; the plague came, and the
necessity of avoiding the quarantine detention to which I should
have been subjected if I had sailed from Alexandria forced me to
alter my route; I went down into Egypt, and stayed there for a
time, and then crossed the desert once more, and came back to the
mountains of the Lebanon exactly as the prophetess had foretold.

Lady Hester talked to me long and earnestly on the subject of
religion, announcing that the Messiah was yet to come; she strived

to impress me with the vanity and the falseness of all European creeds, as well as with a sense of her own spiritual greatness: throughout her conversation upon these high topics she carefully insinuated, without actually asserting, her heavenly rank.

Amongst other much more marvelous powers, the lady claimed one which most women have, more or less—namely, that of reading men's characters in their faces; she examined the line of my features very attentively, and told me the result: this, however, I mean to keep hidden.

One favored subject of discourse was that of "race": upon this she was very diffuse and yet rather mysterious; she set great value upon the ancient French* (not Norman blood, for that she vilified), but professed to despise our English notion of "an old family." She had a vast idea of the Cornish miners, on account of their race, and said if she chose she could give me the means of rousing them to the most tremendous enthusiasm.

Such are the topics on which the lady mainly conversed, but very often she would descend to more worldly chat, and then she was no longer the prophetess, but the sort of woman that you sometimes see, I am told, in London drawing-rooms—cool, decisive in manner, unsparing of enemies, full of audacious fun, and saying the downright things that the sheepish society around her is afraid to utter. I am told that Lady Hester was in her youth a capital mimic, and she showed me that not all the queenly dullness to which she had condemned herself, not all her fasting and solitude, had destroyed this terrible power. The first whom she crucified in my presence was poor Lord Byron; she had seen him, it appeared, I know not where, soon after his arrival in the East, and was vastly amused at his little affectations; he had picked up a few

---

* In a letter which I afterwards received from Lady Hester, she mentioned incidentally Lord Hardwicke, and said that he was "the kindest-hearted man existing,—a most manly, firm character. He comes from a good breed,—all the Yorkes excellent, with *ancient* French blood in their veins." The underscoring of the word "ancient" is by the writer of the letter, who had certainly no great love or veneration for the French of the present day: she did not consider them as descended from her favorite stock.

sentences of the Romaic, and with these he affected to give orders to his Greek servant in a *ton d'apameibomenos* style; I can't tell whether Lady Hester's mimicry of the bard was at all close, but it was amusing; she attributed to him a curiously coxcombical lisp.

Another person whose style of speaking the lady took off very amusingly was one who would scarcely object to suffer by the side of Lord Byron—I mean Lamartine. The peculiarity which attracted her ridicule was an over-refinement of manner. According to my lady's imitation of Lamartine (I have never seen him myself), he had none of the violent grimace of his countrymen, and not even their usual way of talking, but rather bore himself mincingly, like the humbler sort of English dandy.*

Lady Hester seems to have heartily despised everything approaching to exquisiteness; she told me, by the by (and her opinion upon that subject is worth having), that a downright manner, amounting even to brusqueness, is more effective than any other with the Oriental; and that amongst the English, of all ranks and all classes, there is no man so attractive to the Orientals, no man who can negotiate with them half so effectively, as a good, honest, open-hearted, and positive naval officer of the old school.

I have told you, I think, that Lady Hester could deal fiercely with those she hated; one man above all others (he is now uprooted from society) she blasted with her wrath; you would have thought that in the scornfulness of her nature she must have sprung upon her foe with more of fierceness than of skill, but this was not so, for with all the force and vehemence of her invective, she displayed a sober, patient, and minute attention to the details of vituperation, which contributed to its success a thousand times more than mere violence.

---

* It is said that deaf people can hear what is said concerning themselves, and it would seem that those who live without books or newspapers know all that is written about them. Lady Hester Stanhope, though not admitting a book or newspaper into her fortress, seems to have known the way in which M. Lamartine mentioned her in his book, for in a letter which she wrote to me after my return to England she says: "Although neglected, as Monsieur Le M." (referring, as I believe, to M. Lamartine) "describes, and without books, yet my head is organized to supply the want of them, as well as acquired knowledge."

During the hours that this sort of conversation, or rather discourse, was going on our chibouks were from time to time replenished, and the lady as well as I continued to smoke with little or no intermission until the interview ended. I think that the fragrant fumes of the latakia must have helped to keep me on my good behavior as a patient disciple of the prophetess.

It was not till after midnight that my visit for the evening came to an end; when I quitted my seat the lady rose and stood up in the same formal attitude (almost that of a soldier in a state of "attention") which she had assumed on my entrance; at the same time she pushed the loose drapery from her lap and let it fall down upon the floor.

The next morning, after breakfast, I was visited by my lady's secretary—the only European, except the doctor, whom she retained in her household. This secretary, like the doctor, was Italian, but he preserved more signs of European dress and European pretensions than his medical fellow-slave. He spoke little or no English, though he wrote it pretty well, having been formerly employed in a mercantile house connected with England. The poor fellow was in an unhappy state of mind. In order to make you understand the extent of his spiritual anxieties, I ought to have told you that the doctor (who had sunk into the complete Asiatic, and had condescended accordingly to the performance of even menial services) had adopted the common faith of all the neighboring people, and had become a firm and happy believer in the divine power of his mistress. Not so the secretary: when I had strolled with him to such a distance from being overheard by human ears, he told me in a hollow voice, trembling with emotion, that there were times at which he doubted the divinity of Miladi. I said nothing to encourage the poor fellow in his frightful state of skepticism, for I saw that, if indulged, it might end in positive infidelity. Lady Hester, it seemed, had rather arbitrarily abridged the amusements of her secretary, and especially she had forbidden him from shooting small birds on the mountain side. This oppression had aroused in him a spirit of inquiry that might end fatally— perhaps for himself, perhaps for the "religion of the place."

The secretary told me that his mistress was strongly disliked by the surrounding people, and that she oppressed them a good deal by her exactions. I know not whether this statement had any truth in it; but whether it was or was not well founded, it is certain that in Eastern countries hate and veneration are very commonly felt for the same object, and the general belief in the superhuman power of this wonderful white lady, her resolute and imperious character, and above all, perhaps, her fierce Albanians (not backward to obey an order for the sacking of a village), inspired sincere respect amongst the surrounding inhabitants. Now the being "respected" amongst Orientals is not an empty or merely honorary distinction, but carries with it a clear right to take your neighbor's corn, his cattle, his eggs, and his honey, and almost anything that is his, except his wives. This law was acted upon by the Princess of Djoun, and her establishment was supplied by contributions apportioned amongst the nearest villages.

I understood that the Albanians (restrained, I suppose, by the dread of being delivered up to Ibrahim) had not given any very troublesome proofs of their unruly natures. The secretary told me that their rations, including a small allowance of coffee and tobacco, were served out to them with tolerable regularity.

I asked the secretary how Lady Hester was off for horses, and said that I would take a look at the stable; the man did not raise any opposition to my proposal, and affected no mystery about the matter, but said that the only two steeds which then belonged to Miladi were of a very humble sort; this answer, and a storm of rain then beginning to descend, prevented me at the time from undertaking my journey to the stables, and I don't know that I ever thought of the matter afterwards until my return to England, when I saw Lamartine's eye-witnessing account of the strange horse saddled, as he pretends, by the hands of his Maker!

When I returned to my room (this, as my hostess told me, was the only one in the whole building that kept out the rain) Lady Hester sent to say she would be glad to receive me again; I was rather surprised at this, for I had understood that she reposed during the day, and it was now little later than noon. "Really,"

[79]

said she, when I had taken my seat and my pipe, "we were together for hours last night, and still I have heard nothing at all of
my old friends; now *do* tell me something of your dear mother and
her sister; I never knew your father—it was after I left Burton
Pynsent that your mother married." I began to make slow answer,
but my questioner soon went off again to topics more sublime, so
that this second interview, though it lasted two or three hours,
was all occupied by the same sort of varied discourse as that which
I have been describing.

In the course of the afternoon the captain of an English man-
of-war arrived at Djoun, and Lady Hester determined to receive
him for the same reason as that which had induced her to allow
my visit—namely, an early intimacy with his family. I and the new
visitor—he was a pleasant, amusing man—dined together, and we
were afterwards invited to the presence of my lady, and with her
we sat smoking till midnight. The conversation turned chiefly, I
think, upon magical science. I had determined to be off at an early
hour the next morning, and so at the end of this interview I bade
my lady farewell. With her parting words she once more advised
me to abandon Europe and seek my reward in the East, and she
urged me, too, to give the like counsels to my father, and tell him
that *"she had said it."*

Lady Hester's unholy claim to supremacy in the spiritual kingdom was, no doubt, the suggestion of fierce and inordinate pride
most perilously akin to madness; but I am quite sure that the mind
of the woman was too strong to be thoroughly overcome by even
this potent feeling. I plainly saw that she was not an unhesitating
follower of her own system, and I even fancied that I could distinguish the brief moments during which she contrived to believe
in herself from those long and less happy intervals in which her
own reason was too strong for her.

As for the lady's faith in astrology and magic science, you are
not for a moment to suppose that this implied any aberration of
intellect. She believed these things in common with those around
her, and it could scarcely be otherwise, for she seldom spoke to
anybody, except crazy old dervishes, who at once received her

alms and fostered her extravagances, and even when (as on the occasion of my visit) she was brought into contact with a person entertaining different notions, she still remained uncontradicted. This entourage and the habit of fasting from books and newspapers were quite enough to make her a facile recipient of any marvelous story.

I think that in England we scarcely acknowledge to ourselves how much we owe to the wise and watchful press which presides over the formation of our opinions, and which brings about this splendid result—namely, that in matters of belief the humblest of us are lifted up to the level of the most sagacious, so that really a simple cornet in the Blues is no more likely to entertain a foolish belief about ghosts, or witchcraft, or any other supernatural topic, than the Lord High Chancellor, or the Leader of the House of Commons. How different is the intellectual régime of Eastern countries! In Syria and Palestine and Egypt you might as well dispute the efficacy of grass or grain as of magic. There is no controversy about the matter. The effect of this, the unanimous belief of an ignorant people, upon the mind of a stranger is extremely curious and well worth noticing. A man coming freshly from Europe is at first proof against the nonsense with which he is assailed; but often it happens that after a little while the social atmosphere of Asia will begin to infect him, and if he has been unaccustomed to the cunning of fence by which reason prepares the means of guarding herself against fallacy, he will yield himself at last to the faith of those around him, and this he will do by sympathy, it would seem, rather than from conviction. I have been much interested in observing that the mere "practical man," however skilful and shrewd in his own way, has not the kind of power that will enable him to resist the gradual impression made upon his mind by the common opinion of those whom he sees and hears from day to day. Even amongst the English, though their good sense and sound religious knowledge would be likely to guard them from error, I have known the calculating merchant, the inquisitive traveler, and the post-captain, with his bright, wakeful eye of command,—I have known all these surrender themselves to the *really* magic-like influence of other people's minds; their language at first is that they are "staggered," leading you by that expression to suppose that they had been witnesses to some phenomenon which it was very difficult to account for otherwise than by supernatural causes; but when I have questioned further, I have always found that these "staggering" wonders were not even specious enough to be looked upon as good "tricks." A man in England who gained his whole livelihood as a conjurer would soon be starved to death if he could perform no better miracles than those which are wrought with so much effect in Syria and Egypt; *sometimes*, no doubt, a magician will make a good hit (Sir John once said a "good thing"), but all such successes range, of course, under the head of mere "tentative miracles," as distinguished by the strong-brained Paley.

CHAPTER
IX

The Sanctuary.

I CROSSED the plain of Esdraelon, and entered amongst the hills of beautiful Galilee. It was at sunset that my path brought me sharply round into the gorge of a little valley, and close upon a gray mass of dwellings that lay happily nestled in the lap of the mountain. There was one only shining point still touched with the light of the sun, who had set for all besides: a brave sign this to "holy" Shereef and the rest of my Moslem men, for the one glittering summit was the head of a minaret, and the rest of the seeming village that had veiled itself so meekly under the shades of evening was Christian Nazareth!

Within the precincts of the Latin convent there stands the great Catholic church which incloses the Sanctuary—the dwelling of the Blessed Virgin.* This is a grotto of about ten feet either way, forming a little chapel or recess, and reached by descending steps. It is decorated with splendor; on the left hand a column of granite

---

* The Greek Church does not recognize this as the true Sanctuary, and many Protestants look upon all the traditions by which it is attempted to ascertain the holy places of Palestine as utterly fabulous. For myself, I do not mean either to affirm or deny the correctness of the opinion which has fixed upon this as the true site, but merely to mention it as a belief entertained, without question, by my brethren of the Latin Church whose guest I was at the time. It would be a great aggravation of the trouble of writing about these matters if I were to stop in the midst of every sentence for the purpose of saying "so-called," or "so it is said," and would besides sound very ungraciously; yet I am anxious to be literally true in all I write. Now, thus it is that I mean to get over my difficulty. Whenever in this great bundle of papers, or book (if book it is to be), you see any words about matters of religion which would seem to involve the assertion of my own opinion, you are to understand me just as if one or other of the qualifying phrases above mentioned had been actually inserted in every sentence. My general direction for you to construe me thus will render all that I write as strictly and actually true as if I had every time lugged in a formal declaration of the fact that I was merely expressing the notions of other people.

hangs from the top of the grotto to within a few feet of the ground; immediately beneath another column of the same size rises from the ground as if to meet the one above; but between this and the suspended pillar there is an interval of more than a foot; these fragments once formed a single column, on which the angel leant when he spoke and told to Mary the mystery of her awful blessedness. Hard by, near the altar, the Holy Virgin was kneeling.

I had been journeying, cheerily indeed, for the voices of my followers were ever within my hearing, but yet, as it were, in solitude, for I had no comrade to whet the edge of my reason or wake me from my noon-day dreams. I was left all alone to be taught and swayed by the beautiful circumstances of Palestine traveling, by the clime and the land and the name of the land with all its mighty import, by the glittering freshness of the sward, and the abounding masses of flowers that furnished my sumptuous pathway, by the bracing and fragrant air that seemed to poise me in my saddle and to lift me along as a planet appointed to glide through space.

And the end of my journey was Nazareth—the home of the Blessed Virgin! In the first dawn of my manhood the old painters of Italy had taught me their dangerous worship of the beauty that is more than mortal, but those images all seemed shadowy now, and floated before me so dimly, the one overcasting the other, that they left me no one sweet idol on which I could look, and look again, and say, "Maria mia!" Yet they left me more than an idol—they left me (for to them I am wont to trace it) a faint apprehension of beauty not compassed with lines and shadows—they touched me (forgive, proud Marie of Anjou!)—they touched me with a faith in loveliness transcending mortal shapes.

I came to Nazareth and was led from the convent to the Sanctuary. Long fasting will sometimes heat a man's brain and draw him away out of the world, will disturb his judgment, confuse his notions of right and wrong, and weaken his power of choosing the right. I had fasted, perhaps too long, for I was fevered with the zeal of an insane devotion to the Heavenly Queen of Christendom. But I knew the feebleness of this gentle malady, and knew how easily my watchful reason, if ever so slightly provoked, would drag me back to life; let there but come one chilling breath of the outer world, and all this loving piety would cower and fly before the sound of my own bitter laugh. And so as I went I trod tenderly, not looking to the right nor to the left, but bending my eyes to the ground.

The attending friar served me well: he led me down quietly and all but silently to the Virgin's home. The mystic air was so burned with the consuming flames of the altar, and so laden with incense, that my chest labored strongly and heaved with luscious pain. There—there, with beating heart, the Virgin knelt and listened! I strived to grasp and hold with my riveted eyes some one of the feigned Madonnas, but of all the heaven-lit faces imagined by men, there was none that would abide with me in this the very Sanctuary. Impatient of vacancy, I grew madly strong against nature, and if by some awful spell, some impious rite, I could— Oh! most sweet religion that bid me fear God, and be pious, and yet not cease from loving! Religion and gracious custom commanded me that I fall down loyally and kiss the rock that blessed Mary pressed. With a half consciousness, with the semblance of a thrilling hope that I was plunging deep, deep into my first knowledge of some most holy mystery, or of some new, rapturous, and daring sin, I knelt and bowed down my face till I met the smooth rock with my lips. One moment—one moment—my heart, or some old pagan demon within me, woke up and fiercely bounded; my bosom was lifted and swung, as though I had touched her warm robe. One moment—one more, and then the fever had left me. I rose from my knees. I felt hopelessly sane. The mere world reappeared. My good old monk was there, dangling his key with listless patience, and as he guided me from the church and talked of the refectory and the coming repast, I listened to his words with some attention and pleasure.

CHAPTER
X

The monks of Palestine.

WHENEVER you come back to me from Palestine, we will find some "golden wine"* of Lebanon, that we may celebrate with apt libations the monks of the Holy Land, and though the poor fellows be theoretically "dead to the world," we will drink to every man of them a good, long life and a merry one! Graceless is the traveler who forgets his obligations to these saints upon earth, little love has he for merry Christendom if he has not rejoiced with great joy to find in the very midst of water-drinking infidels those lowly monasteries, where the blessed juice of the grape is quaffed in peace. Aye, aye! We will fill our glasses till they look like cups of amber, and drink profoundly to our gracious hosts in Palestine.

Christianity permits and sanctions the drinking of wine, and of all the holy brethren in Palestine there are none who hold fast to this gladsome rite so strenuously as the monks of Damascus; not that they are more zealous Christians than the rest of their fellows in the Holy Land, but that they have better wine. Whilst I was at Damascus I had my quarters at the Franciscan convent there, and very soon after my arrival I asked one of the monks to let me know something of the spots that deserved to be seen: I made my inquiry in reference to the associations with which the city had been hallowed by the sojourn and adventures of St. Paul. "There is nothing in all Damascus," said the good man, "half so well worth seeing as our cellars," and forthwith he invited me to go, see, and admire the long range of liquid treasure that he and his brethren had laid up for themselves on earth. And these, I soon found, were not as the treasures of the miser that lie in unprofit-

---

* "Vino d'oro."

able disuse, for day by day, and hour by hour, the golden juice ascended from the dark recesses of the cellar to the uppermost brains of the friars. Dear old fellows! in the midst of that solemn land their Christian laughter rang loudly and merrily, their eyes kept flashing with joyful fire, and their heavy woolen petticoats could no more weigh down the springiness of their paces than the filmy gauze of a danseuse can clog her bounding step.

You would be likely enough to fancy that these monastics are men who have retired to the sacred sites of Palestine from an enthusiastic longing to devote themselves to the exercise of religion in the midst of the very land on which its first seeds were cast, and this is partially, at least, the case with the monks of the Greek Church; but it is not with enthusiasts that the Catholic establishments are filled. The monks of the Latin convents are chiefly persons of the peasant class from Italy and Spain, who have been handed over to these remote asylums by order of their ecclesiastical superiors, and can no more account for their being in the Holy Land than men of marching regiments can explain why they are in "stupid quarters." I believe that these monks are for the most part well conducted men, punctual in their ceremonial duties, and altogether humble-minded Christians; their humility is not at all misplaced, for you see at a glance (poor fellows!) that they belong to the "lag remove" of the human race. If the taking of the cowl does not imply a complete renouncement of the world, it is, at least in these days, a thorough farewell to every kind of useful and entertaining knowledge, and accordingly the low bestial brow and the animal caste of those almost Bourbon features show plainly enough that all the intellectual vanities of life have been really and truly abandoned. But it is hard to quench altogether the spirit of inquiry that stirs in the human breast, and accordingly these monks inquire,—they are *always* inquiring— inquiring for "news"! Poor fellows! they could scarcely have yielded themselves to the sway of any passion more difficult of gratification, for they have no means of communicating with the busy world, except through European travelers; and these, in consequence, I suppose, of that restlessness and irritability that generally haunt their wanderings, seem to have always avoided the bore of giving any information to their hosts; as for me, I am more patient and good-natured, and when I found that the kind monks who gathered round me at Nazareth were longing to know the real truth about General Bonaparte who had recoiled from the siege of Acre, I softened my heart down to the good humor of Herodotus, and calmly began to "sing history," telling my eager hearers of the French Empire and the greatness of its glory, and of Waterloo, and the fall of Napoleon! Now my story of this marvelous ignorance on the part of the poor monks is one upon which (though depending on my own testimony) I look "with considerable suspicion"; it is quite true (how silly it would be to *invent* anything so witless!), and yet I think I could satisfy the mind of a "reasonable man" that it is false. Many of the older monks must have been in Europe at the time when the Italy and the Spain from which they came were in act of taking their French lessons, or had parted so lately with their teachers that not to know of "the Emperor" was impossible, and these men could scarcely, therefore, have failed to bring with them some tidings of Napoleon's career. Yet I say that that which I have written is true, the one who believes because I have said it will be right (she always is), whilst poor Mr. "Reasonable Man," who is convinced by the weight of my argument, will be completely deceived.

In Spanish politics, however, the monks are better instructed; the revenues of the monasteries, which had been principally supplied by the bounty of their most Catholic Majesties, have been withheld since Ferdinand's death, and the interests of these establishments being thus closely involved in the destinies of Spain, it is not wonderful that the brethren should be a little more knowing in Spanish affairs than in other branches of history. Besides, a large proportion of the monks were natives of the Peninsula; to these, I remember, Mysseri's familiarity with the Spanish language and character was a source of immense delight; they were always gathering around him, and it seemed to me that they treasured like gold the few Castilian words which he deigned to spare them.

The monks do a world of good in their way, and there can be

no doubting that previously to the arrival of Bishop Alexander, with his numerous young family and his pretty English nurse-maids, they were the chief propagandists of Christianity in Palestine. My old friends of the Franciscan convent at Jerusalem some time since gave proof of their goodness by delivering themselves up to the peril of death for the sake of duty. When I was their guest they were forty, I believe, in number, and I don't recollect that there was one of them whom I should have looked upon as a desirable life-holder of any property to which I might be entitled in expectancy. Yet these forty were reduced in a few days to nineteen; the plague was the messenger that summoned them to a taste of real death, but the circumstances under which they perished are rather curious, and though I have no authority for the story except an Italian newspaper, I harbor no doubt of its truth, for the facts were detailed with minuteness, and strictly corresponded with all that I knew of the poor fellows to whom they related.

It was about three months after the time of my leaving Jerusalem that the plague set his spotted foot on the Holy City. The monks felt great alarm; they did not shrink from their duty, but for its performance they chose a plan most sadly well fitted for bringing down upon them the very death which they were striving to ward off. They imagined themselves almost safe so long as they remained within their walls; but then it was quite needful that the Catholic Christians of the place, who had always looked to the convent for the supply of their spiritual wants, should receive the aids of religion in the hour of death. A single monk, therefore, was chosen either by lot or by some other fair appeal to Destiny; being thus singled out, he was to go forth into the plague-stricken city, and to perform with exactness his priestly duties; then he was to return, not to the interior of the convent, for fear of infecting his brethren, but to a detached building (which I remember) belonging to the establishment, but at some little distance from the inhabited rooms; he was provided with a bell, and at a certain hour in the morning he was ordered to ring it, *if he could:* but if no sound was heard at the appointed time, then knew his brethren that he was either delirious or dead, and another martyr was sent forth to take his place. In this way twenty-one of the monks were carried off. One cannot well fail to admire the steadiness with which the dismal scheme was carried through; but if there be any truth in the notion that disease may be invited by a frightening imagination, it is difficult to conceive a more dangerous plan than that which was chosen by these poor fellows. The anxiety with which they must have expected each day the sound of the bell, the silence that reigned instead of it, and then the drawing of the lots (the odds against death being one point lower than yesterday) and the going forth of the newly doomed man,—all this must have widened the gulf that opens to the shades below. When his victim had already suffered so much of mental torture, it was but easy work for big, bullying pestilence to follow a forlorn monk from the beds of the dying, and wrench away his life from him as he lay all alone in an outhouse.

In most—I believe in all—of the Holy Land convents there are two personages so strangely raised above their brethren in all that dignifies humanity, that their bearing the same habit, their dwelling under the same roof, their worshiping the same God (consistent as all this is with the spirit of their religion), yet strikes the mind with a sense of wondrous incongruity. The men I speak of are the "Padre Superiore" and the "Padre Missionario." The former is the supreme and absolute governor of the establishment over which he is appointed to rule; the latter is intrusted with the more active of the spiritual duties attaching to the pilgrim church. He is the shepherd of the good Catholic flock whose pasture is prepared in the midst of Mussulmans and schismatics; he keeps the light of the true faith ever vividly before their eyes, reproves their vices, supports them in their good resolves, consoles them in their afflictions, and teaches them to hate the Greek Church. Such are his labors, and you may conceive that great tact must be needed for conducting with success the spiritual interests of the Church under circumstances so odd as those which surround it in Palestine.

But the position of the Padre Superiore is still more delicate: he is almost unceasingly in treaty with the powers that be, and the worldly prosperity of the whole establishment is in great measure dependent upon the extent of diplomatic skill which he can employ in its favor. I know not from what class of churchmen these personages are chosen, for there is a mystery attending their origin and the circumstance of their being stationed in these convents which Rome does not suffer to be penetrated: I have heard it said that they are men of great note and, perhaps, of too high ambition in the Catholic hierarchy, who, having fallen under the grave censure of the Church, are banished for fixed periods to these distant monasteries. I believe that the term during which they are condemned to remain in the Holy Land is from eight to twelve years. By the natives of the country as well as by the rest of the brethren they are looked upon as superior beings, and rightly, too, for nature seems to have crowned them in her own true way.

The chief of the Jerusalem convent was a noble creature; his worldly and spiritual authority seemed to have surrounded him, as it were, with a kind of "court," and the manly gracefulness of his bearing did honor to the throne he filled. There were no lords of the bedchamber, and no gold sticks and stones in waiting, yet everybody who approached him looked as though he were being "presented." Every interview which he granted wore the air of an "audience"; the brethren, as often as they came near, bowed low and kissed his hand; and if he went out, the Catholics of the place that hovered about the convent would crowd around him with devout affection, and almost scramble for the blessing which his touch could give. He bore his honors all serenely, as though calmly conscious of his power to "bind and to loose."

CHAPTER
XI

Galilee.

N EITHER old "Sacred"* himself nor any of his helpers knew
the road which I meant to take from Nazareth to the Sea of
Galilee, and from thence to Jerusalem, so I was forced to add
another to my party by hiring a guide. The associations of Nazareth, as well as my kind feeling towards the hospitable monks,
whose guest I had been, inclined me to set at naught the advice
which I had received against employing Christians. I accordingly
engaged a lithe, active young Nazarene who was recommended to
me by the monks, and who affected to be familiar with the line of
country through which I intended to pass. My disregard of the
popular prejudices against Christians was not justified in this particular instance by the result of my choice. This you will see by and
by.

I passed by Cana and the house of the marriage feast prolonged
by miraculous wine. I came to the field in which our Saviour had
rebuked the Scotch Sabbath-keepers of that period by suffering his
disciples to pluck corn on the Lord's day. I rode over the ground
where the fainting multitude had been fed, and they showed me
some massive fragments—the relics, they said, of that wondrous
banquet now turned into stone. The petrifaction was most complete.

I ascended the height where our Lord was standing when he
wrought the miracle. The hill rose lofty enough to show me the
fairness of the land on all sides, but I have an ancient love for the
mere features of a lake, and so, forgetting all else when I reached
the summit, I looked away eagerly to the eastward. There she
lay—the Sea of Galilee. Less stern than Wastwater, less fair than

---

* Shereef.

gentle Windermere, she had still the winning ways of an English lake; she caught from the smiling heavens unceasing light and changeful phases of beauty, and with all this brightness on her face, she yet clung fondly to the dull he-looking mountain at her side, as though she would

"Soothe him with her finer fancies,
Touch him with her lighter thought."*

If one might judge of men's real thoughts by their writings, it would seem that there are people who can visit an interesting locality and follow up continuously the exact train of thought that ought to be suggested by the historical associations of the place. A person of this sort can go to Athens and think of nothing later than the age of Pericles; can live with the Scipios as long as he stays in Rome. I am not thus docile: it is only by snatches and for few moments together that I can really associate a place with its proper history.

"There at Tiberias, and along this western shore towards the north, and upon the bosom, too, of the lake, our Saviour and his disciples—" Away flew those recollections and my mind strained eastward, because that farthest shore was the end of the world that belongs to man the dweller—the beginning of the other and veiled world that is held by the strange race, whose life (like the pastime of Satan) is a "going to and fro upon the face of the earth." From those gray hills right away to the gates of Bagdad stretched forth the mysterious "Desert"—not a pale, void, sandy tract, but a land abounding in rich pastures; a land without cities or towns, without any "respectable" people, or any "respectable" things, yet yielding its eighty thousand cavalry to the beck of a few old men. But once more—"Tiberias—the plain of Gennesareth— the very earth on which I stood—that the deep, low tones of the Saviour's voice should have gone forth into Eternity from out of the midst of these hills and these valleys!" Aye, aye! but yet again the calm face of the lake was uplifted and smiled upon my eyes with such familiar gaze that the "deep low tones" were hushed,

---

* Tennyson.

the listening multitudes all passed away, and instead there came to me a loving thought from over the seas in England—a thought more sweet than Gospel to a wilful mortal like this.

I went to Tiberias and soon got afloat upon the water. In the evening I took up my quarters in the Catholic church, and the building being large enough, the whole of my people were admitted to the benefit of the same shelter. With portmanteaus and carpet-bags and books and maps and fragrant tea, Mysseri soon made me a home on the southern side of the church. One of old Shereef's helpers was an enthusiastic Catholic, and was greatly delighted at having so sacred a lodging. He lit up the altar with a number of tapers, and when his preparations were complete he began to perform strange orisons: his lips muttered the prayers of the Latin Church, but he bowed himself down and laid his forehead to the stones beneath him, after the manner of a Mussulman. The universal aptness of a religious system for all stages of civilization, and for all sorts and conditions of men, well befits its claim of divine origin. She is of all nations and of all times, that wonderful Church of Rome!

Tiberias is one of the four holy cities,* according to the Talmud, and it is from this place, or the immediate neighborhood of it, that the Messiah is to arise.

Except at Jerusalem, never think of attempting to sleep in a "holy city." Old Jews from all parts of the world go to lay their bones upon the sacred soil, and since these people never return to their homes, it follows that any domestic vermin they may bring with them are likely to become permanently resident, so that the population is continually increasing. No recent census had been taken when I was at Tiberias, but I know that the congregations of fleas which attended at my church alone must have been something enormous. It was a carnal, self-seeking congregation, wholly inattentive to the service which was going on, and devoted to the one object of having my blood. The fleas of all nations were there. The smug, steady, importunate flea from Holywell Street; the pert,

---

* The other three cities held holy by Jews are Jerusalem, Hebron, and Safet.

jumping "puce" from hungry France; the wary, watchful "pulce," with his poisoned stiletto; the vengeful "pulga" of Castile, with his ugly knife; the German "floh," with his knife and fork, insatiate, not rising from table; whole swarms from all the Russias and Asiatic hordes unnumbered,—all these were there, and all rejoiced in one great international feast. I could not more defend myself against my enemies than if I had been *pain à discretion* in the hands of a French communist. After passing a night like this you are glad to gather up the remains of your body long, long before morning dawns. Your skin is scorched, your temples throb, your lips feel withered and dried, your burning eyeballs are screwed inwards against the brain. You have no hope but only in the saddle and the freshness of the morning air.

CHAPTER
XII

My first bivouac.

THE course of the Jordan is from the north to the south, and in that direction, with very little of devious winding, it carries the shining waters of Galilee straight down into the solitudes of the Dead Sea. Speaking roughly, the river in that meridian is a boundary between the people living under roofs and the tented tribes that wander on the farther side. And so, as I went down in my way from Tiberias towards Jerusalem along the western bank of the stream, my thinking all propended to the ancient world of herdsmen and warriors that lay so close over my bridle-arm.

If a man and an Englishman be not born of his mother with a Chiffney-bit in his mouth, there comes to him a time for loathing the wearisome ways of society—a time for not liking tamed people—a time for not sitting in pews—a time for impugning the foregone opinions of men, and haughtily dividing truth from falsehood—a time, in short, for questioning, scoffing, and railing, for speaking lightly of the very opera and all our most cherished institutions. It is from nineteen to two or three and twenty, perhaps, that this war of the man against men is like to be waged most sullenly. You are yet in this smiling England, but you find yourself bending away to the dark sides of her mountains, climbing the dizzy crags, exulting in the fellowship of mists and clouds, and watching the storms how they gather, or proving the mettle of your mare upon the broad and dreary downs, because that you feel congenially with the yet unparceled earth. A little while you are free and unlabeled like the ground that you compass, but Civilization is watching to throw her lasso; you will be surely inclosed, and sooner or later brought down to a state of mere usefulness, your gray hills will be curiously sliced into acres and roods and perches, and you, for all you sit so wilful in your saddle, you will be caught, you will be taken up from travel as a colt from grass, to be trained and tried and matched and run. This in time, but first come Continental tours and the moody longing for Eastern travel: the downs and the moors of England can hold you no longer; with larger stride you burst away from these slips and patches of free land, you thread your path through the crowds of Europe, and at last on the banks of Jordan you joyfully know that you are upon the very frontier of all accustomed respectabilities. There, on the other side of the river (you can swim it with one arm), there reigns the people that will be like to put you to death for *not* being a vagrant, for *not* being a robber, for *not* being armed and houseless. There is comfort in that—health, comfort, and strength to one who is aching from very weariness of that poor, dear, middle-aged, deserving, accomplished, pedantic, and painstaking governess, Europe.

I had ridden for some hours along the right bank of Jordan, when I came to the Djesr el Medjamè (an old Roman bridge, I believe), which crossed the river. My Nazarene guide was riding ahead of the party, and now, to my surprise and delight, he turned leftwards and led on over the bridge. I knew that the true road to Jerusalem must be mainly by the right bank of Jordan, but I supposed that my guide was crossing the bridge at this spot in order to avoid some bend in the river, and that he knew of a ford lower down by which we should regain the western bank. I made no question about the road, for I was but too glad to set my horse's hoofs upon the land of the wandering tribes. None of my people, except the Nazarene, knew the country. On we went through rich pastures upon the eastern side of the water. I looked for the expected bend of the river, but, far as I could see, it kept a straight southerly course; I still left my guide unquestioned.

The Jordan is not a perfectly accurate boundary betwixt roofs and tents, for soon after passing the bridge I came upon a cluster of huts. Some time afterwards the guide, upon being closely questioned by my servants, confessed that the village which we had left behind was the last that we should see, but he declared that he knew a spot at which we should find an encampment of friendly

Bedouins, who would receive me with all hospitality. I had long determined not to leave the East without seeing something of the wandering tribes, but I had looked forward to this as a pleasure to be found in the desert between El Arish and Egypt; I had no idea that the Bedouins on the east of Jordan were accessible. My delight was so great at the near prospect of bread and salt in the tent of an Arab warrior, that I wilfully allowed my guide to go on and mislead me; I saw that he was taking me out of the straight route towards Jerusalem, and was drawing me into the midst of the Bedouins, but the idea of his betraying me seemed (I know not why) so utterly absurd that I could not entertain it for a moment; I fancied it possible that the fellow had taken me out of my route in order to attempt some little mercantile enterprise with the tribe for which he was seeking, and I was glad of the opportunity which I might thus gain of coming in contact with the wanderers.

Not long after passing the village a horseman met us; it appeared that some of the cavalry of Ibrahim Pasha had crossed the river for the sake of the rich pastures on the eastern bank, and that this man was one of the troopers; he stopped and saluted; he was obviously surprised at meeting an unarmed or half-armed cavalcade, and at last he fairly told us that we were on the wrong side of the river, and that if we went on we must lay our account with falling amongst robbers. All this while, and throughout the day, my Nazarene kept well ahead of the party and was constantly up in his stirrups, straining forward, and searching the distance for some objects which still remained unseen.

For the rest of the day we saw no human being; we pushed on eagerly in the hope of coming up with the Bedouins before nightfall. Night came, and we still went on in our way till about ten o'clock. Then the thorough darkness of the night and the weariness of our beasts (they had already done two good days' journey in one) forced us to determine upon coming to a standstill. Upon the heights to the eastward we saw lights; these shone from caves on the mountain side, inhabited, as the Nazarene told us, by rascals of a low sort—not real Bedouins—men whom we might frighten into harmlessness, but from whom there was no willing hospitality to be expected.

We heard at a little distance the brawling of a rivulet, and on the banks of this it was determined to establish our bivouac; we soon found the stream, and following its course for a few yards, came to a spot which was thought to be fit for our purpose. It was a sharply cold night in February, and when I dismounted I found myself standing upon some wet, rank herbage that promised ill for the comfort of our resting-place. I had bad hopes of a fire, for the pitchy darkness of the night was a great obstacle to any successful search for fuel, and, besides, the boughs of trees or bushes would be so full of sap in this early spring that they would not easily burn. However, we were not likely to submit to a dark and cold bivouac without an effort, and my fellows groped forward through the darkness till, after advancing a few paces, they were happily stopped by a complete barrier of dead, prickly bushes. Before our swords could be drawn to reap this welcome harvest, it was found to our surprise that the fuel was already hewn and strewed along the ground in a thick mass. A spot for the fire was found with some difficulty, for the earth was moist and the grass high and rank. At last there was a clicking of flint and steel, and presently there stood out from darkness one of the tawny faces of my muleteers bent down to near the ground, and suddenly lit up by the glowing of the spark, which he courted with careful breath. Before long there was a particle of dry fiber of leaf that kindled to a tiny flame; then another was lit from that, and then another. Then small, crisp twigs, little bigger than bodkins, were laid athwart the glowing fire. The swelling cheeks of the muleteer, laid level with the earth, blew tenderly at first, then more boldly, and the young flame was daintily nursed and fed, and fed more plentifully till it gained good strength. At last a whole armful of dry bushes was piled up over the fire, and presently, with a loud, cheery cracking and crackling, a royal tall blaze shot up from the earth, and showed me once more the shapes and faces of my men, and the dim outlines of the horses and mules that stood grazing hard by.

My servants busied themselves in unpacking the baggage, as though we had arrived at an hotel; Shereef and his helpers unsaddled their cattle. We had left Tiberias without the slightest idea that we were to make our way to Jerusalem along the desolate side of the Jordan, and my servants (generally provident in those matters) had brought with them only, I think, some unleavened bread and a rocky fragment of goat's-milk cheese. These treasures were produced. Tea and the contrivances for making it were always a standing part of my baggage. My men gathered in circle around the fire. The Nazarene was in a false position from having misled us so strangely, and he would have shrunk back—poor devil!— into the cold and outer darkness, but I made him draw near and share the luxuries of the night. My quilt and my pelisse were spread, and the rest of my people had all their capotes, or pelisses, or robes of some sort, which furnished their couches. The men gathered in circle, some kneeling, some sitting, some lying reclined around our common hearth. Sometimes on one, sometimes on another, the flickering light would glare more fiercely. Sometimes it was the good Shereef that seemed the foremost, as he sat with venerable beard, the image of manly piety, unknowing of all geography, unknowing where he was or whither he might go, but trusting in the goodness of God, and the clenching power of fate, and the good star of the Englishman. Sometimes, like marble, the classic face of the Greek Mysseri would catch the sudden light, and then again, by turns, the ever-perturbed Dthemetri, with his odd Chinaman's eye and bristling, terrier-like mustache, shone forth illustrious.

I always liked the men who attended me on these Eastern travels, for they were all of them brave, cheery-hearted fellows, and although their following my career brought upon them a pretty large share of those toils and hardships which are so much more amusing to gentlemen than to servants, yet not one of them ever uttered or hinted a syllable of complaint, or even affected to put on an air of resignation. I always liked them, but never, perhaps, so much as when they were thus grouped together under the light of the bivouac fire. I felt towards them as my comrades rather than as my servants, and took delight in breaking bread with them and merrily passing the cup.

The love of tea is a glad source of fellow-feeling between the Englishman and the Asiatic; in Persia it is drunk by all, and although it is a luxury that is rarely within the reach of the Osmanlis, there are few of them who do not know and love the blessed *tchäi*. Our camp-kettle, filled from the brook, hummed doubtfully for a while, then busily bubbled under the sidelong glare of the flames; cups clinked and rattled, the fragrant steam ascended, and soon this little circlet in the wilderness grew warm and genial as my lady's drawing-room.

And after this there came the chibouk—great comforter of those that are hungry and wayworn. And it has this virtue—it helps to destroy the *gêne* and awkwardness which one sometimes feels at being in company with one's dependents; for whilst the amber is at your lips there is nothing ungracious in your remaining silent, or speaking pithily in short, inter-whiff sentences. And for us that night there was pleasant and plentiful matter of talk; for the where we should be on the morrow, and the wherewithal we should be fed, whether by some ford we should regain the western bank of Jordan, or find bread and salt under the tents of a wandering tribe, or whether we should fall into the hands of the Philistines, and so come to see Death, the last and greatest of all the "fine sights" that there be—these were questionings not dull nor wearisome to us, for we were all concerned in the answers. And it was not an all-imagined morrow that we probed with our sharp guesses, for the lights of those low Philistines—the men of the caves—still shone on the rock above, and we knew by their yells that the fire of our bivouac had shown us.

At length we thought it well to seek for sleep. Our plans were laid for keeping up a good watch through the night. My quilt, and my pelisse, and my cloak were spread out so that I might lie spokewise, with my feet towards the central fire. I wrapped my limbs daintily round, and gave myself orders to sleep like a veteran soldier. But I found that my attempt to sleep upon the earth that God gave me was more new and strange than I had fancied it. I had grown used to the scene which was before me whilst I was sitting or reclining by the side of the fire, but now that I laid myself down at full length, it was the deep black mystery of the heavens that hung over my eyes—not an earthly thing in the way from my own very forehead right up to the end of all space. I grew proud of my boundless bed-chamber. I might have "found sermons" in all this greatness (if I had I should surely have slept), but such was not then my way. If this cherished self of mine had built the universe, I should have dwelt with delight on the "wonders of creation." As it was, I felt rather the vainglory of my promotion from out of mere rooms and houses into the midst of that grand, dark, infinite palace.

And then, too, my head, far from the fire, was in cold latitudes, and it seemed to me strange that I should be lying so still and passive, whilst the sharp night breeze walked free over my cheek, and the cold damp clung to my hair, as though my face grew in the earth, and must bear with the footsteps of the wind, and the falling of the dew, as meekly as the grass of the field. And so, when from time to time the watch quietly and gently kept up the languishing fire, he seldom, I think, was unseen to my restless eyes. Yet, at last, when they called me, and said that the morn would soon be dawning, I rose from a state of half-oblivion not much unlike to sleep, though sharply qualified by a sort of vegetable's consciousness of having been growing still colder and colder for many and many an hour.

CHAPTER
XIII

The Dead Sea.

THE gray light of the morning showed us for the first time the ground we had chosen for our resting-place. We found that we had bivouacked upon a little patch of barley plainly belonging to the men of the caves. The dead bushes which we found so happily placed in readiness for our fire had been strewn as a fence for the protection of the little crop. This was the only cultivated spot of ground which we had seen for many a league, and I was rather sorry to find that our night fire and our cattle had spread so much ruin upon this poor, solitary slip of corn-land.

The saddling and loading of our beasts was a work which generally took nearly an hour, and before this was half over daylight came. We could now see the men of the caves. They collected in a body, amounting, I thought, to nearly fifty, and rushed down towards our quarters with fierce shouts and yells. But the nearer they got the slower they went; their shouts grew less resolute in tone, and soon ceased altogether. The fellows, however, advanced to a thicket within thirty yards of us, and behind this "took up their position." My men without premeditation did exactly that which was best: they kept steadily to their work of loading the beasts without fuss or hurry, and whether it was that they instinctively felt the wisdom of keeping quiet, or that they merely obeyed the natural inclination to silence which one feels in the early morning, I cannot tell, but I know that, except when they exchanged a syllable or two relative to the work they were about, not a word was said. I now believe that this quietness of our party created an undefined terror in the minds of the cave-holders, and scared them from coming on; it gave them a notion that we were relying on some resources which they knew not of. Several times the fellows tried to lash themselves into a state of excitement which might do instead of pluck. They would raise a great shout, and sway forward in a dense body from behind the thicket; but when they saw that their bravery, thus gathered to a head, did not even suspend the strapping of a portmanteau or the tying of a hat-box, their shout lost its spirit, and the whole mass was irresistibly drawn back like a wave receding from the shore.

These attempts at an onset were repeated several times, but always with the same result. I remained under the apprehension of an attack for more than half an hour, and it seemed to me that the work of packing and loading had never been done so slowly. I felt inclined to tell my fellows to make their best speed, but just as I was going to speak, I observed that every one was doing his duty already; I therefore held my peace, and said not a word, till at last Mysseri led up my horse, and asked me if I were ready to mount.

We all marched off without hindrance.

After some time, we came across a party of Ibrahim's cavalry, which had bivouacked at no great distance from us. The knowledge that such a force was in the neighborhood may have conduced to the forbearance of the cave-holders.

We saw a scraggy-looking fellow, nearly black, and wearing nothing but a cloth round the loins; he was tending flocks. Afterwards I came up with another of these goatherds, whose helpmate was with him. They gave us some goat's milk, a welcome present. I pitied the poor devil of a goatherd for having such a very plain wife. I spend an enormous quantity of pity upon that particular form of human misery.

About midday I began to examine my map, and to question my guide; he at first tried to elude inquiry, then suddenly fell on his knees and confessed that he knew nothing of the country. I was thus thrown upon my own resources, and calculating that on the preceding day we had nearly performed a two days' journey, I concluded that the Dead Sea must be near. In this I was right, for at about three or four o'clock in the afternoon I caught a first sight of its dismal face.

I went on and came near to those waters of Death. They stretched deeply into the southern desert, and before me, and all around, as far away as the eye could follow, blank hills piled high over hills, pale, yellow, and naked, walled up in her tomb forever the dead and damned Gomorrah. There was no fly that hummed in the forbidden air, but instead a deep stillness; no grass grew from the earth, no weed peered through the void sand, but, in mockery of all life, there were trees borne down by Jordan in some ancient flood, and these, grotesquely planted upon the forlorn shore, spread out their grim skeleton arms, all scorched and charred to blackness by the heats of the long, silent years.

I now struck off towards the debouchure of the river; but I found that the country, though seemingly quite flat, was intersected by deep ravines, which did not show themselves until nearly approached. For some time my progress was much obstructed; but at last I came across a track leading towards the river, and which might, as I hoped, bring me to a ford. I found, in fact, when I came to the river's side, that the track reappeared upon the opposite bank, plainly showing that the stream had been fordable at this place. Now, however, in consequence of the late rains, the river was quite impracticable for baggage-horses. A body of waters about equal to the Thames at Eton, but confined to a narrower channel, poured down in a current so swift and heavy that the idea of passing with laden baggage-horses was utterly forbidden. I could have swum across myself, and I might, perhaps, have succeeded in swimming a horse over. But this would have been useless, because in such case I must have abandoned not only my baggage, but all my attendants, for none of them were able to swim, and without that resource it would have been madness for them to rely upon the swimming of their beasts across such a powerful stream. I still hoped, however, that there might be a chance of passing the river at the point of its actual junction with the Dead Sea, and I therefore went on in that direction.

Night came upon us whilst laboring across gullies and sandy mounds, and we were obliged to come to a standstill quite suddenly upon the very edge of a precipitous descent. Every step towards the Dead Sea had brought us into a country more and more dreary; and this sand-hill which we were forced to choose for our resting-place was dismal enough. A few slender blades of grass, which here and there singly pierced the sand, mocked bitterly the hunger of our jaded beasts, and with our small remaining fragment of goat's-milk rock, by way of supper, we were not much better off than our horses; we wanted, too, the great requisite of a cheery bivouac—fire. Moreover, the spot on which we had been so suddenly brought to a standstill was relatively high and unsheltered, and the night wind blew swiftly and cold.

The next morning I reached the debouchure of the Jordan, where I had hoped to find a bar of sand that might render its passage possible. The river, however, rolled its eddying waters fast down to the "sea," in a strong, deep stream that shut out all hope of crossing.

It now seemed necessary either to contruct a raft of some kind or else to retrace my steps and remount the banks of the Jordan. I had once happened to give some attention to the subject of military bridges—a branch of military science which includes the construction of rafts and contrivances of the like sort; and I should have been very proud indeed if I could have carried my people and my baggage across by dint of any idea gathered from Sir Howard Douglas or Robinson Crusoe. But we were all faint and languid from want of food, and, besides, there were no materials. Higher up the river there were bushes and river plants, but nothing like timber, and the cord with which my baggage was tied to the pack-saddles amounted altogether to a very small quantity—not nearly enough to haul any sort of craft across the stream.

And now it was, if I remember rightly, that Dthemetri submitted to me a plan for putting to death the Nazarene whose misguidance had been the cause of our difficulties. There was something fascinating in this suggestion, for the slaying of the guide was, of course, easy enough, and would look like an act of what politicians call "vigor." If it were only to become known to my friends in England that I had calmly killed a fellow-creature for taking me out of my way, I might remain perfectly quiet and tranquil for all the rest of my days, quite free from the danger of being considered "slow"; I might ever after live on upon my reputation, like "single-speech Hamilton" in the last century, or "single-sin ——" in this, without being obliged to take the trouble of doing any more harm in the world. This was a great temptation to an indolent person, but the motive was not strengthened by any sincere feeling of anger with the Nazarene. Whilst the question of his life and death was debated, he was riding in front of our party, and there was something in the anxious writhing of his supple limbs that seemed to express a sense of his false position, and struck me as highly comic. I had no crotchet at the time against the punishment of death, but I was unused to blood, and the proposed victim looked so thoroughly capable of enjoying life (if he could only get to the other side of the river) that I thought it would be hard for him to die merely in order to give me a character of energy. Acting on the result of these considerations, and reserving to myself a free and unfettered discretion to have the poor villain shot at any future moment, I magnanimously decided that for the present he should live, and not die.

I bathed in the Dead Sea. The ground covered by the water sloped so gradually that I was not only forced to "sneak in," but to walk through the water nearly a quarter of a mile before I could get out of my depth. When at last I was able to attempt to dive, the salts held in solution made my eyes smart so sharply that the pain I thus suffered, joined with the weakness occasioned by want of food, made me giddy and faint for some moments, but I soon grew better. I knew beforehand the impossibility of sinking in this buoyant water, but I was surprised to find that I could not swim at my accustomed pace; my legs and feet were lifted so high and dry out of the lake that my stroke was baffled, and I found myself kicking against the thin air instead of the dense fluid upon which I was swimming. The water is perfectly bright and clear, its taste detestable. After finishing my attempts at swimming and diving, I took some time in regaining the shore, and before I began to dress I found that the sun had already evaporated the water which clung to me, and that my skin was thickly incrusted with salts.

CHAPTER
XIV

The black tents.

MY steps were reluctantly turned towards the north. I had ridden some way, and still it seemed that all life was fenced and barred out from the desolate ground over which I was journeying. On the west there flowed the impassable Jordan, on the east stood an endless range of barren mountains, and on the south lay that desert sea that knew not the plashing of an oar; greatly, therefore, was I surprised when suddenly there broke upon my ear the long, ludicrous, persevering bray of a donkey. I was riding at this time some few hundred yards ahead of all my party, except the Nazarene (who by a wise instinct kept closer to me than to Dthemetri), and I instantly went forward in the direction of the sound, for I fancied that where there were donkeys, there, too, most surely would be men. The ground on all sides of me seemed thoroughly void and lifeless, but at last I got down into a hollow, and presently a sudden turn brought me within thirty yards of an Arab encampment. The low, black tents which I had so long lusted to see were right before me, and they were all teeming with live Arabs—men, women, and children.

I wished to have let my people behind know where I was, but I recollected that they would be able to trace me by the prints of my horse's hoofs in the sand, and having to do with Asiatics, I felt the danger of the slightest movement which might be looked upon as a sign of irresolution. Therefore, without looking behind me, without looking to the right or to the left I rode straight up towards the foremost tent. Before it was strewed a semicircular fence of dead boughs; through this and about opposite to the front of the tent there was a narrow opening. As I advanced, some twenty or thirty of the most uncouth-looking fellows imaginable came forward to meet me. In their appearance they showed nothing of the Bedouin blood; they were of many colors, from dingy brown to jet-black, and some of these last had much of the negro look about them. They were tall, powerful fellows, but repulsively ugly. They wore nothing but the Arab shirts, confined at the waist by leather belts.

I advanced to the gap left in the fence, and at once alighted from my horse. The chief greeted me after his fashion by alternately touching first my hand and then his own forehead, as if he were conveying the virtue of the touch like a spark of electricity. Presently I found myself seated upon a sheepskin, spread for me under the sacred shade of Arabian canvas. The tent was of a long, narrow, oblong form, and contained a quantity of men, women, and children so closely huddled together that there was scarcely one of them who was not in actual contact with his neighbor. The moment I had taken my seat, the chief repeated his salutations in the most enthusiastic manner, and then the people, having gathered densely about me, got hold of my unresisting hand and passed it round like a claret jug for the benefit of everybody. The women soon brought me a wooden bowl full of buttermilk, and welcome indeed came the gift to my hungry and thirsty soul.

After some time my people, as I had expected, came up, and when poor Dthemetri saw me on my sheepskin, "the life and soul" of this ragamuffin party, he was so astounded that he even failed to check his cry of horror; he plainly thought that now at last, the Lord had delivered me (interpreter and all) into the hands of the lowest Philistines.

Mysseri carried a tobacco-pouch slung at his belt, and as soon as its contents were known, the whole population of the tent began begging like spaniels for bits of the beloved weed. I concluded, from the abject manner of these people, that they could not possibly be thoroughbred Bedouins, and I saw, too, that they must be in the very last stage of misery, for poor indeed is the man in these climes who cannot command a pipeful of tobacco. I began to think that I had fallen amongst thorough savages, and it seemed likely enough that they would gain their very first knowledge of civilization by seizing and studying the contents of my dearest portmanteaus; but still my impression was that they would hardly

venture upon such an attempt. I observed, indeed, that they did
not offer me the bread and salt (the pledges of peace amongst
wandering tribes), but I fancied that they refrained from this act
of hospitality, not in consequence of any hostile determination,
but in order that the notion of robbing me might remain for the
present an "open question." I afterwards found that the poor
fellows had no bread to offer. They were literally "out at grass."
It is true that they had a scanty supply of milk from goats, but they
were living almost entirely upon certain grass-stems, which were
just in season at that time of the year. These, if not highly nour-
ishing, are pleasant enough to the taste, and their acid juices come
gratefully to thirsty lips.

CHAPTER
XV

Passage of the Jordan.

A ND now Dthemetri began to enter into a negotiation with my hosts for a passage over the river. I never interfered with my worthy dragoman upon these occasions, because, from my entire ignorance of the Arabic, I should have been quite unable to exercise any real control over his words, and it would have been silly to break the stream of his eloquence to no purpose. I have reason to fear, however, that he lied transcendently, and especially in representing me as the bosom friend of Ibrahim Pasha. The mention of that name produced immense agitation and excitement and the sheik explained to Dthemetri the grounds of the infinite respect which he and his tribe entertained for the Pasha. Only a few weeks before Ibrahim had craftily sent a body of troops across the Jordan. The force went warily round to the foot of the mountains on the east, so as to cut off the retreat of this tribe, and then surrounded them as they lay encamped in the vale; their camels, and indeed all their possessions worth taking, were carried off by the soldiery, and moreover the then sheik, together with every tenth man of the tribe, was brought out and shot. You would think that this conduct on the part of the Pasha might not procure for his "friend" a very gracious reception amongst the people whom he had thus despoiled and decimated; but the Asiatic seems to be animated with a feeling of profound respect, almost bordering upon affection, for those who have done him any bold and violent wrong, and there is always, too, so much of vague and undefined apprehension mixed up with his really well-founded alarms that I can see no limit to the yielding and bending of his mind when it is worked upon by the idea of power.

After some discussion the Arabs agreed, as I thought, to conduct me to a ford, and we moved on towards the river, followed by seventeen of the most able-bodied of the tribe, under the guidance of several gray-bearded elders, and Sheik Ali Djourban at the head of the whole detachment. Upon leaving the encampment a sort of ceremony was performed, for the purpose, it seemed, of insuring, if possible, a happy result for the undertaking. There was an uplifting of arms, and a repeating of words that sounded like formulae, but there were no prostrations, and I did not understand that the ceremony was of a religious charaacter. The tented Arabs are looked upon as very bad Mohammedans.

We arrived upon the banks of the river,—not at a ford, but at a deep and rapid part of the stream,—and I now understood that it was the plan of these men, if they helped me at all, to transport me across the river by some species of raft. But a reaction had taken place in the opinions of many, and a violent dispute arose, upon a motion which seemed to have been made by some honorable member with a view to robbery. The fellows all gathered together in circle, at a little distance from my party, and there disputed with great vehemence and fury for nearly two hours. I can't give a correct report of the debate, for it was held in a barbarous dialect of the Arabic unknown to my dragoman. I recollect I sincerely felt, at the time, that the arguments in favor of robbing me must have been almost unanswerable, and I gave great credit to the speakers on my side for the ingenuity and sophistry which they must have shown in maintaining the fight so well.

During the discussion I remained lying in front of my baggage, for this had been already taken from the pack-saddles and placed upon the ground. I was so languid from want of food that I had scarcely animation enough to feel as deeply interested as you would suppose in the result of the discussion. I thought, however, that the pleasantest toys to play with, during this interval, were my pistols, and now and then, when I listlessly visited my loaded barrels with the swivel ramrods, or drew a sweet, musical click from my English firelocks, it seemed to me that I exercised a slight and gentle influence on the debate. Thanks to Ibrahim Pasha's terrible visitation, the men of the tribe were wholly unarmed, and my advantage in this respect might have counterbalanced in some measure the superiority of numbers.

Mysseri (not interpreting in Arabic) had no duty to perform, and he seemed to be faint and listless as myself. Shereef looked perfectly resigned to any fate. But Dthemetri (faithful terrier!) was bristling with zeal and watchfulness. He could not understand the debate, for it was carried on at a distance too great to be easily heard, even if the language had been familiar; but he was always on the alert, and now and then conferring with men who had straggled out of the assembly. At last he found an opportunity of making an offer which at once produced immense sensation: he proposed, on my behalf, that the tribe should bear themselves loyally towards me, and take my people and my baggage in safety to the other bank of the river, and that I on my part should give such a *teskeri*, or written certificate of their good conduct, as might avail them hereafter in the hour of their direst need. This proposal was received and instantly accepted by all the men of the tribe there present with the utmost enthusiasm. I was to give the men, too, a "bakshish," that is, a present of money, usually made upon the conclusion of any sort of treaty; but although the people of the tribe were so miserably poor, they seemed to look upon the pecuniary part of the arrangement as a matter quite trivial in comparison with the teskeri. Indeed, the sum which Dthemetri promised them was extremely small, and no attempt was made to extort any further reward.

The council broke up, and most of the men rushed madly towards me, overwhelming me with vehement gratulations, and kissing my hands and my boots.

The Arabs then earnestly began their attempt to effect the passage of the river. They had brought with them a great number of skins used for carrying water in the desert; these they filled with air, and fastened several of them to small boughs cut from the banks of the river. In this way they constructed a raft not more than about four or five feet square, but rendered buoyant by the inflated skins. Upon this a portion of my baggage was placed, and was firmly tied to it by the cords used on my pack-saddles. The little raft, with its weighty cargo, was then gently lifted into the water, and I had the satisfaction to see that it floated well.

Twelve of the Arabs now stripped, and tied inflated skins to their loins; six of the men went down into the river, got in front of the little raft, and pulled it off a few feet from the bank. The other six then dashed into the stream with loud shouts, and swam along after the raft, pushing it from behind. Off went the craft in capital style at first, for the stream was easy on the eastern side; but I saw the tug was to come, for the main torrent swept round in a bend near the western bank of the river.

The old men, with their long gray grisly beards, stood shouting and cheering, praying and commanding. At length the raft entered upon the difficult part of its course; the whirling stream seized and twisted it about, and then bore it rapidly downwards; the swimmers flagged, and seemed to be beaten in the struggle. But now the old men on the bank, with their rigid arms uplifted straight, sent forth a cry and a shout that tore the wide air, and then, to make their urging yet more strong, they shrieked out the dreadful syllables, "Brahim Pasha!" The swimmers, one moment before so blown and so weary, found lungs to answer the cry, and shouted back the name of their great destroyer; they dashed on through the torrent, and bore the raft in safety to the western bank.

Afterwards the swimmers returned with the raft, and attached to it the rest of my baggage. I took my seat upon the top of the cargo, and the raft, thus laden, passed the river in the same way, and with the same struggle as before. The skins, however, not being perfectly air-tight, had lost a great part of their buoyancy, so that I, as well as the luggage that passed on this last voyage, got wet in the waters of Jordan. The raft could not be trusted for another trip, and the rest of my people passed the river in a different and (for them) much safer way. Inflated skins were fastened to their loins, and thus supported they were tugged across by Arabs swimming on either side of them. The horses and mules were thrown into the water and forced to swim over. The poor beasts had a hard struggle for their lives in that swift stream, and I thought that one of the horses would have been drowned, for he was too weak to gain a footing on the western bank, and the stream bore him down. At last, however, he swam back to the side from which he had come. Before night all had passed the river except this one horse and old Shereef. He, poor fellow, was shivering on the eastern bank, for his dread of the passage was so great that he delayed it as long as he could, and at last it became so dark that he was obliged to wait till the morning.

I lay that night on the bank of the river. The Arabs at a little distance from me contrived to kindle a fire, and sat all around in a circle. They were made most savagely happy by the tobacco with which I supplied them, and they soon determined that the whole night should be one smoking festival. The poor fellows had only a cracked bowl, without any tube at all; but this morsel of a pipe they handed round from one to the other, allowing to each a fixed number of whiffs. In that way they passed the whole night.

The next morning old Shereef was brought across. It was strange to see this solemn old Mussulman, with his shaven head and his sacred beard, sprawling and puffing upon the surface of the water. When at last he reached the bank, the people told him that by his baptism in Jordan he had surely become a mere Christian. Poor Shereef! the holy man! the descendant of the Prophet! He was sadly hurt by the taunt, and the more so as he seemed to feel there was some foundation for it, and that he really might have absorbed some Christian errors.

When all was ready for departure, I wrote the teskeri in French, and delivered it to Sheik Ali Djourban, together with the promised bakshish. He was exceedingly grateful, and I parted in a very friendly way from this ragged tribe.

In two or three hours I gained Rihah, a village said to occupy the site of ancient Jericho. There was one building there which I observed with some emotion, for although it may not have been actually standing in the days of Jericho, it contained at this day a most interesting collection of—modern loaves.

Some hours after sunset I reached the convent of Santa Saba, and there remained for the night.

CHAPTER
XVI

Terra Santa.

THE enthusiasm that had glowed, or seemed to glow, within me, for one blessed moment, when I knelt by the shrine of the Virgin at Nazareth was not rekindled at Jerusalem. In the stead of the solemn gloom and the deep stillness rightfully belonging to the Holy City, there was the hum and bustle of active life. It was the "height of the season." The Easter ceremonies drew near; the pilgrims were flocking in from all quarters, and although their objects were, partly at least, of a religious character, yet their "arrivals" brought as much stir and liveliness to the city as if they had come up to marry their daughters.

The votaries who every year crowd to the Holy Sepulcher are chiefly of the Greek and Armenian churches. They are not drawn into Palestine by a mere sentimental longing to stand upon the ground trodden by our Saviour, but rather they perform the pilgrimage as a plain duty, strongly inculcated by their religion. A very great proportion of those who belong to the Greek Church contrive at some time or other, in the course of their lives, to achieve the enterprise. Many in their infancy and childhood are brought to the holy sites by their parents, but those who have not had this advantage will often make it the main object of their lives to save money enough for this holy undertaking.

The pilgrims begin to arrive in Palestine some weeks before the Easter festival of the Greek Church; they come from Egypt, from all parts of Syria, from Armenia and Asia Minor, from Stamboul, from Rumelia, from the provinces of the Danube, and from all the Russias. Most of these people bring with them some articles of merchandise, but I myself believe (notwithstanding the common taunt against pilgrims) that they do this rather as a mode of paying the expenses of their journey than from a spirit of mercenary speculation. They generally travel in families, for the women are, of course, more ardent than their husbands in undertaking these pious enterprises, and they take care to bring with them all their children, however young. They do this because the efficacy of the rites is quite independent of the age of the votary, and people whose careful mothers have obtained for them the benefit of the pilgrimage in early life are saved from the expense and trouble of undertaking the journey at a later age. The superior veneration so often excited by objects that are distant and unknown shows not, perhaps, the wrong-headedness of a man, but rather the transcendent power of his imagination. However this may be, and whether it is by mere obstinacy that they force their way through intervening distance, or whether they come by the winged strength of fancy, quite certainly the pilgrims who flock to Palestine from remote homes are the people most eager in the enterprise, and in number, too, they bear a very high proportion to the whole mass.

The great bulk of the pilgrims make their way by sea to the port of Jaffa. A number of families will charter a vessel amongst them, all bringing their own provisions: these are of the simplest and cheapest kind. On board every vessel thus freighted there is, I believe, a priest, who helps the people in their religious exercises, and tries (and fails) to maintain something like order and harmony. The vessels employed in the service are usually Greek brigs or brigantines and schooners, and the number of passengers stowed in them is almost always horribly excessive. The voyages are sadly protracted, not only by the land-seeking, storm-flying habits of the Greek seamen, but also by the endless schemes and speculations forever tempting them to touch at the nearest port. The voyage, too, must be made during winter, in order that Jerusalem may be reached some weeks before the Greek Easter.

When the pilgrims have landed at Jaffa, they hire camels, horses, mules, or donkeys, and make their way as well as they can to the Holy City. The space fronting the Church of the Holy Sepulcher soon becomes a kind of bazaar, or rather, perhaps, reminds you of an English fair. On this spot the pilgrims display their merchandise, and there, too, the trading residents of the place offer their goods for sale. I have never, I think, seen elsewhere in Asia so much commercial animation as upon this square of ground by the church door: the "money-changers" seemed to be almost as brisk and lively as if they had been *within* the temple.

When I entered the church, I found a Babel of worshipers. Greek, Roman, and Armenian priests were performing their different rites in various nooks and corners, and crowds of disciples were rushing about in all directions, some laughing and talking, some begging, but most of them going round in a regular and methodical way to kiss the sanctified spots, and speak the appointed syllables, and lay down the accustomed coin. If this kissing of the shrines had seemed as though it were done at the bidding of enthusiasm, or of any poor sentiment even feebly approaching to it, the sight would have been less odd to English eyes; but as it was, I felt shocked at the sight of grown men thus steadily and carefully embracing the sticks and the stones—not from love or from zeal (else God forbid that I should have blamed), but from a calm sense of duty. They seemed to be, not "working out," but *transacting*, the great business of salvation.

Dthemetri, however (he generally came with me when I went out, in order to do duty as interpreter), really had in him some enthusiasm. He was a zealous and almost fanatical member of the Greek Church, and had long since performed the pilgrimage, so now, great indeed was the pride and delight with which he guided me from one holy spot to another. Every now and then, when he came to an unoccupied shrine, he fell down on his knees and performed devotion. He was almost distracted by the temptations that surrounded him. There were so many stones absolutely requiring to be kissed that he rushed about, happily puzzled and sweetly teased, like "Jack among the maidens."

A Protestant, familiar with the Holy Scripture, but ignorant of tradition and the geography of modern Jerusalem, finds himself a good deal "mazed" when he first looks for the sacred sites. The Holy Sepulcher is not in a field without the walls, but in the midst and in the best part of the town, under the roof of the great church which I have been talking about. It is a handsome tomb of oblong form, partly subterranean and partly above ground, and closed in on all sides except the one by which it is entered. You descend into the interior by a few steps, and there find an altar with burning tapers. This is the spot held in greater sanctity than any other in Jerusalem. When you have seen enough of it, you feel perhaps weary of the busy crowd and inclined for a gallop; you ask your dragoman whether there will be time before sunset to send for horses and take a ride to Mount Calvary. "Mount Calvary, signor? *Eccolo!* it is *up-stairs—on the first floor.*" In effect you ascend, if I remember rightly, just thirteen steps, and then you are shown the now golden sockets in which the crosses of our Lord and the two thieves were fixed. All this is startling, but the truth is that the city, having gathered round the Sepulcher (the main point of interest), has gradually crept northward, and thus in great measure are occasioned the many geographical surprises that puzzle the "Bible Christian."

The Church of the Holy Sepulcher comprises very compendiously almost all the spots associated with the closing career of our Lord. Just there, on your right, he stood and wept; by the pillar on your left he was scourged; on the spot just before you he was crowned with the crown of thorns; up there he was crucified, and down here he was buried. A locality is assigned to every the minutest event connected with the recorded history of our Saviour; even the spot where the cock crew when Peter denied his master is ascertained, and surrounded by the walls of an Armenian convent. Many Protestants are wont to treat these traditions contemptuously, and those who distinguish themselves from their brethren by the appellation of "Bible Christians" are almost fierce in their denunciation of these supposed errors.

It is admitted, I believe, by everybody that the formal sanctification of these spots was the act of the Empress Helena, the mother of Constantine, but I think it is fair to suppose that she was guided by a careful regard to the then prevailing traditions. Now, the nature of the ground upon which Jerusalem stands is such that the localities belonging to the events there enacted might have been more easily and permanently ascertained by tradition than

those of any city that I know of. Jerusalem, whether ancient or
modern, was built upon and surrounded by sharp, salient rocks,
intersected by deep ravines. Up to the time of the siege, Mount
Calvary, of course, must have been well enough known to the
people of Jerusalem. The destruction of the mere buildings could
not have obliterated from any man's memory the names of those
steep rocks and narrow ravines in the midst of which the city had
stood. It seems to me, therefore, highly probable that in fixing the
site of Calvary the Empress was rightly guided. Recollect, too, that
the voice of tradition at Jerusalem is quite unanimous, and that
Romans, Greeks, Armenians, and Jews, all hating each other sincerely, concur in assigning the same localities to the events told in
the Gospel. I concede, however, that the attempt of the Empress to
ascertain the sites of the minor events cannot be safely relied upon.
With respect, for instance, to the certainty of the spot where the
cock crew I am far from being convinced.

Supposing that the Empress acted arbitrarily in fixing the holy
sites, it would seem that she followed the Gospel of St. John, and
that the geography sanctioned by her can be more easily reconciled with that history than with the accounts of the other Evan-
gelists.

The authority exercised by the Mussulman Government in relation to the holy sites is in one view somewhat humbling to the
Christians, for it is almost as an arbitrator between the contending
sects (this always, of course, for the sake of pecuniary advantage)
that the Mussulman lends his contemptuous aid. He not only
grants, but enforces, toleration. All persons, of whatever religion,
are allowed to go as they will into every part of the Church of the
Holy Sepulcher, but in order to prevent indecent contests, and also
from motives arising out of money payments, the Turkish Government assigns the peculiar care of each sacred spot to one of the
ecclesiastic bodies. Since this guardianship carries with it the re-
ceipt of all the coins deposited by the pilgrims upon the sacred
shrines, it is strenuously fought for by all rival churches, and the
artifices of intrigue are busily exerted at Stamboul in order to
procure the isssue or revocation of the firmans by which the cov-

eted privilege is granted. In this strife the Greek Church has of late years signally triumphed, and the most famous of the shrines are committed to the care of their priesthood. They possess the golden socket in which stood the cross of our Lord, whilst the Latins are obliged to content themselves with the apertures in which were inserted the crosses of the two thieves. They are naturally discontented with that poor privilege, and sorrowfully look back to the days of their former glory—the days when Napoleon was emperor, and Sebastiani ambassador at the Porte.

Although the pilgrims perform their devotions at the several shrines with so little apparent enthusiasm, they are driven to the verge of madness by the miracle displayed before them on Easter Saturday. Then it is that the heaven-sent fire issues from the Holy Sepulcher. The pilgrims assemble in the great church, and already, long before the wonder is worked, they are wrought by anticipation of God's sign, as well as by their struggles for room and breathing-space, to a most frightful state of excitement. At length the Chief Priest of the Greeks, accompanied (of all people in the world) by the Turkish Governor, enters the tomb. After this there is a long pause, but at last and suddenly from out of the small apertures on either side of the Sepulcher there issue long, shining flames. The pilgrims now rush forward, madly struggling to light their tapers at the holy fire. This is the dangerous moment, and many lives are often lost.

The year before that of my going to Jerusalem, Ibrahim Pasha, from some whim or motive of policy, chose to witness the miracle. The vast church was, of course, thronged, as it always is on that awful day. It seems that the appearance of the fire was delayed for a very long time, and that the growing frenzy of the people was heightened by suspense. Many, too, had already sunk under the effect of the heat and the stifling atmosphere, when at last the fire flashed from the Sepulcher. Then a terrible struggle ensued. Many sank and were crushed. Ibrahim had taken his station in one of the galleries; but now, feeling, perhaps, his brave blood warmed by the sight and sound of such strife, he took upon himself to quiet the people by his personal presence, and descended into the body of the church with only a few guards. He had forced his way into the midst of the dense crowd, when, unhappily, he fainted away. His guards shrieked out, and the event instantly became known. A body of soldiers recklessly forced their way through the crowd, trampling over every obstacle that they might save the life of their general. Nearly two hundred people were killed in the struggle.

The following year, however, the Government took better measures for the prevention of these calamities. I was not present at the ceremony, having gone away from Jerusalem some time before, but I afterwards returned into Palestine, and I then learned that the day had passed off without any disturbance of a fatal kind. It is, however, almost too much to expect that so many ministers of peace can assemble without finding some occasion for strife, and in that year a tribe of wild Bedouins became the subject of discord. These men, it seems, led an Arab life in some of the desert tracts bordering on the neighborhood of Jerusalem, but were not connected with any of the great ruling tribes. Some whim or notion of policy had induced them to embrace Christianity, but they were grossly ignorant of the rudiments of their adopted faith, and having no priest with them in their desert, they had as little knowledge of religious ceremonies as of religion itself; they were not even capable of conducting themselves in a place of worship with ordinary decorum, but would interrupt the service with scandalous cries and warlike shouts. Such is the account the Latins give of them, but I have never heard the other side of the question. These wild fellows, notwithstanding their entire ignorance of all religion, are yet claimed by the Greeks, not only as proselytes who have embraced Christianity generally, but as converts to the particular doctrines and practice of their Church. The people thus alleged to have concurred with the Greeks in rejecting the great Roman Catholic schism, are never, I believe, within the walls of a church, or even of any building at all, except upon this occasion of Easter, and as they then never fail to find a row of some kind going on by the side of the Sepulcher, they fancy, it seems, that the ceremonies there enacted are funeral games of a martial character, held in honor of a deceased chieftain, and that a Christian festival is a peculiar kind of battle fought between walls and without cavalry. It does not appear, however, that these men are guilty of any ferocious acts, or that they attempt to commit depredations. The charge against them is merely that by their way of applauding the performance—by their horrible cries and frightful gestures— they destroy the solemnity of divine service, and upon this ground the Franciscans obtained a firman for the exclusion of such tumultuous worshipers. The Greeks, however, did not choose to lose the aid of their wild converts merely because they were a little backward in their religious education, and they therefore persuaded them to defy the firman by entering the city en masse and overawing their enemies. The Franciscans, as well as the Government authorities, were obliged to give way, and the Arabs triumphantly marched into the church. The festival, however, must have seemed to them rather flat, for although there may have been some "casualties" in the way of eyes black, and noses bloody, and women "missing," there was no return of "killed."

Formerly the Latin Catholics concurred in acknowledging (but not, I hope, in working) the annual miracle of the heavenly fire, but they have for many years withdrawn their countenance from this exhibition, and they now repudiate it as a trick of the Greek Church. Thus, of course, the violence of feeling with which the rival churches meet at the Holy Sepulcher, on Easter Saturday, is greatly increased, and a disturbance of some kind is certain. In the year I speak of, though no lives were lost, there was, as it seems, a tough struggle in the church. I was amused at hearing of a taunt that was thrown that day upon an English traveler: he had taken his station in a convenient part of the church, and was no doubt displaying that peculiar air of serenity and gratification with which an English gentleman usually looks on at a row, when one of the Franciscans came by, all reeking from the fight, and was so disgusted at the coolness and placid contentment of the Englishman that he forgot his monkish humility, as well as the duties of hospitality (the Englishman was a guest at the convent), and plainly said: "You sleep under our roof, you eat our bread, you drink our wine, and then, when Easter Saturday comes, you don't fight for us!"

Yet these rival churches go on quietly enough till their blood is up. The terms on which they live remind one of the peculiar relation subsisting at Cambridge between "town and gown."

The contests waged by the priests and friars certainly do not originate with the lay pilgrims, for the great body of these are quiet and inoffensive people. It is true, however, that their pious enterprise is believed by them to operate as a counterpoise for a multitude of sins, whether past or future, and perhaps they exert themselves in after life to restore the balance of good and evil. The Turks have a maxim which, like most cynical apothegms, carries with it the buzzing trumpet of falsehood, as well as the small, fine "sting of truth." "If your friend has made the pilgrimage once, distrust him; if he has made the pilgrimage twice, cut him dead!" The caution is said to be as applicable to the visitants of Jerusalem as to those of Mecca; but I cannot help believing that the frailties of all the hadjis,* whether Christian or Mohammedan, are greatly exaggerated. I certainly regarded the pilgrims to Palestine as a well disposed, orderly body of people, not strongly enthusiastic, but desirous to comply with the ordinances of their religion, and to attain the great end of salvation as quietly and economically as possible.

When the solemnities of Easter are concluded, the pilgrims move off in a body to complete their good work by visiting the sacred scenes in the neighborhood of Jerusalem, including the wilderness of John the Baptist, Bethlehem, and, above all, the Jordan, for to bathe in those sacred waters is one of the chief objects of the expedition. All the pilgrims—men, women, and children—are submerged *en chemise*, and the saturated linen is carefully wrapped up and preserved as a burial dress that shall inure for salvation in the realms of death.

I saw the burial of a pilgrim; he was a Greek—miserably poor, and very old. He had just crawled into the Holy City, and had reached at once the goal of his pious journey and the end of his sufferings upon earth. There was no coffin, nor wrapper, and as I

---

* Hadji—a pilgrim.

looked full upon the face of the dead, I saw how deeply it was rutted with the ruts of age and misery. The priest, strong and portly, fresh, fat, and alive with the life of the animal kingdom, unpaid or ill paid for his work, would scarcely deign to mutter out his forms, but hurried over the words with shocking haste. Presently he called out impatiently: "Yalla! Goor!" ("Come! Look sharp!"), and then the dead Greek was seized. His limbs yielded inertly to the rude men that handled them, and down he went into his grave, so roughly bundled in that his neck was twisted by the fall—so twisted that if the sharp malady of life were still upon him, the old man would have shrieked and groaned, and the lines of his face would have quivered with pain. The lines of his face were not moved, and the old man lay still and heedless—so well cured of that tedious life-ache that nothing could hurt him now. His clay was *itself again*—cool, firm, and tough. The pilgrim had found great rest. I threw the accustomed handful of the holy soil upon his patient face, and then, and in less than a minute, the earth closed coldly round him.

I did not say "Alas!" (Nobody ever does that I know of, though the word is so frequently written.) I thought the old man had got rather well out of the scrape of being alive, and poor.

The destruction of the mere buildings in such a place as Jerusalem would not involve the permanent dispersion of the inhabitants, for the rocky neighborhood in which the town is situate abounds in caves, and these would give an easy refuge to the people until they gained an opportunity of rebuilding their dwellings. Therefore I could not help looking upon the Jews of Jerusalem as being in some sort the representatives, if not the actual descendants, of the men who crucified our Saviour. Supposing this to be the case, I felt that there would be some interest in knowing how the events of the Gospel history were regarded by the Israelites of modern Jerusalem. The result of my inquiry upon this subject was, so far as it went, entirely favorable to the truth of Christianity. I understood that *the performance of the miracles was not doubted by any of the Jews in the place.* All of them concurred in attributing the works of our Lord to the influence of magic, but they were divided as to the species of the enchantment from which the power proceeded; the great mass of the Jewish people believed, I fancy, that the miracles had been wrought by aid of the powers of darkness, but many, and those the more enlightened, would call Jesus "the good Magician." To Europeans repudiating the notion of all magic, good or bad, the opinion of the Jews as to the agency by which the miracles were worked is a matter of no importance, but the circumstance of their admitting that those miracles *were in fact performed* is certainly curious, and perhaps not quite immaterial.

If you stay in the Holy City long enough to fall into anything like regular habits of amusement and occupation, and to become, in short, for the time a "man about town" at Jerusalem, you will necessarily lose the enthusiasm which you may have felt when you trod the sacred soil for the first time, and it will then seem almost strange to you to find yourself so entirely surrounded in all your daily pursuits by the signs and sounds of religion. Your hotel is a monastery, your rooms are cells, the landlord is a stately abbot, and the waiters are hooded monks. If you walk out of the town, you find yourself on the Mount of Olives, or in the Valley of Jehoshaphat, or on the Hill of Evil Counsel. If you mount your horse and extend your rambles, you will be guided to the wilderness of St. John, or the birthplace of our Saviour. Your club is the great Church of the Holy Sepulcher, where everybody meets everybody every day. If you lounge through the town, your Pall Mall is the Via Dolorosa, and the object of your hopeless affections is some maid or matron all forlorn, and sadly shrouded in her pilgrim's robe. If you would hear music, it must be the chanting of friars; if you look at pictures, you see Virgins with misforeshortened arms, or devils out of drawing, or angels tumbling up the skies in impious perspective. If you would make any purchases, you must go again to the church doors, and when you inquire for the manufactures of the place, you find that they consist of double-blessed beads and sanctified shells. These last are the favorite tokens which the pilgrims carry off with them. The shell is graven or rather scratched on the white side with a rude drawing of the Blessed Virgin, or of the Crucifixion, or some other scriptural subject; having passed this stage, it goes into the hands of a priest; by him it is subjected to some process for rendering it efficacious against the schemes of our ghostly enemy; the manufacture is then complete, and is deemed to be fit for use.

The village of Bethlehem lies prettily couched on the slope of a hill. The sanctuary is a subterranean grotto, and is committed to the joint guardianship of the Romans, Greeks, and Armenians: these vie with each other in adorning it. Beneath an altar gorgeously decorated and lit with everlasting fires there stands the low slab of stone which marks the holy site of the Nativity; and near to this is a hollow scooped out of the living rock. Here the infant Jesus was laid. Near the spot of the Nativity is the rock against which the Blessed Virgin was leaning when she presented her babe to the adoring shepherds.

Many of those Protestants who are accustomed to despise tradition consider that this sanctuary is altogether unscriptural—that a grotto is not a stable, and that mangers are made of wood. It is perfectly true, however, that the many grottoes and caves which are found among the rocks of Judea were formerly used for the reception of cattle; they are so used at this day. I have myself seen grottoes appropriated to this purpose.

You know what a sad and somber decorum it is that outwardly reigns through the lands oppressed by Moslem sway. The Mohammedans make beauty their prisoner, and enforce such a stern and gloomy morality, or, at all events, such a frightfully close semblance of it, that far and long the wearied traveler may go without catching one glimpse of outward happiness. By a strange chance in these latter days, it happened that, alone of all the places in the land, this Bethlehem, the native village of our Lord, escaped the moral yoke of the Mussulmans, and heard again, after ages of dull oppression, the cheering clatter of social freedom, and the voices of laughing girls. It was after an insurrection which had been raised against the authority of Mehemet Ali that Bethlehem was freed from the hateful laws of Asiatic decorum. The Mussulmans of the village had taken an active part in the movement, and when Ibrahim had quelled it, his wrath was still so hot that he put to death every one of the few Mohammedans of Bethlehem who had not already fled. The effect produced upon the Christian inhabitants by the sudden removal of this restraint was immense. The village smiled once more. It is true that such sweet freedom could not long endure. Even if the population of the place should continue to be entirely Christian, the sad decorum of the Mussulmans, or rather of the Asiatics, would sooner of later be restored by the force of opinion and custom. But for a while the sunshine would last, and when I was at Bethlehem, though long after the flight of the Mussulmans, the cloud of Moslem propriety had not yet come back to cast its cold shadow upon life. When you reach that gladsome village, pray Heaven there still may be heard there the voice of free, innocent girls. It will sound so dearly welcome!

To a Christian and thoroughbred Englishman not even the licentiousness generally accompanying it can compensate for the oppressiveness of that horrible outward decorum which turns the cities and the palaces of Asia into deserts and jails. So I say, when you see and hear them, those romping girls of Bethlehem will gladden your very soul. Distant at first, and then nearer and nearer, the timid flock will gather round you, with their large burning eyes gravely fixed against yours, so that they see into your brain; and if you imagine evil against them, they will know of your ill thought before it is yet well born, and will fly and be gone in the moment. But presently, if you will only look virtuous enough to prevent alarm, and vicious enough to avoid looking silly, the blithe maidens will draw nearer and nearer to you, and soon there will be one, the bravest of the sisters, who will venture right up to your side, and touch the hem of your coat, in playful defiance of the danger; and then the rest will follow the daring of their youthful leader, and gather close round you, and hold a shrill controversy on the wondrous formation that you call a hat, and the cunning of the hands that clothed you with cloth so fine; and then, growing more profound in their researches, they will pass from the study of your mere dress to a serious contemplation of your stately height, and your nut-brown hair, and the ruddy glow

[133]

of your English cheeks. And if they catch a glimpse of your un-gloved fingers, then again will they make the air ring with their sweet screams of delight and amazement, as they compare the fairness of your hand with their own warmer tints. Instantly the ringleader of the gentle rioters imagines a new sin: with tremulous boldness she touches, then grasps, your hand, and smoothes it gently betwixt her own, and pries curiously into its make and color, as though it were silk of Damascus, or shawl of Cashmere. And when they see you even then still sage and gentle, the joyous girls will suddenly and screamingly, and all at once, explain to each other that you are surely quite harmless and innocent—a lion that makes no spring, a bear that never hugs; and upon this faith, one after the other, they will take your passive hand, and strive to explain it, and make it a theme and a controversy. But the one—the fairest and the sweetest of all—is yet the most timid; she shrinks from the daring deeds of her playmates, and seeks shelter behind their sleeves, and strives to screen her glowing conscious-ness from the eyes that look upon her. But her laughing sisters will have none of this cowardice; they vow that the fair one *shall* be their complice, *shall* share their dangers, *shall* touch the hand of the stranger; they seize her small wrist, and drag her forward by force, and at last, whilst yet she strives to turn away, and to cover up her whole soul under the folds of downcast eyelids, they van-quish her utmost strength, they vanquish her utmost modesty, and marry her hand to yours. The quick pulse springs from her fingers and throbs like a whisper upon your listening palm. For an instant her large, timid eyes are upon you; in an instant they are shrouded again, and there comes a blush so burning that the frightened girls stay their shrill laughter, as though they had played too perilously and harmed their gentle sister. A moment, and all, with a sudden intelligence, turn away and fly like deer; yet soon, again like deer, they wheel round and return, and stand, and gaze upon the dan-ger, until they grow brave once more.

"I regret to observe that the removal of the moral restraint imposed by the presence of the Mohammedan inhabitants has led to a certain degree of boisterous though innocent levity in the

bearing of the Christians, and more especially in the demeanor of
those who belong to the younger portion of the female population; but I feel assured that a more thorough knowledge of the
principles of their own pure religion will speedily restore these
young people to habits of propriety even more strict than those
which were imposed upon them by the authority of their Mohammedan brethren." Bah! thus you might chant, if you choose; but,
loving the truth, you will not so disown sweet Bethlehem—you
will not disown nor dissemble your right good hearty delight
when you find, as though in a desert, this gushing spring of fresh
and joyous girlhood.

CHAPTER
XVII

The desert.

GAZA stands upon the verge of the desert, and bears towards it the same kind of relation as a seaport bears to the sea. It is there that you *charter* your camels ("the ships of the desert").

These preparations kept me in the town for some days; disliking restraint, I declined making myself the guest of the Governor (as it is usual and proper to do), but took up my quarters at the caravansary, or khan, as they call it in that part of Asia.

Dthemetri had to make the arrangements for my journey, and in order to arm himself with sufficient authority for doing all that was required, he found it necessary to put himself in communication with the Governor. The result of this diplomatic intercourse was that the Governor, with his train of attendants, came to me one day at my caravansary, and formally complained that Dthemetri had grossly insulted him. I was shocked at this, for the man had been always attentive and civil to me, and I was disgusted at the idea of his being rewarded with insult. Dthemetri was present when the complaint was made, and I angrily asked him whether it was true that he had really insulted the Governor, and what the deuce he meant by it. This I asked with the full certainty that Dthemetri, as a matter of course, would deny the charge—would swear that a "wrong construction had been put upon his words, and that nothing was further from his thoughts," etc., after the manner of the parliamentary people; but, to my surprise, he very plainly answered that he certainly *had* insulted the Governor, and that rather grossly, but, he said, it was quite necessary to do this in order to "strike terror and inspire respect." "Terror and respect! What on earth do you mean by that nonsense?" "Yes, but without striking terror and inspiring respect, he (Dthemetri) would never be able to force on the arrangements for

my journey, and Vossignoria would be kept at Gaza for a month!"
This would have been awkward, and certainly I could not deny
that poor Dthemetri had succeeded in his odd plan of inspiring
respect, for at the very time that this explanation was going on in
Italian, the Governor seemed more than ever and more anxiously
disposed to overwhelm me with assurances of good will and prof-
fers of his best services. All this kindness, or promise of kindness,
I naturally received with courtesy—a courtesy that greatly per-
turbed Dthemetri, for he evidently feared that my civility would
undo all the good that his insults had achieved.

You will find, I think, that one of the greatest drawbacks to the
pleasure of traveling in Asia is the being obliged more or less to
make your way by bullying. It is true that your own lips are not
soiled by the utterance of all the mean words that are spoken for
you, and that you don't even know of the sham threats, and the
false promises, and the vainglorious boasts put forth by your
dragoman; but now and then there happens some incident of the
sort which I have just been mentioning, which forces you to believe, or suspect, that your dragoman is habitually fighting your
battles for you in a way you can hardly bear to think of.

A caravansary is not ill adapted to the purposes for which it is
meant. It forms the four sides of a large quadrangular court. The
ground floor is used for warehouses, the first floor for guests, and
the open court for the temporary reception of the camels, as well
as for the loading and unloading of their burdens, and the transaction of mercantile business generally. The apartments used for
the guests are small cells opening into a kind of corridor which
runs through the inner sides of the court.

Whilst I lay near the opening of my cell, looking down into the
court below, there arrived from the desert a caravan—that is, a
large assemblage of travelers. It consisted chiefly of Moldavian
pilgrims, who, to make their good work even more than complete,
had begun by visiting the shrine of the Virgin in Egypt, and were
now going on to Jerusalem. They had been overtaken in the desert
by a gale of wind, which so drove the sand, and raised up such
mountains before them, that their journey had been terribly per-

plexed and obstructed, and their provisions (including water, the most precious of all) had been exhausted long before they reached the end of their toilsome march. They were sadly wayworn. The arrival of the caravan drew many and various groups into the court. There was the Moldavian pilgrim with his sable dress, and cap of fur, and heavy masses of bushy hair; the Turk with his various and brilliant garments; the Arab superbly stalking under his striped blanket, that hung like royalty upon his stately form; the jetty Ethiopian in his slavish frock; the sleek, smooth-faced scribe with his comely pelisse, and his silver ink-box stuck in like a dagger at his girdle. And mingled with these were the camels—some standing, some kneeling and being unladen, some twisting round their long necks and gently stealing straw from out of their own pack-saddles.

In a couple of days I was ready to start. The way of providing for the passage of the desert is this: there is an agent in the town who keeps himself in communication with some of the desert Arabs that are hovering within a day's journey of the place; a party of these, upon being guaranteed against seizure or other ill-treatment at the hands of the Governor, come into the town, bringing with them the number of camels which you require, and then they stipulate for a certain sum to take you to the place of your destination in a given time; the agreement thus made by them includes a safe-conduct through their country, as well as the hire of the camels. According to the contract made with me, I was to reach Cairo within ten days from the commencement of the journey. I had four camels, one for my baggage, one for each of my servants and one for myself. Four Arabs, the owners of the camels, came with me on foot. My stores were a small soldier's tent, two bags of dried bread brought from the convent at Jerusalem, and a couple of bottles of wine from the same source, two goatskins filled with water, tea, sugar, a cold tongue, and (of all things in the world) a jar of Irish butter which Mysseri had purchased from some merchant. There was also a small sack of charcoal, for the greater part of the desert through which we were to pass is void of fuel.

The camel kneels to receive her load, and for a while she will allow the packing to go on with silent resignation; but when she begins to suspect that her master is putting more than a just burden upon her poor hump, she turns round her supple neck, and looks sadly upon the increasing load, and then gently remonstrates against the wrong with the sigh of a patient wife. If sighs will not move you, she can weep; you soon learn to pity and soon to love her for the sake of her gentle and womanish ways.

You cannot, of course, put an English or any other riding-saddle upon the back of the camel, but your quilt, or carpet, or whatever you carry for the purpose of lying on at night, is folded, and fastened on to the pack-saddle upon the top of the hump, and on this you ride, or rather sit. You sit as a man sits on a chair when he sits astride. I made an improvement on this plan: I had my English stirrups strapped on to the cross-bars of the pack-saddle, and thus by gaining rest for my dangling legs, and gaining, too, the power of varying my position more easily than I could otherwise have done, I added very much to my comfort.

The camel, like the elephant, is one of the old-fashioned sort of animals that still walk along upon the (now nearly exploded) plan of the ancient beasts that lived before the flood; she moves forward both her near legs at the same time, and then awkwardly swings round her off shoulder and haunch, so as to repeat the manœuver on that side; her pace, therefore, is an odd, disjointed, and disjoining sort of movement that is rather disagreeable at first, but you soon grow reconciled to it. The height to which you are raised is of great advantage to you in passing the burning sands of the desert, for the air at such a distance from the ground is much cooler, and more lively than that which circulates beneath.

For several miles beyond Gaza the land, freshened by the rains of the last week, was covered with rich verdure, and thickly jeweled with meadow flowers so bright and fragrant that I began to grow almost uneasy—to fancy that the very desert was receding before me, and that the long-desired adventure of passing its "burning sands" was to end in a mere ride across a field. But as I advanced, the true character of the country began to display itself with sufficient clearness to dispel my apprehensions, and before the close of my first day's journey I had the gratification of finding that I was surrounded on all sides by a tract of real sand, and had nothing at all to complain of, except that there peeped forth at intervals a few isolated blades of grass, and many of those stunted shrubs which are the accustomed food of the camel.

Before sunset I came up with an encampment of Arabs (the encampment from which my camels had been brought), and my tent was pitched amongst theirs. I was now amongst the true Bedouins. Almost every man of this race closely resembles his brethren; almost every man has large and finely formed features, but his face is so thoroughly stripped of flesh, and the white folds from his head-gear fall down by his haggard cheeks so much in the burial fashion, that he looks quite sad and ghastly; his large, dark orbs roll slowly and solemnly over the white of his deep-set eyes; his countenance shows painful thought and long suffering—the suffering of one fallen from a high estate. His gait is strangely majestic, and he marches along with his simple blanket as though he were wearing the purple. His common talk is a series of piercing screams and cries,* very painful to hear.

The Bedouin women are not treasured up like the wives and daughters of other Orientals, and indeed they seemed almost entirely free from the restraints imposed by jealousy. The feint which they made of concealing their faces from me was always slight. When they first saw me, they used to hold up a part of their drapery with one hand across their faces, but they seldom persevered very steadily in subjecting me to this privation. They were sadly plain. The awful haggardness that gave something of character to the faces of the men was sheer ugliness in the poor women. It is a great shame, but the truth is that, except when we refer to the beautiful devotion of the mother to her child, all the fine things we say and think about woman apply only to those who are tolerably good-looking or graceful. These Arab women were not

---

* Milnes cleverly goes to the French for the exact word which conveys the impression produced by the voice of the Arabs, and calls them "un peuple *criard*."

within the scope of the privilege, and indeed were altogether much too plain and clumsy for this vain and lovesome world. They may have been good women enough, so far as relates to the exercise of the minor virtues, but they had so grossly neglected the prime duty of looking pretty in this transitory life that I could not at all forgive them; they seemed to feel the weight of their guilt, and to be truly and humbly penitent. I had the complete command of their affections, for at any moment I could make their young hearts bound and their old hearts jump by offering a handful of tobacco; yet, believe me, it was not in the first soirée that my store of latakia was exhausted!

The Bedouin women have no religion. This is partly the cause of their clumsiness. Perhaps if from Christian girls they would learn how to pray, their souls might become more gentle, and their limbs be clothed with grace.

You who are going into their country have a direct personal interest in knowing something about "Arab hospitality"; but the deuce of it is that the poor fellows with whom I have happened to pitch my tent were scarcely ever in a condition to exercise that magnanimous virtue with much éclat; indeed, Mysseri's canteen generally enabled me to outdo my hosts in the matter of entertainment. They were always courteous, however, and were never backward in offering me the *youart*, a kind of whey, which is the principal delicacy to be found amongst the wandering tribes.

Practically, I think, Childe Harold would have found it a dreadful bore to make "the desert his dwelling-place," for, at all events, if he adopted the life of the Arabs he would have tasted no solitude. The tents are partitioned, not so as to divide the Childe and the "fair spirit" who is his "minister" from the rest of the world, but so as to separate the twenty or thirty brown men that sit screaming in the one compartment from the fifty or sixty brown women and children that scream and squeak in the other. If you adopt the Arab life for the sake of seclusion, you will be horribly disappointed, for you will find yourself in perpetual contact with a mass of hot fellow-creatures. It is true that all who are inmates

of the same tent are related to each other, but I am not quite sure
that that circumstance adds much to the charm of such a life.

In passing the desert you will find your Arabs wanting to start
and to rest at all sorts of odd times; they like, for instance, to be
off at one in the morning, and to rest during the whole of the
afternoon. You must not give way to their wishes in this respect;
I tried their plan once, and found it very harassing and unwhole-
some. An ordinary tent can give you very little protection against
heat, for the fire strikes fiercely through single canvas, and you
soon find that whilst you lie crouching and striving to hide yourself from the blazing face of the sun, his power is harder to bear
than it is when you boldly defy him from the airy heights of your
camel.

It had been arranged with my Arabs that they were to bring
with them all the food which they would want for themselves
during the passage of the desert, but as we rested, at the end of the
first day's journey, by the side of an Arab encampment, my camel-
men found all that they required for that night in the tents of their
own brethren. On the evening of the second day, however, just
before we encamped for the night, my four Arabs came to Dthemetri, and formally announced that they had not brought with them
one atom of food, and that they looked entirely to my supplies for
their daily bread. This was awkward intelligence. We were now
just two days deep in the desert, and I had brought with me no
more bread than might be reasonably required for myself and my
European attendants. I believed at the moment (for it seemed
likely enough) that the men had really mistaken the terms of the
arrangement, and feeling that the bore of being put upon half-
rations would be a less evil (and even to myself a less inconvenience) than the starvation of my Arabs, I at once told Dthemetri
to assure them that my bread should be equally shared with all.
Dthemetri, however, did not approve of this concession; he assured me quite positively that the Arabs thoroughly understood
the agreement, and that if they were now without food, they had
wilfully brought themselves into this strait for the wretched purpose of bettering their bargain by this value of a few paras' worth

of bread. This suggestion made me look at that affair in a new light. I should have been glad enough to put up with the slight privation to which my concession would subject me, and could have borne to witness the semi-starvation of poor Dthemetri with a fine, philosophical calm; but it seemed to me that the scheme, if scheme it were, had something of audacity in it, and was well enough calculated to try the extent of my softness. I knew the danger of allowing such a trial to result in a conclusion that I was one who might be easily managed; and therefore, after thoroughly satisfying myself, from Dthemetri's clear and repeated assertions, that the Arabs had really understood the arrangement, I determined that they should not now violate it by taking advantage of my position in the midst of their big desert; so I desired Dthemetri to tell them that they should touch no bread of mine. We stopped, and the tent was pitched; the Arabs came to me and prayed loudly for bread; I refused them.

"Then we die!"

"God's will be done."

I gave the Arabs to understand that I regretted their perishing by hunger, but that I should bear this calmly, like any other misfortune not my own—that, in short, I was happily resigned to *their* fate. The men would have talked a great deal, but they were under the disadvantage of addressing me through a hostile interpreter; they looked hard upon my face, but they found no hope there, so at last they retired, as they pretended to lay them down and die.

In about ten minutes from this time I found that the Arabs were busily cooking their bread! Their pretense of having brought no food was false, and was only invented for the purpose of saving it. They had a good bag of meal which they had contrived to stow away under the baggage, upon one of the camels, in such a way as to escape notice. In Europe the detection of a scheme like this would have occasioned a disagreeable feeling between the master and the delinquent, but you would no more recoil from an Oriental on account of a matter of this sort than in England you would reject a horse that had tried, and failed, to throw you. Indeed, I felt quite good-humoredly towards my Arabs, because they had so woefully failed in their wretched attempt, and because, as it turned out, I had done what was right; they, too, poor fellows, evidently began to like me immensely, on account of the hard-heartedness which had enabled me to baffle their scheme.

The Arabs adhere to those ancestral principles of bread-baking which have been sanctioned by the experience of ages. The very first baker of bread that ever lived must have done his work exactly as the Arab does at this day. He takes some meal, and holds it out in the hollow of his hands, whilst his comrade pours over it a few drops of water; he then mashes up the moistened flour into a paste, pulls the lump of dough so made into small pieces and thrusts them into the embers. His way of baking exactly resembles the craft or mystery of roasting chestnuts as practised by children; there is the same prudence and circumspection in choosing a good berth for the morsel—the same enterprise and self-sacrificing valor in pulling it out with the fingers.

The manner of my daily march was this: At about an hour before dawn, I rose and made the most of about a pint of water which I allowed myself for washing. Then I breakfasted upon tea and bread. As soon as the beasts were loaded, I mounted my camel and pressed forward. My poor Arabs, being on foot, would sometimes moan with fatigue, and pray for rest; but I was anxious to enable them to perform their contract for bringing me to Cairo within the stipulated time, and I did not, therefore, allow a halt until the evening came. About mid-day, or soon after, Mysseri used to bring up his camel alongside of mine, and supply me with a piece of the dried bread softened in water, and also (as long as it lasted) with a piece of the tongue; after this there came into my hand (how well I remember it!) the little tin cup half filled with wine and water.

As long as you are journeying in the interior of the desert you have no particular point to make for as your resting-place. The endless sands yield nothing but small stunted shrubs; even these fail after the first two or three days, and from that time you pass over broad plains, you pass over newly reared hills, you pass through valleys dug out by the last week's storm; and the hills and

[145]

the valleys are sand, sand, sand, still sand, and only sand, and sand, and sand again. The earth is so samely that your eyes turn towards heaven—towards heaven, I mean, in sense of sky. You look to the sun, for he is your taskmaster, and by him you know the measure of the work that you have done, and the measure of the work that remains for you to do. He comes when you strike your tent in the early morning, and then, for the first hour of the day, as you move forward on your camel, he stands at your near side, and makes you know that the whole day's toil is before you; then for a while, and a long while, you see him no more, for you are veiled, and shrouded, and dare not look upon the greatness of his glory, but you know where he strides overhead, by the touch of his flaming sword. No words are spoken, but your Arabs moan, your camels sigh, your skin glows, your shoulders ache, and for sights you see the pattern and the web of the silk that veils your eyes, and the glare of the outer light. Time labors on; your skin glows, your shoulders ache, your Arabs moan, your camels sigh, and you see the same pattern in the silk, and the same glare of light beyond; but conquering time marches on, and by and by the descending sun has compassed the heaven, and now softly touches your right arm, and throws your lank shadow over the sand, right along on the way for Persia. Then again you look upon his face, for his power is all veiled in his beauty, and the redness of flames has become the redness of roses; the fair, wavy cloud that fled in the morning now comes to his sight once more—comes blushing, yet still comes on, comes burning with blushes, yet comes and clings to his side.

Then begins your season of rest. The world about you is all your own, and there, where you will, you pitch your solitary tent; there is no living thing to dispute your choice. When at last the spot had been fixed upon, and we came to a halt, one of the Arabs would touch the chest of my camel, and utter at the same time a peculiar gurgling sound. The beast instantly understood and obeyed the sign, and slowly sank under me till she brought her body to a level with the ground. Then gladly enough I alighted. The rest of the camels were unloaded, and turned loose to browse upon the shrubs of the desert, where shrubs there were, or, where these failed, to wait for the small quantity of food that was allowed them out of our stores.

My servants, helped by the Arabs, busied themselves in pitching the tent and kindling the fire. Whilst this was doing I used to walk away towards the east, confiding in the print of my foot as a guide for my return. Apart from the cheering voices of my attendants I could better know and feel the loneliness of the desert. The influence of such scenes, however, was not of a softening kind, but filled me rather with a sort of childish exultation in the self-sufficiency which enabled me to stand thus alone in the wideness of Asia—a short-lived pride, for wherever man wanders, he still remains tethered by the chain that links him to his kind; and so when the night closed round me I began to return—to return, as it were, to my own gate. Reaching at last some high ground, I could see, and see with delight, the fire of our small encampment, and when at last I regained the spot, it seemed a very home that had sprung up for me in the midst of these solitudes. My Arabs were busy with their bread, Mysseri rattling tea-cups; the little kettle, with her odd, old-maidish looks, sat humming away old songs about England; and two or three yards from the fire my tent stood prim and tight, with open portal and with welcoming look—a look like "the own arm-chair" of our lyrist's "sweet Lady Anne."

Sometimes in the earlier part of my journey the night breeze blew coldly; when that happened, the dry sand was heaped up outside round the skirts of the tent, and so the wind that everywhere else could sweep as he listed along those dreary plains was forced to turn aside in his course, and make way, as he ought, for the Englishman. Then, within my tent, there were heaps of luxuries—dining-rooms, dressing-rooms, libraries, bedrooms, drawing-rooms, oratories, all crowded into the space of a hearth-rug. The first night, I remember, with my books and maps about me, I wanted a light. They brought me a taper, and immediately from out of the silent desert there rushed in a flood of life unseen before. Monsters of moths, of all shapes and hues, that never before perhaps had looked upon the shining of a flame, now madly thronged into my tent, and dashed through the fire of the candle till they fairly extinguished it with their burning limbs. Those who had failed in attaining this martyrdom suddenly became serious, and clung despondingly to the canvas.

By and by there was brought to me the fragrant tea, and big masses of scorched and scorching toast, and the butter that had come all the way to me in this desert of Asia from out of that poor, dear, starving Ireland. I feasted like a king—like four kings—like a boy in the fourth form.

When the cold, sullen morning dawned, and my people began to load the camels, I always felt loath to give back to the waste this little spot of ground that had glowed for a while with the cheerfulness of a human dwelling. One by one, the cloaks, the saddles, the baggage, the hundred things that strewed the ground and made it look so familiar—all these were taken away and laid upon the camels. A speck in the broad tracts of Asia remained still impressed with the mark of patent portmanteaus and the heels of London boots; the embers of the fire lay black and cold upon the sand; and these were the signs we left.

My tent was spared to the last, but when all else was ready for the start, then came its fall; the pegs were drawn, the canvas shivered, and in less than a minute there was nothing that remained of my genial home but only a pole and a bundle. The encroaching Englishman was off, and instant upon the fall of the canvas, like an owner who had waited and watched, the Genius of the Desert stalked in.

To servants, as I suppose to any other Europeans not much accustomed to amuse themselves by fancy or memory, it often happens that after a few days' journeying the loneliness of the desert will become frightfully oppressive. Upon my poor fellows the access of melancholy came heavy and all at once, as a blow from above. They bent their necks and bore it as best they could, but their joy was great on the fifth day, when we came to an oasis called Gatieh, for here we found encamped a caravan (that is, an assemblage of travelers) from Cairo. The Orientals living in cities never pass the desert, except in this way; many will wait for weeks, and even for months, until a sufficient number of persons can be found ready to undertake the journey at the same time— until the flock of sheep is big enough to fancy itself a match for wolves. They could not, I think, really secure themselves against any serious danger by this contrivance; for, though they have arms, they are so little accustomed to use them, and so utterly unorganized, that they never could make good their resistance to robbers of the slightest respectability. It is not of the Bedouins that such travelers are afraid, for the safe-conduct granted by the chief of the ruling tribe is never, I believe, violated; but it is said that there are deserters and scamps of various sorts who hover about the skirts of the desert, particularly on the Cairo side, and are anxious to succeed to the property of any poor devils whom they may find more weak and defenseless than themselves.

These people from Cairo professed to be amazed at the ludicrous disproportion between their numerical forces and mine. They could not understand, and they wanted to know, by what strange privilege it is that an Englishman with a brace of pistols and a couple of servants rides safely across the desert, whilst they, the natives of the neighboring cities, are forced to travel in troops, or rather in herds. One of them got a few minutes of private conversation with Dthemetri, and ventured to ask him anxiously whether the English did not travel under the protection of evil demons. I had previously known (from Methley, I think, who had traveled in Persia) that this notion, so conducive to the safety of our countrymen, is generally prevalent amongst Orientals; it owes its origin partly to the strong wilfulness of the English gentleman (a quality which, not being backed by any visible authority, either civil or military, seems perfectly superhuman to the soft Asiatic), but partly, too, to the magic of the banking system, by force of which the wealthy traveler will make all his journeys without carrying a handful of coin, and yet, when he arrives at a city, will rain down showers of gold. The theory is that the English traveler has committed some sin against God and his conscience, and that for this the Evil Spirit has hold of him, and drives him from his home, like a victim of the old Grecian Furies, and forces him to travel over countries far and strange, and most chiefly over deserts and desolate place, and to stand upon the sites of cities that once were and are now no more, and to grope among the tombs of dead men. Often enough there is something of truth in this notion; often enough the wandering Englishman is guilty (if guilt it be) of some pride or ambition, big or small, imperial or parochial, which, being offended, has made the lone places more tolerable than ballrooms to him, a sinner.

I can understand the sort of amazement of the Orientals at the scantiness of the retinue with which an Englishman passes the desert, for I was somewhat struck myself when I saw one of my countrymen making his way across the wilderness in this simple style. At first there was a mere moving speck in the horizon. My party, of course, became all alive with excitement, and there were many surmises. Soon it appeared that three laden camels were approaching, and that two of them carried riders; in a little while we saw that one of the riders wore the European dress, and at last the travelers were pronounced to be an English gentleman and his servant. By their side there were a couple of Arabs on foot, and this, if I rightly remember, was the whole party.

You,—you love sailing,—in returning from a cruise to the English coast, you see often enough a fisherman's humble boat far away from all shores, with an ugly, black sky above, and an angry sea beneath. You watch the grisly old man at the helm, carrying his craft with strange skill through the turmoil of waters; and the boy, supple-limbed, yet weather-worn already, and with steady eyes that look through the blast—you see him understanding commandments from the jerk of his father's white eyebrow—now belaying, and now letting go, now scrunching himself down into mere ballast, or bailing out death with a pipkin. Familiar enough is the sight, and yet when I see it I always stare anew, and with a kind of Titanic exultation, because that a poor boat with the brain of a man and the hands of a boy on board can match herself so bravely against black heaven and ocean. Well, so when you have traveled for days and days over an Eastern desert, without meeting the likeness of a human being, and then at last see an English shooting-jacket and a single servant come listlessly slouching along from out of the forward horizon, you stare at the wide unproportion between this slender company, and the boundless plains of sand through which they are keeping their way.

This Englishman, as I afterwards found, was a military man returning to his country from India, and crossing the desert at this part in order to go through Palestine. As for me, I had come pretty straight from England, and so here we met in the wilderness at about half-way from our respective starting-points. As we approached each other, it became with me a question whether we should speak. I thought it likely that the stranger would accost me, and in the event of his doing so I was quite ready to be as sociable and chatty as I could be, according to my nature; but still I could not think of anything particular that I had to say to him. Of course, among civilized people, the not having anything to say is no excuse at all for not speaking, but I was shy and indolent, and I felt no great wish to stop and talk like a morning visitor in the midst of those broad solitudes. The traveler, perhaps, felt as I did, for, except that we lifted our hands to our caps and waved our arms in courtesy, we passed each other quite as distantly as if we had passed in Pall Mall. Our attendants, however, were not to be cheated of the delight that they felt in speaking to new listeners and hearing fresh voices once more. The masters, therefore, had no sooner passed each other than their respective servants quietly stopped and entered into conversation. As soon as my camel found that her companions were not following her, she caught the social feeling and refused to go on. I felt the absurdity of the situation, and determined to accost the stranger, if only to avoid the awkwardness of remaining stuck fast in the desert whilst our servants were amusing themselves. When with this intent I turned round my camel, I found that the gallant officer had passed me by about thirty or forty yards, and was exactly in the same predicament as myself. I put my now willing camel in motion, and rode up towards the stranger. Seeing this, he followed my example, and came forward to meet me. He was the first to speak. Too courteous to address me as if he admitted the possibility of my wishing to accost him from any feeling of mere sociability or civilian-like love of vain talk, he at once attributed my advances to a laudable wish of acquiring statistical information, and accordingly, when we got within speaking distance, he said, "I dare say you wish to know how the plague is going on at Cairo?" And then he went on to say he regretted that his information did not enable him to give me in numbers a perfectly accurate statement of the daily deaths; he afterwards talked pleasantly enough upon other and less ghastly subjects. I though him manly and intelligent—a worthy one of the few thousand strong Englishmen to whom the Empire of India is committed.

The night after the meeting with the people of the caravan, Dthemetri, alarmed by their warnings, took upon himself to keep watch all night in the tent. No robbers came, except a jackal that poked his nose into my tent from some motive of rational curiosity. Dthemetri did not shoot him, for fear of waking me. These brutes swarm in every part of Syria; and there were many of them even in the midst of those void sands, which would seem to give such poor promise of food; I can hardly tell what prey they could be hoping for, unless it were that they might find, now and then, the carcass of some camel that had died on the journey. They do not marshal themselves into great packs like the wild dogs of Eastern cities, but follow their prey in families, like place-hunters of Europe; their voices are frightfully like to the shouts and cries of human beings. If you lie awake in your tent at night, you are almost continually hearing some hungry family as it sweeps along in full cry; you hear the exulting scream with which the sagacious dam first winds the carrion, and the shrill response of the unanimous cubs as they snuff the tainted air: "Wha! wha! wha! wha! wha! wha! Whose gift is it in, mama?"

Once, during the passage, my Arabs lost their way among the hills of loose sand that surrounded us, but after a while we were lucky enough to recover our right line of march. The same day we fell in with a sheik, the head of a family, that actually dwells at no great distance from this part of the desert during nine months of the year. The man carried a matchlock, and of this he was inordinately proud on account of the supposed novelty and ingenuity of the contrivance. We stopped, and sat down and rested awhile for the sake of a little talk. There was much that I should have liked to ask this man, but he could not understand Dthemetri's language, and the process of getting at his knowledge by double interpretation through my Arabs was tedious. I discovered, however (and my Arabs knew of that fact), that this man and his family lived habitually for nine months of the year without touching or seeing either bread or water. The stunted shrub growing at intervals through the sand in this part of the desert enables the camel mares to yield a little milk, and this furnishes the sole food and drink of their owner and his people. During the other three months (the hottest, I suppose) even this resource fails, and then the sheik and his people are forced to pass into another district. You would ask me why the man should not remain always in that district which supplies him with water during three months of the year, but I don't know enough of Arab politics to answer the question. The sheik was not a good specimen of the effect produced by his way of living. He was very small, very spare, and sadly shriveled—a poor over-roasted snipe, a mere cinder of a man. I made him sit down by my side, and gave him a piece of bread and a cup of water from out of my goatskins. This was not very tempting drink to look at, for it had become turbid, and was deeply reddened by some coloring matter contained in the skins, but it kept its sweetness and tasted like a strong decoction of Russian leather. The sheik sipped this, drop by drop, with ineffable relish, and rolled his eyes solemnly round between every draught, as though the drink were the drink of the Prophet, and had come from the seventh heaven.

An inquiry about distance led to the discovery that this sheik had never heard of the division of time into hours.

About this part of my journey I saw the likeness of a freshwater lake. I saw, as it seemed, a broad sheet of calm water stretching far and fair towards the south—stretching deep into winding creeks, and hemmed in by jutting promontories, and shelving smooth off towards the shallow side; on its bosom the reflected fire of the sun lay playing, and seeming to float as though upon deep, still waters.

Though I knew of the cheat, it was not till the spongy foot of my camel had almost trodden in the seeming lake that I could undeceive my eyes, for the shore-line was quite true and natural. I soon saw the cause of the phantasm. A sheet of water, heavily impregnated with salts, had gathered together in a vast hollow between the sand-hills, and, when dried up by evaporation, had left a white saline deposit; this exactly marked the space which the waters had covered, and so traced out a good shore-line. The minute crystals of the salt, by their way of sparkling in the sun, were made to seem like the dazzled face of a lake that is calm and smooth.

The pace of the camel is irksome, and makes your shoulders and loins ache from the peculiar way in which you are obliged to suit yourself to the movements of the beast; but one soon, of course, becomes inured to the work, and after my first two days this way of traveling became so familiar to me that (poor sleeper as I am) I now and then slumbered for some moments together on the back of my camel. On the fifth day of my journey, the air above lay dead, and all the whole earth that I could reach with my utmost sight and keenest listening was still and lifeless as some dispeopled and forgotten world that rolls round and round in the heavens through wasted floods of light. The sun, growing fiercer and fiercer, shone down more mightily now than ever on me he shone before, and as I drooped my head under his fire, and closed my eyes against the glare that surrounded me, I slowly fell asleep, for how many minutes or moments I cannot tell; but after a while I was gently awakened by a peal of church bells—my native bells— the innocent bells of Marlen, that never before sent forth their music beyond the Blaygon hills! My first idea naturally was that I still remained fast under the power of a dream. I roused myself, and drew aside the silk that covered my eyes, and plunged my bare face into the light. Then, at least, I was well enough awakened, but still those old Marlen bells rang on, not ringing for joy, but properly, prosily, steadily, merrily ringing "for church." After a while the sound died away slowly. It happened that neither I nor any in my party had a watch by which to measure the exact time of its lasting, but it seemed to me that about ten minutes had passed before the bells ceased. I attributed the effect to the great heat of the sun, the perfect dryness of the clear air through which I moved, and the deep stillness of all around me. It seemed to me that these causes, by occasioning a great tension and consequent susceptibility of the hearing organs, had rendered them liable to tingle under the passing touch of some mere memory that must have swept across my brain in a moment of sleep. Since my return to England it has been told me that like sounds have been heard at sea, and that the sailor, becalmed under a vertical sun in the midst of the wide ocean, has listened in trembling wonder to the chime of his own village bells.

During my travels I kept a journal—a journal sadly meager and intermittent, but one which enabled me to find out the day of the month and the week, according to the European calendar. Referring to this, I found that the day was Sunday, and roughly allowing for the difference of longitude, I concluded that at the moment of my hearing that strange peal the church-going bells of Marlen must have been actually calling the prim congregation of the parish to morning prayer. The coincidence amused me faintly, but I could not allow myself a hope that the effect I had experienced was anything other than illusion—an illusion liable to be explained (as every illusion is in these days) by some of the philosophers who guess at nature's riddles. It would have been sweeter to believe that my kneeling mother, by some pious enchantment, had asked and found this spell to rouse me from my scandalous forgetfulness of God's holy day, but my fancy was too weak to carry a faith like that. Indeed, the vale through which the bells of Marlen send their song is a highly respectable vale, and its people (save one, two, or three) are wholly unaddicted to the practice of magical arts.

After the fifth day of my journey I no longer traveled over shifting hills, but came upon a dead level—a dead level bed of sand, quite hard, and studded with small shining pebbles.

The heat grew fierce; there was no valley nor hollow, no hill, no mound, no shadow of hill nor of mound, by which I could mark the way I was making. Hour by hour I advanced, and saw no change—I was still the very center of a round horizon; hour by hour I advanced, and still there was the same, and the same, and the same—the same circle of flaming sky, the same circle of sand still glaring with light and fire. Over all the heaven above, over all the earth beneath, there was no visible power that could balk the fierce will of the sun. "He rejoiced as a strong man to run a race. His going forth was from the end of the heaven, and his circuit unto the ends of it: and there was nothing hid from the heat thereof." From pole to pole, and from the east to the west, he brandished his fiery scepter as though he had usurped all heaven and earth. As he bid the soft Persian in ancient times, so now, and fiercely, too, he bid me bow down and worship him; so now in his pride he seemed to command me and say, "Thou shalt have none other gods but me." I was all alone before him. There were these two pitted together, and face to face—the mighty sun for one, and for the other this poor, pale, solitary self of mine that I always carry about with me.

But on the eighth day, and before I had yet turned away from Jehovah for the glittering god of the Persians, there appeared a dark line upon the edge of the forward horizon, and soon the line deepened into a delicate fringe, that sparkled here and there as though it were sown with diamonds. There, then, before were the gardens and the minarets of Egypt, and the mighty works of the Nile, and I (the eternal Ego that I am!)—I had lived to see, and I saw them.

When evening came I was still within the confines of the desert, and my tent was pitched as usual, but one of my Arabs stalked away rapidly towards the west, without telling me of the errand on which he was bent. After a while he returned. He had toiled on a graceful service: he had traveled all the way on to the border of the living world, and brought me back for a token an ear of rice, full, fresh, and green.

The next day I entered upon Egypt, and floated along (for the delight was as the delight of bathing) through green, wavy fields of rice, and pastures fresh and plentiful, and dived into the cold verdure of groves and gardens, and quenched my hot eyes in shade, as though in a bed of deep waters.

CHAPTER
XVIII

*Cairo and the plague.**

CAIRO and Plague! During the whole time of my stay the plague was so master of the city, and stared so plain in every street and every alley, that I can't now affect to dissociate the two ideas.

When, coming from the desert, I rode through a village lying near to the city on the eastern side, there approached me, with busy face and earnest gestures, a personage in the Turkish dress. His long flowing beard gave him rather a majestic look, but his briskness of manner and his visible anxiety to accost me seemed strange in an Oriental. The man, in fact, was French, or of French origin, and his object was to warn me of the plague, and prevent me from entering the city.

"Arrêtez-vous, monsieur, je vous en prie—arrêtez-vous; il ne faut pas entrer dans la ville; la peste y règne partout."

---

* There is some semblance of bravado in my manner of talking about the plague. I have been more careful to describe the terrors of other people than my own. The truth is that during the whole period of my stay at Cairo I remained thoroughly impressed with a sense of my danger. I may almost say that I lived under perpetual apprehension, for even in sleep, as I fancy, there remained with me some faint notion of the peril with which I was encompassed. But fear does not necessarily damp the spirits; on the contrary, it will often operate as an excitement, giving rise to unusual animation, and thus it affected me. If I had not been surrounded at this time by new faces, new scenes, and new sounds, the effect produced upon my mind by one unceasing cause of alarm may have been very different. As it was, the eagerness with which I pursued my rambles among the wonders of Egypt was sharpened and increased by the sting of the fear of death. Thus my account of the matter plainly conveys an impression that I remained at Cairo without losing my cheerfulness and buoyancy of spirits. And this is the truth; but it is also true, as I have freely confessed, that my sense of danger during the whole period was lively and continuous.

[159]

"Oui, je sais,* mais—"

"Mais, monsieur, je dis la peste—la peste; c'est de LA PESTE qu'il est question."

"Oui, je sais, mais—"

"Mais, monsieur, je dis encore LA PESTE—LA PESTE. Je vous conjure de ne pas entrer dans la ville—vous seriez dans une ville empestée."

"Oui, je sais, mais—"

"Mais, monsieur, je dois donc vous avertir tout bonnement que si vous entrez dans la ville, vous serez—enfin vous serez COMPRO-MIS!"†

"Oui, je sais, mais—"

The Frenchman was at last convinced that it was vain to reason with a mere Englishman, who could not understand what it was to be "compromised." I thanked him most sincerely for his kindly meant warning; in hot countries it is very unusual indeed for a man to go out in the glare of the sun and give free advice to a stranger.

When I arrived at Cairo I summoned Osman Effendi, who was, as I knew, the owner of several houses, and would be able to provide me with apartments; he had no difficulty in doing this, for there was not one European traveler in Cairo besides myself. Poor Osman! he met me with a sorrowful countenance, for the fear of the plague sat heavily on his soul; he seemed as if he felt that he was doing wrong in lending me a resting-place, and he betrayed such a listlessness about temporal matters as one might look for in a man who believed that his days were numbered. He caught me, too, soon after my arrival, coming out from the public baths,‡ and

---

* *Anglicè* for "je le sais." These answers of mine as given above are not meant as specimens of mere French, but of that fine, terse, nervous *Continental English* with which I and my compatriots make our way through Europe.

† The import of the word "compromised," when used in reference to contagion, is explained in page 2.

‡ It is said that when a Mussulman finds himself attacked by the plague, he goes and takes a bath. The couches on which the bathers recline would carry infection, according to the notions of the Europeans. Whenever, therefore, I took the bath at Cairo (except the first time of my doing so), I avoided that part of the luxury which consists in being "put up to dry" upon a kind of bed.

from that time forward he was sadly afraid of me, for upon the subject of contagion he held European opinions.

Osman's history is a curious one. He was a Scotchman born, and when very young, being then a drummer-boy, he landed in Egypt with Fraser's force. He was taken prisoner, and, according to Mohammedan custom, the alternative of death or the Koran was offered to him. He did not choose death, and, therefore, went through the ceremonies necessary for turning him into a good Mohammedan. But what amused me most in his history was this: that very soon after having embraced Islam he was obliged in practice to become curious and discriminating in his new faith—to make war upon Mohammedan dissenters, and follow the ortho-dox standard of the Prophet in fierce campaigns against the Wa-habis, the Unitarians of the Mussulman world. The Wahabis were crushed, and Osman, returning home in triumph from his holy wars, began to flourish in the world; he acquired property, and became "effendi," or gentleman. At the time of my visit to Cairo, he seemed to be much respected by his brother Mohammedans, and gave pledge of his sincere alienation from Christianity by keeping a couple of wives. He affected the same sort of reserve in mentioning them as is generally shown by Orientals. He invited me, indeed, to see his harem, but he made both his wives bundle out before I was admitted; he felt, as it seemd to me, that neither of them would bear criticism, and I think that this idea, rather than any motive of sincere jealousy, induced him to keep them out of sight. The rooms of the harem reminded me of an English nursery rather than a Mohammedan paradise. One is apt to judge of a woman before one sees her by the air of elegance or coarse-ness with which she surrounds her home. I judged Osman's wives by this test, and condemned them both. But the strangest feature in Osman's character was his inextinguishable nationality. In vain they had brought him over the seas in early boyhood; in vain had he suffered captivity, conversion, circumcision; in vain they had passed him through fire in their Arabian campaigns: they could not cut away or burn out poor Osman's inborn love of all that was Scotch. In vain men called him effendi; in vain he swept along in

Eastern robes; in vain the rival wives adorned his harem: the joy of his heart still plainly lay in this, that he had three shelves of books, and that the books were thoroughbred Scotch—the Edinburgh this, the Edinburgh that, and above all, I recollect, he prided himself upon the "Edinburgh Cabinet Library."

The fear of the plague is its forerunner. It is likely enough that at the time of my seeing poor Osman the deadly taint was beginning to creep through his veins, but it was not till after I had left Cairo that he was visibly stricken. He died.

As soon as I had seen all that interested me in Cairo and its neighborhood, I wished to make my escape from a city that lay under the terrible curse of the plague; but Mysseri fell ill—in consequence, I believe of the hardships which he had been suffering in my service; after a while he recovered sufficiently to undertake a journey, but then there was some difficulty in procuring beasts of burden, and it was not till the nineteenth day of my sojourn that I quitted the city.

During all this time the power of the plague was rapidly increasing. When I first arrived, it was said that the daily number of "accidents" by plague, out of a population of about two hundred thousand, did not exceed four or five hundred; but before I went away, the deaths were reckoned at twelve hundred a day. I had no means of knowing whether the numbers (given out, as I believe they were, by officials) were at all correct, but I could not help knowing that from day to day the number of the dead was increasing. My quarters were in one of the chief thoroughfares of the city, and as the funerals in Cairo take place between daybreak and noon (a time during which I generally stayed in my rooms), I could form some opinion as to the briskness of the plague. I don't mean that I got up every morning with the sun. It was not so. But the funerals of most people in decent circumstances at Cairo are attended by singers and howlers, and the performances of these people woke me in the early morning, and prevented me from remaining in ignorance of what was going on in the street below.

These funerals were very simply conducted. The bier was a shallow wooden tray carried upon a light and weak wooden frame. The tray had, in general, no lid, but the body was more or less hidden from view by a shawl or scarf. The whole was borne upon the shoulders of men, and hurried forward at a great pace. Two or three singers generally preceded the bier; the howlers (these are paid for their vocal labors) followed after; and last of all came such of the dead man's friends and relations as could keep up with such a rapid procession; these, especially the women, would get terribly blown, and would struggle back into the rear; many were fairly "beaten off." I never observed any appearance of mourning in the mourners; the pace was too severe for any solemn affectation of grief.

When first I arrived at Cairo, the funerals that daily passed under my windows were many, but still there were frequent and long intervals without a single howl. Every day, however (except one, when I fancied that I observed a diminution of funerals), these intervals became less frequent and shorter, and at last the passing of the howlers from morn to noon was almost incessant. I believe that about one half of the whole people was carried off by this visitation. The Orientals, however, have more quiet fortitude than Europeans under afflictions of this sort, and they never allow the plague to interfere with their religious usages. I rode, one day, round the great burial-ground. The tombs are strewed over a great expanse, among the vast mountains of rubbish (the accumulation of many centuries) which surround the city. The ground, unlike the Turkish "cities of the dead," which are made so beautiful by their dark cypresses, has nothing to sweeten melancholy—nothing to mitigate the hatefulness of death. Carnivorous beasts and birds possess the place by night, and now in the fair morning it was all alive with fresh comers—alive with dead. Yet at this very time when the plague was raging so furiously, and on this very ground which resounded so mournfully with the howls of arriving funerals, preparations were going on for the religious festival called the Kourban Bairam. Tents were pitched, and *swings hung for the amusement of children*. A ghastly holiday! but the Mohammedans take a pride, and a just pride, in following their ancient customs undisturbed by the shadow of death.

I did not hear, whilst I was at Cairo, that any prayer for a remission of the plague had been offered up in the mosques. I believe that, however frightful the ravages of the disease may be, the Mohammedans refrain from approaching Heaven with their complaints until the plague has endured for a long space, and then at last they pray God, not that the plague may cease, but that it may go to another city!

A good Mussulman seems to take pride in repudiating the European notion that the will of God can be eluded by shunning the touch of a sleeve. When I went to see the Pyramids of Sakkara, I was the guest of a noble old fellow—an Osmanli (how sweet it was to hear his soft, rolling language after suffering as I had suffered of late from the shrieking tongue of the Arabs!). This man was aware of the European ideas about contagion, and his first care, therefore, was to assure me that not a single instance of plague had occurred in his village. He then inquired as to the progress of the plague at Cairo. I had but a bad account to give. Up to this time my host had carefully refrained from touching me, out of respect to the European theory of contagion; but as soon as it was made plain that he, and not I, would be the person endangered by contact, he gently laid his hand upon my arm, in order to make me feel sure that the circumstance of my coming from an infected city did not occasion him the least uneasiness. In that touch there was true hospitality.

Very different is the faith and the practice of the Europeans, or rather, I mean, of the Europeans settled in the East, and commonly called Levantines. When I came to the end of my journey over the desert, I had been so long alone that the prospect of speaking to somebody at Cairo seemed almost a new excitement. I felt a sort of consciousness that I had a little of the wild beast about me, but I was quite in the humor to be charmingly tame, and to be quite engaging in my manners, if I should have an opportunity of holding communion with any of the human race whilst at Cairo. I knew no one in the place, and had no letters of introduction, but I carried letters of credit, and it often happens, in places remote from England, that those "advices" operate as a sort of introduction, and obtain for the bearer (if disposed to receive them) such ordinary civilities as it may be in the power of the banker to offer.

Very soon after my arrival, I found out the abode of the Levantine to whom my credentials were addressed. At his door several persons (all Arabs) were hanging about and keeping guard. It was not till after some delay, and the interchange of some communications with those in the interior of the citadel, that I was admitted. At length, however, I was conducted through the court, and up a flight of stairs, and finally into the apartment where business was transacted. The room was divided by a good, substantial fence of iron bars, and behind these defenses the banker had his station. The truth was that from fear of the plague he had adopted the course usually taken by European residents, and had shut himself up "in strict quarantine"—that is to say, that he had, as he hoped, cut himself off from all communication with infecting substances. The Europeans long resident in the East, without any or with scarcely any exception, are firmly convinced that the plague is propagated by contact, and by contact only—that if they can but avoid the touch of an infecting substance they are safe, and that if they cannot they die. This belief induces them to adopt the contrivance of putting themselves in that state of siege which they call "quarantine." It is a part of their faith that metals, and hempen rope, and also, I fancy, one or two other substances, will not carry the infection; and they likewise believe that the germ of pestilence lying in an infected substance may be destroyed by submersion in water, or by the action of smoke. They, therefore, guard the doors of their houses with the utmost care against intrusion, and condemn themselves, with all the members of their family, including European servants, to a strict imprisonment within the walls of their dwelling. Their native attendants are not allowed to enter at all, but they make the necessary purchases of provisions; these are hauled up through one of the windows by means of a rope, and are afterwards soaked in water.

I knew nothing of these mysteries, and was not, therefore, prepared for the sort of reception I met with. I advanced to the iron fence, and putting my letter between the bars, politely proffered it to Mr. Banker. Mr. Banker received me with a sad and dejected look, and not "with open arms," or with any arms at all, but with—a pair of tongs! I placed my letter between the iron fingers. These instantly picked it up as it were a viper, and conveyed it away to be scorched and purified by fire and smoke. I was disgusted at this reception, and at the idea that anything of mine could carry infection to the poor wretch who stood on the other side of the bars—pale and trembling, and already meet for death. I looked with something of the Mohammedan's feeling upon these little contrivances for eluding fate; and in this instance at least they were vain: a little while, and the poor money-changer, who had strived to guard the days of his life (as though they were coins) with bolts and bars of iron—he was seized by the plague, and he died.

To people entertaining such opinions as these respecting the fatal effect of contact, the narrow and crowded streets of Cairo were terrible as the easy slope that leads to Avernus. The roaring ocean and the beetling crags owe something of their sublimity to this—that if they be tempted they can take the warm life of a man. To the contagionist, filled as he is with the dread of final causes, having no faith in destiny, nor in the fixed will of God, and with none of the devil-may-care indifference which might stand him instead of creeds—to such one every rag that shivers in the breeze of a plague-stricken city has this sort of sublimity. If, by any terrible ordinance, he be forced to venture forth, he sees death dangling from every sleeve, and as he creeps forward, he poises his shuddering limbs between the imminent jacket that is stabbing at his right elbow, and the murderous pelisse that threatens to mow him clean down as it sweeps along on his left. But most of all he dreads that which most of all he should love—the touch of a woman's dress; for mothers and wives, hurrying forth on kindly errands from the bedsides of the dying, go slouching along through the streets more wilfully and less courteously than the men. For a while it may be that the caution of the poor Levantine may enable him to avoid contact, but sooner or later, perhaps, the dreaded chance arrives. That bundle of linen, with the dark, tearful eyes at the top of it, that labors along with the voluptuous clumsiness of Grisi—she has touched the poor Levantine with the hem of her sleeve! From that dread moment his peace is gone; his mind forever hanging upon the fatal touch, invites the blow which he fears; he watches for the symptoms of plague so carefully that, sooner or later, they come in truth. The parched mouth is a sign—his mouth *is* parched. The throbbing brain—his brain *does* throb. The rapid pulse—he touches his own wrist (for he dares not ask counsel of any man, lest he be deserted), he touches his wrist, and feels how his frighted blood goes galloping out of his heart. There is nothing but the fatal swelling that is wanting to make his sad conviction complete. Immediately he has an odd feel under the arm—no pain, but a little straining of the skin. He would to God it were his fancy that were strong enough to give him that sensation! This is the worst of all. It now seems to him that he could be happy and contented with his parched mouth, and his throbbing brain, and his rapid pulse, if only he could know that there were no swelling under the left arm; but dares he try? In a moment of calmness and deliberation he dares not, but when for a while he has writhed under the torture of suspense, a sudden strength of will drives him to seek and know his fate. He touches the gland, and finds the skin sane and sound, but under the cuticle there lies a small lump, like a pistol bullet, that moves as he pushes it. Oh! but is this for all certainty? is this the sentence of death? Feel the gland of the other arm; there is not the same lump exactly, yet something a little like it. Have not some people glands naturally enlarged? Would to Heaven he were one! So he does for himself the work of the plague, and when the Angel of Death, thus courted, does indeed and in truth come, he has only to finish that which has been so well begun. He passes his fiery hand over the brain of the victim, and lets him rave for a season, but all chance-wise, of people and things once dear, or of people and things indifferent. Once more the poor fellow is back at his home in fair Provence, and sees the sun-dial that stood in his childhood's garden—sees part of his mother, and the long since forgotten face of that dear little sister

[167]

(he sees her, he says, on a Sunday morning, for all the church bells are ringing); he looks up and down through the universe, and owns it well piled with bales upon bales of cotton and cotton eternal—so much so that he feels—he knows—he swears he could make that winning hazard, if the billiard-table would not slant upwards, and if the cue were a cue worth playing with; but it is not; it's a cue that won't move—his own arm won't move. In short, there's the devil to pay in the brain of the poor Levantine; and perhaps the next night but one he becomes the "life and the soul" of some squalling jackal family, who fish him out by the foot from his shallow and sandy grave.

Better fate was mine. By some happy perverseness (occasioned, perhaps, by my disgust at the notion of being received with a pair of tongs), I took it into my pleasant head that all the European notions about contagion were thoroughly unfounded—that the plague might be providential, or "epidemic" (as they phrase it), but was not contagious, and that I could not be killed by the touch of a woman's sleeve, nor yet by her blessed breath. I, therefore, determined that the plague should not alter my habits and amusements in any one respect. Though I came to this resolve from impulse, I think that I took the course which was in effect the most prudent; for the cheefulness of spirits which I was thus enabled to retain discouraged the yellow-winged angel, and prevented him from taking a shot at me. I, however, so far respected the opinion of the Europeans that I avoided touching, when I could do so without privation or inconvenience. This endeavor furnished me with a sort of amusement as I passed through the streets. The usual mode of moving from place to place in the city of Cairo is upon donkeys. Of these great numbers are always in readiness, with donkey-boys attached. I had two who constantly (until one of them died of the plague) waited at my door upon the chance of being wanted. I found this way of moving about exceedingly pleasant, and never attempted any other. I had only to mount my beast, and tell my donkey-boy the point for which I was bound, and instantly I began to glide on at a capital pace. The streets of Cairo are not paved in any way, but strewed with a dry, sandy soil, so deadening to sound that the footfall of my donkey could scarcely be heard. There is no trottoir, and as you ride through the streets you mingle with the people on foot. Those who are in your way, upon being warned by the shout of the donkey-boy, move very slightly aside, so as to leave you a narrow lane for your passage. Through this you move at a gallop, gliding on delightfully in the very midst of crowds, without being inconvenienced or stopped for a moment; it seems to you that it is not the donkey, but the donkey-boy, who wafts you along with his shouts through pleasant groups and air that comes thick with the fragrance of burial spice. "Eh, sheik! Eh, bint! reggalek, shumalek," etc. ("O old man, O virgin, get out of the way on the right! O virgin, O old man, get out of the way on the left! This Englishman comes, he comes, he comes!") The narrow alley which these shouts cleared for my passage made it possible, though difficult, to go on for a long way without touching a single person, and my endeavors to avoid such contact were a sort of game for me in my loneliness. If I got through a street without being touched, I won; if I was touched, I lost—lost a deuce of a stake, according to the theory of the Europeans, but that I deemed to be all nonsense; I only lost that game, and would certainly win the next.

There is not much in the way of public buildings to admire at Cairo, but I saw one handsome mosque, and to this an instructive history is attached. A Hindustani merchant, having amassed an immense fortune, settled in Cairo, and soon found that his riches in the then state of the political world gave him vast power in the city—power, however, the exercise of which was much restrained by the counteracting influence of other wealthy men. With a view to extinguish every attempt at rivalry, the Hindustani merchant built this magnificent mosque at his own expense; when the work was complete, he invited all the leading men of the city to join him in prayer within the walls of the newly built temple, and he then caused to be massacred all those who were sufficiently influential to cause him any jealousy or uneasiness—in short, all the "respectable men" of the place. After this he possessed undisputed power in the city, and was greatly revered—he is revered to this day. It struck me that there was a touching simplicity in the mode which this man so successfully adopted for gaining the confidence and good will of his fellow-citizens. There seems to be some improbability in the story (though not nearly so gross as it might appear to an European ignorant of the East, for witness Mehemet Ali's destruction of the Mamelukes, a closely similar act, and attended with the like brilliant success*; but even if the story be false as a mere fact, it is perfectly true as an illustration—it is a true exposition of the means by which the respect and affection of Orientals may be conciliated.

I ascended, one day, to the citadel, and gained from its ramparts a superb view of the town. The fanciful and elaborate gilt-work of the many minarets gives a light and florid grace to the city as seen from this height, but before you can look for many seconds at such things, your eyes are drawn westward—drawn westward and over the Nile, till they rest upon the massive enormities of the Gizeh Pyramids.

I saw within the fortress many yoke of men, all haggard and woebegone, and a kennel of very fine lions, well fed and flourishing; I say *yoke* of men, for the poor fellows were working together in bonds; I say a *kennel* of lions, for the beasts were not inclosed in cages, but simply chained up like dogs.

I went round the bazaars; it seemed to me that pipes and arms were cheaper here than at Constantinople, and I should advise you, therefore, if you reach both places, to prefer the market of Cairo. In the open slave market I saw about fifty girls exposed for sale, but all of them black or "invisible" brown. A slave agent took me to some rooms in the upper story of the building, and also into several obscure houses in the neighborhood, with a view to show me some white women. The owners raised various objections to the display of their ware, and well they might, for I had not the least notion of purchasing; some refused on account of the

---

* Mehemet Ali invited the Mamelukes to a feast, and murdered them whilst preparing to enter the banquet-hall

illegality of selling to unbelievers,* and others declared that all
transactions of this sort were completely out of the question as
long as the plague was raging. I only succeeded in seeing one white
slave who was for sale, but on this treasure the owner affected to
set an immense value, and raised my expectations to a high pitch
by saying that the girl was Circassian, and was "fair as the full
moon." There was a good deal of delay, but at last I was led into
a long, dreary room, and there, after marching timidly forward for
a few paces, I descried at the farther end that mass of white linen
which indicates an Eastern woman. She was bid to uncover her
face, and I presently saw that, though very far from being good-
looking according to my notion of beauty, she had not been in-
aptly described by the man who compared her to the full moon,
for her large face was perfectly round and perfectly white. Though
very young, she was nevertheless extremely fat. She gave me the
idea of having been got up for sale—of having been fattened and
whitened by medicines or by some peculiar diet. I was firmly
determined not to see any more of her than the face. She was
perhaps disgusted at this my virtuous resolve, as well as with my
personal appearance; perhaps she saw my distaste and disappoint-
ment; perhaps she wished to gain favor with her owner by showing her attachment to his faith; at all events, she holloed out very
lustily and very decidedly that "she would not be bought by the
infidel."

Whilst I remained at Cairo I thought it worth while to see
something of the magicians, because I considered that these men
were in some sort the descendants of those who contended so
stoutly against the superior power of Aaron. I therefore sent for an
old man who was held to be the chief of the magicians, and
desired him to show me the wonders of his art. The old man
looked and dressed his character exceedingly well. The vast turban, the flowing beard, and the ample robes were all that one
could wish in the way of appearance. The first experiment (a very
stale one) which he attempted to perform for me was that of

---

* It is not strictly lawful to sell *white* slaves to a Christian.

showing the forms and faces of my absent friends, not to me, but to a boy brought in from the streets for the purpose, and said to be chosen at random. A mangal (pan of burning charcoal) was brought into my room, and the magician, bending over it, sprinkled upon the fire some substances consisting, I suppose, of spices or sweetly burning woods, for immediately a fragrant smoke arose that curled around the bending form of the wizard the while that he pronounced his first incantations. When these were over, the boy was made to sit down, and a common green shade was bound over his brow. Then the wizard took ink and, still continuing his incantations, wrote certain mysterious figures upon the boy's palm, and directed him to rivet his attention to these marks, without looking aside for an instant. Again the incantations proceeded, and after a while the boy, being seemingly a little agitated, was asked whether he saw anything on the palm of his hand. He declared that he saw—and he described it rather minutely—a kind of military procession with royal flags and warlike banners flying. I was then called upon to name the absent person whose form was to be made visible. I named Keate. You were not at Eton, and I must tell you, therefore, what manner of man it was that I named, though I think you must have some idea of him already, for wherever, from utmost Canada to Bundelcund, wherever there was the whitewashed wall of an officer's room, or of any other apartment in which English gentlemen are forced to kick their heels, there, likely enough (in the days of his reign), the head of Keate would be seen, scratched or drawn with those various degrees of skill which one observes in the representation of saints. Anybody without the least notion of drawing could still draw a speaking, nay, scolding likeness of Keate. If you had no pencil you could draw him well enough with a poker, or the leg of a chair, or the smoke of a candle. He was little more (if more at all) than five feet in height, and was not very great in girth, but within this space was concentrated the pluck of ten battalions. He had a really noble voice, and this he could modulate with great skill; but he had also the power of quacking like an angry duck, and he almost always adopted this mode of communication in order to inspire respect.

He was a capital scholar, but his ingenuous learning had *not* "softened his manners," and *had* "permitted them to be fierce"—tremendously fierce. He had such a complete command over his temper—I mean over his *good* temper—that he scarcely ever allowed it to appear. You could not put him out of humor—that is, out of the *ill* humor which he thought to be fitting for a headmaster. His red, shaggy eyebrows were so prominent that he habitually used them as arms and hands for the purpose of pointing out any object towards which he wished to direct attention. The rest of his features were equally striking in their way, and were all and all his own. He wore a fancy dress, partly resembling the costume of Napoleon, and partly that of a widow woman. I could not have named anybody more decidedly differing in apprecance from the rest of the human race.

"Whom do you name?" "I name John Keate." "Now, what do you see?" said the wizard to the boy. "I see," answered the boy, "I see a fair girl with golden hair, blue eyes, pallid face, rosy lips." *There* was a shot! I shouted out my laughter with profane exultation, and the wizard, perceiving the grossness of his failure, declared that the boy must have known sin (for none but the innocent can see truth), and accordingly kicked him down-stairs.

One or two other boys were tried, but none could "see truth."

Notwithstanding the failure of these experiments, I wished to see what sort of mummery my magician would practise if I called upon him to show me some performances of a higher order than those already attempted. I therefore made a treaty with him, in virtue of which he was to descend with me into the tombs near the Pyramids, and there evoke the devil. The negotiation lasted some time, for Dthemetri, as in duty bound, tried to beat down the wizard as much as he could and the wizard, on his part, manfully stuck up for his price, declaring that to raise the devil was really no joke, and insinuating that to do so was an awesome crime. I let Dthemetri have his way in the negotiation, but I felt in reality very indifferent about the sum to be paid, and for this reason, namely, that the payment (except a very small present, which I might make, or not, as I chose) was to be *contingent on success*. At length the bargain was finished, and it was arranged that, after a few days to be allowed for preparation, the wizard should raise the devil for £2 10s., play or pay—no devil, no piasters.

The wizard failed to keep his appointment. I sent to know why the deuce he had not come to raise the devil. The truth was that my Mohammed had gone to the mountain. The plague had seized him, and he died.

Although the plague was now spreading quick and terrible havoc around him, I did not see very plainly any corresponding change in the looks of the streets until the seventh day after my arrival; I then first observed that the city was *silenced*. There were no outward signs of despair, nor of violent terror, but many of the voices that had swelled the busy hum of men were already hushed in death, and the survivors, so used to scream and screech in their earnestness whenever they bought or sold, now showed an unwonted indifference about the affairs of this world; it was less worth while for men to haggle and haggle, and crack the sky with noisy bargains, when the Great Commander was there, who could "pay all their debts with the roll of his drum."

At this time I was informed that of twenty-five thousand people at Alexandria, twelve thousand had died already; the Destroyer had come rather later to Cairo, but there was nothing of weariness in his strides. The deaths came faster than ever they befell in the plague of London; but the calmness of Orientals under such visitations, and their habit of using biers for interment, instead of burying coffins along with the bodies, rendered it practicable to dispose of the dead in the usual way, without shocking the people by any unaccustomed spectacle of horror. There was no tumbling of bodies into carts, as in the plague of Florence and the plague of London; every man, according to his station, was properly buried, and that in the accustomed way, except that he went to his grave at a pace more than usually rapid.

The funerals pouring through the streets were not the only public evidence of deaths. In Cairo this custom prevails: at the instant of a man's death (if his property is sufficient to justify the expense) professional howlers are employed. I believe that these persons are brought near to the dying man when his end appears to be approaching, and the moment that life is gone, they lift up their voices and send forth a loud wail from the chamber of death. Thus I knew when my near neighbors died. Sometimes the howls were near, sometimes more distant. Once I was awakened in the night by the wail of death in the next house, and another time by a like howl from the house opposite; and there were two or three minutes, I recollect, during which the howl seemed to be actually *running* along the street.

I happened to be rather teased at this time by a sore throat, and I thought it would be well to get it cured, if I could, before I again started on my travels. I therefore inquired for a Frank doctor, and was informed that the only one then at Cairo was a Bolgnese refugee, a very young practitioner, and so poor that he had not been able to take flight, as the other medical men had done. At such a time as this it was out of the question to *send* for an European physician; a person thus summoned would be sure to suppose that the patient was ill of the plague, and would decline to come. I therefore rode to the young doctor's residence, ascended a flight or two of stairs, and knocked at his door. No one came immediately, but after some little delay the medico himself opened the door and admitted me. I, of course, made him understand that I had come to consult him, but before entering upon my throat grievance, I accepted a chair and exchanged a sentence or two of commonplace conversation. Now the natural commonplace of the city at this season was of a gloomy sort: "Comme va la peste?" ("How goes the plague?") And this was precisely the question I put. A deep sigh, and the words, "Sette cento per giorno, signor" ("Seven hundred a day"), pronounced in a tone of the deepest sadness and dejection, were the answer I received. The day was not oppressively hot, yet I saw that the doctor was transpiring profusely, and even the outside surface of the thick shawl dressing-gown in which he had wrapped himself appeared to be moist. He was a handsome, pleasant-looking young fellow, but the deep melancholy of his tone did not tempt me to prolong the conversation, and without further delay, I requested that my throat might be looked at. The medico held my chin in the usual way, and examined my throat; he then wrote me a prescription, and almost immediately afterwards I bade him farewell; but as he conducted me towards the door I observed an expression of strange and unhappy watchfulness in his rolling eyes. It was not the next day, but the next day but one, if I rightly remember, that I sent to request another interview with my doctor. In due time Dthemetri, my messenger, returned, looking sadly aghast; he had "*met* the medico," for so he phrased it, "coming out from his house—in a bier!"

It was, of course, plain that when the poor Bolognese stood looking down my throat, and almost mingling his breath with mine, he was already stricken of the plague. I suppose that his violent sweat must have been owing to some medicine administered by himself in the faint hope of a cure. The peculiar rolling of his eyes which I had remarked is, I believe, to experienced observers, a pretty sure test of the plague. A Russian acquaintance of mine, speaking from the information of men who had made the Turkish campaigns of 1828 and 1829, told me that by this sign the officers of Sabalkansky's force were able to make out the plague-stricken soldiers with a good deal of certainty.

It so happened that most of the people with whom I had anything to do, during my stay at Cairo, were seized with plague, and all these died. Since I had been for a long time en route before I reached Egypt, and was about to start again for another long journey over the desert, there were of course, many little matters touching my wardrobe and my traveling equipments which required to be attended to whilst I remained in the city. It happened so many times that Dthemetri's orders in respect to these matters were frustrated by the deaths of the tradespeople and others whom he employed that at last I became quite accustomed to the peculiar manner of the man when he prepared to announce a new death to me. The poor fellow naturally supposed that I should feel some uneasiness at hearing of the "accidents" continually happening to persons employed by me, and he therefore communicated their deaths as though they were the deaths of friends. He would cast

down his eyes and look like a man abashed, and then gently and
with a mournful gesture allow the words, "Morto, signor," to
come through his lips. I don't know how many of such instances
occurred, but they were several, and besides these (as I told you
before), my banker, my doctor, my landlord, and my magician all
died of the plague. A lad who acted as a helper in the house I
occupied lost a brother and a sister within a few hours. Out of my
established donkey-boys one died. I did not hear of any instance
in which a plague-stricken patient had recovered.

Going out one morning, I met unexpectedly the scorching
breath of the khamsin wind, and fearing that I should faint under
the infliction, I returned to my rooms. Reflecting, however, that I
might have to encounter this wind in the desert, where there would
be no possibility of avoiding it, I thought it would be better to
brave it once more in the city, and to try whether I could really
bear it or not. I therefore mounted my ass, and rode to old Cairo
and along the gardens by the banks of the Nile. The wind was hot
to the touch, as though it came from a furnace; it blew strongly,
but yet with such perfect steadiness that the trees bending under
its force remained fixed in the same curves without perceptibly
waving. The whole sky was obscured by a veil of yellowish gray,
that shut out the face of the sun. The streets were utterly silent,
being indeed almost entirely deserted, and not without cause, for
the scorching blast, whilst it fevers the blood, closes up the pores
of the skin, and is terribly distressing, therefore, to every animal
that encounters it. I returned to my rooms dreadfully ill. My head
ached with a burning pain, and my pulse bounded quick and
fitfully, but perhaps (as in the instance of the poor Levantine
whose death I was mentioning) the fear and excitement I felt in
trying my own wrist may have made my blood flutter the faster.

It is a thoroughly well believed theory that during the contin-
uance of the plague you can't be ill of any other febrile malady. An
unpleasant privilege that! for ill I was, and ill of fever, and I
anxiously wished that the ailment might turn out to be anything
rather than plague. I had some right to surmise that my illness
might have been merely the effect of the hot wind, and this notion

was encouraged by the elasticity of my spirits, and by a strong forefeeling that much of my destined life in this world was yet to come and yet to be fulfilled. That was my instinctive belief; but when I carefully weighed the probabilities on the one side and on the other, I could not help seeing that the strength of argument was all against me. There was a strong antecedent likelihood in *favor* of my being struck by the same blow as the rest of the people who had been dying around me. Besides, it occurred to me that, after all, the universal opinion of the Europeans upon a medical question, such as that of contagion, might probably be correct, and *if it were,* I was so thoroughly "compromised," especially by the touch and breath of the dying medico, that I had no right to expect any other fate than that which now seemed to have over-taken me. Balancing, then, as well as I could all the considerations suggested by hope and fear, I slowly and reluctantly came to the conclusion that, according to all merely reasonable probability, the plague had come upon me.

You might suppose that this conviction would have induced me to write a few farewell lines to those who were dearest, and that having done that, I should have turned my thoughts towards the world to come. Such, however, was not the case. I believe that the prospect of death often brings with it strong anxieties about mat-ters of comparatively trivial import, and certainly with me the whole energy of the mind was directed towards the one petty object of concealing my illness until the latest possible moment—until the delirious stage. I did not believe that either Mysseri or Dthemetri, who had served me so faithfully in all trials, would have deserted me (as most Europeans are wont to do) when they knew that I was stricken by plague, but I shrank from the idea of putting them to this test, and I dreaded the consternation which the knowledge of my illness would be sure to occasion.

I was very ill indeed at the moment when my dinner was served, and my soul sickened at the sight of the food, but I had luckily the habit of dispensing with the attendance of servants during my meal, and as soon as I was left alone, I made a melancholy cal-culation of the quantity of food I should have eaten if I had been in my usual health, and filled my plates accordingly, and gave myself salt, and so on, as though I were going to dine. I then transferred the viands to a piece of the omnipresent "Times" news-paper, and hid them away in a cupboard, for it was not yet night, and I dared not to throw the food into the street until darkness came. I did not at all relish this process of fictitious dining, but at length the cloth was removed, and I gladly reclined on my divan, (I would not lie down), with the "Arabian Nights" in my hand.

I had a feeling that tea would be a capital thing for me, but I would not order it until the usual hour. When at last the time came, I drank deep draughts from the fragrant cup. The effect was almost instantaneous. A plenteous sweat burst through my skin, and watered my clothes through and through. I kept myself thickly covered. The hot, tormenting weight which had been loading my brain was slowly heaved away. The fever was extinguished. I felt a new buoyancy of spirits, and an unusual activity of mind. I went into my bed under a load of thick covering, and when morning came, and I asked myself how I was, I answered, "Perfectly well."

I was very anxious to procure, if possible, some medical advice for Mysseri, whose illness preventd my departure. Every one of the European practising doctors, of whom there had been many, had either died or fled; it was said, however, that there was an Englishman in the medical service of the Pasha who quietly re-mained at his post, but that he never engaged in private practice. I determined to try if I could obtain assistance in this quarter. I did not venture at first, and at such a time as this, to ask him to visit a servant who was prostrate on the bed of sickness; but thinking that I might thus gain an opportunity of persuading him to attend Mysseri, I wrote a note mentioning my own affair of the sore throat, and asking for the benefit of his medical advice. He in-stantly followed back my messenger, and was at once shown up into my room. I entreated him to stand off, telling him fairly how deeply I was "compromised," and especially by my contact with a person actually ill and since dead of plague. The generous fel-low, with a good-humored laugh at the terror of the contagionists, marched straight up to me, and forcibly seized my hand and shook it with manly violence. I felt grateful indeed, and swelled with fresh pride of race, because that my countryman could carry himself so nobly. He soon cured Mysseri, as well as me, and all this he did from no other motives than the pleasure of doing a kindness and the delight of braving a danger.

At length the great difficulty* I had had in procuring beasts for my departure was overcome, and now, too, I was to have the new excitement of traveling on dromedaries. With two of these beasts and three camels, I gladly wound my way from out of the pest-stricken city. As I passed through the streets, I observed a grave elder stretching forth his arms and lifting up his voice in a speech which seemed to have some reference to me; requiring an interpretation, I found that the man had said: "The Pasha seeks camels, and he finds them not; the Englishman says, 'Let camels be brought,' and behold, there they are!"

I no sooner breathed the free, wholesome air of the desert than I felt that a great burden which I had been scarcely conscious of bearing was lifted away from my mind. For nearly three weeks I had lived under peril of death; the peril ceased, and not till then did I know how much alarm and anxiety I had really been suffering.)

---

* The difficulty was occasioned by the immense exertions which the Pasha was making to collect camels for military purposes.

CHAPTER
XIX

The Pyramids.

I WENT to see and to explore the Pyramids.
Familiar to one from the days of early childhood are the forms
of the Egyptian Pyramids, and now, as I approached them from
the banks of the Nile, I had no print, no picture before me, and yet
the old shapes were there; there was no change: they were just as
I had always known them. I straightened myself in my stirrups,
and strived to persuade my understanding that this was real Egypt,
and that those angles which stood up between me and the west
were of harder stuff and more ancient than the paper pyramids of
the green portfolio. Yet it was not till I came to the base of the
Great Pyramid that reality began to weigh upon my mind. Strange
to say, the bigness of the distinct blocks of stones was the first sign
by which I attained to feel the immensity of the whole pile. When
I came and trod, and touched with my hands, and climbed, in
order that by climbing I might come to the top of one single stone,
then, and almost suddenly, a cold sense and understanding of the
pyramid's enormity came down, overcasting my brain.

Now try to endure this homely, sick-nursish illustration of the
effect produced upon one's mind by the mere vastness of the Great
Pyramid. When I was very young (between the ages, I believe, of
three and five years old), being then of delicate health, I was often
in time of night the victim of a strange kind of mental oppression.
I lay in my bed perfectly conscious and with open eyes, but without power to speak or to move, and all the while my brain was
oppressed to distraction by the presence of a single and abstract
idea—the idea of solid immensity. It seemed to me in my agonies
that the horror of this visitation arose from its coming upon me
without form or shape—that the close presence of the direst monster ever bred in hell would have been a thousand times more

tolerable than that simple idea of solid size; my aching mind was fixed and riveted down upon the mere quality of vastness, vastness, vastness, and was not permitted to invest with it any particular object. If I could have done so, the torment would have ceased. When at last I was roused from this state of suffering, I could not, of course, in those days (knowing no verbal metaphysics, and no metaphysics at all, except by the dreadful experience of an abstract idea)—I could not, of course, find words to describe the nature of my sensations; and even now I cannot explain why it is that the forced contemplation of a mere quality, distinct from matter, should be so terrible. Well, now my eyes saw and knew, and my hands and my feet informed my understanding, that there was nothing at all abstract about the Great Pyramid—it was a big triangle, sufficiently concrete, easy to see, and rough to the touch; it could not, of course, affect me with the peculiar sensation I have been talking of, but yet there was something akin to that old nightmare agony in the terrible completeness with which a mere mass of masonry could fill and load my mind.

And time, too; the remoteness of its origin no less than the enormity of its proportions, screens an Egyptian pyramid from the easy and familiar contact of our modern minds. At its base the common earth ends, and all above is a world—one not created of God, not seeming to be made by men's hands, but rather the sheer giant work of some old dismal age weighing down this younger planet.

Fine sayings! But the truth seems to be, after all, that the Pyramids are quite of this world—that they were piled up into the air for the realization of some kingly crotchets about immortality, some priestly longing for burial fees; and that as for the building— they were built like coral rocks by swarms of insects—by swarms of poor Egyptians, who were not only the abject tools and slaves of power, but who also ate onions for the reward of their immortal labors!* The Pyramids are quite of this world.

I of course ascended to the summit of the Great Pyramid, and

---

* Herodotus, in an after age, stood by with his note-book, and got, as he thought, the exact returns of all the rations served out.

also explored its chambers; but these I need not describe. The first time that I went to the pyramids of Gizeh, there were a number of Arabs hanging about in its neighborhood, and wanting to receive presents on various pretenses. Their sheik was with them. There was also present an ill-looking fellow in soldier's uniform. This man, on my departure, claimed a reward, on the ground that he had maintained order and decorum amongst the Arabs. His claim was not considered valid by my dragoman, and was rejected accordingly. My donkey-boys afterwards said they had overheard this fellow propose to the sheik to put me to death whilst I was in the interior of the Great Pyramid, and to share with him the booty. Fancy a struggle for life in one of those burial-chambers, with acres and acres of solid masonry between one's self and the daylight! I felt exceedingly glad that I had not made the rascal a present.

I visited the very ancient pyramids of Abukir and Sakkara. There are many of these, differing the one from the other in shape as well as size; and it struck me that taken together, they might be looked upon as showing the progress and perfection (such as it is) of pyramidical architecture. One of the pyramids at Sakkara is almost a rival for the full-grown monster at Gizeh; others are scarcely more than vast heaps of brick and stone; and these last suggested to me the idea that, after all, the pyramid is nothing more nor less than a variety of the sepulchral mound so common in most countries (including, I believe, Hindustan, from whence the Egyptians are supposed to have come). Men accustomed to raise these structures for their dead kings or conquerors would carry the usage with them in their migrations; but arriving in Egypt, and seeing the impossibility of finding earth sufficiently tenacious for a mound, they would approximate as nearly as might be to their custom by raising up a round heap of stones—in short, conical pyramids. Of these there are several at Sakara, and the materials of some are thrown together without any order or regularity. The transition from this simple form to that of the square angular pyramid was easy and natural; and it seemed to me that the gradations through which the style passed from infancy up to its mature enormity could plainly be traced at Sakkara.

CHAPTER
XX

The Sphinx.

A ND near the Pyramids, more wondrous and more awful than all else in the land of Egypt, there sits the lonely Sphinx. Comely the creature is, but the comeliness is not of this world. The once worshiped beast is a deformity and a monster to this generation; and yet you can see that those lips, so thick and heavy, were fashioned according to some ancient mold of beauty—some mold of beauty now forgotten—forgotten because that Greece drew forth Cytherea from the flashing foam of the Ægean, and in her image created new forms of beauty, and made it a law among men that the short and proudly wreathed lip should stand for the sign and the main condition of loveliness through all generations to come. Yet still there lives on the race of those who were beautiful in the fashion of the Elder World; and Christian girls of Coptic blood will look on you with the sad, serious gaze, and kiss you your charitable hand with the big pouting lips of the very Sphinx.

Laugh and mock, if you will, at the worship of stone idols; but mark ye this, ye breakers of images: that in one regard the stone idol bears awful semblance of Deity—unchangefulness in the midst of change, the same seeming will and intent for ever and ever inexorable! Upon ancient dynasties of Ethiopian and Egyptian kings, upon Greek and Roman, upon Arab and Ottoman conquerors, upon Napoleon dreaming of an Eastern empire, upon battle and pestilence, upon the ceaseless misery of the Egyptian race, upon keen-eyed travelers,—Herodotus yesterday, and Warburton today,—upon all and more this unworldly Sphinx has watched, and watched like a Providence with the same earnest eyes, and the same sad, tranquil mien. And we, we shall die, and Islam will wither away; and the Englishman, straining far over to hold his loved India, will plant a firm foot on the banks of the Nile and sit in the seats of the Faithful, and still that sleepless rock will lie watching and watching the works of the new busy race with those same sad, earnest eyes, and the same tranquil mien everlasting. You dare not mock at the Sphinx.

CHAPTER
XXI

Cairo to Suez.

T HE "dromedary" of Egypt and Syria is not the two-humped animal described by that name in books of natural history, but is in fact of the same family as the camel, standing towards his more clumsy fellow-slave in about the same relation as a racer to a cart-horse. The fleetness and endurance of this creature are extraordinary. It is not usual to force him into a gallop and I fancy, from his make, that it would be quite impossible for him to maintain that pace for any length of time; but the animal is on so large a scale that the jog-trot at which he is generally ridden implies a progress of perhaps ten or twelve miles an hour, and this pace, it is said, he can keep up incessantly, without food or water or rest, for three whole days and nights.

Of the two dromedaries which I had obtained for this journey, I mounted one myself and put Dthemetri on the other. My plan was to ride on with Dthemetri to Suez as rapidly as the fleetness of the beasts would allow, and to let Mysseri (then still remaining weak from the effects of his late illness) come quietly on with the camels and baggage.

The trot of the dromedary is a pace terribly disagreeable to the rider, until he becomes a little accustomed to it; but after the first half-hour I so far schooled myself to this new exercise that I felt capable of keeping it up (though not without aching limbs) for several hours together. Now, therefore, I was anxious to dart forward and annihilate at once the whole space that divided me from the Red Sea. Dthemetri, however, could not get on at all: every attempt at trotting seemed to threaten the utter dislocation of his whole frame; and indeed I doubt whether any one of Dthemetri's age (nearly forty, I think), and unaccustomed to such exercise, could have borne it at all easily. Besides, the dromedary which fell to his lot was evidently a very bad one; he every now and then came to a dead stop, and coolly knelt down, as though suggesting that the rider had better get off at once, and abandon the experiment as one that was utterly hopeless.

When for the third or fourth time I saw Dthemetri thus planted, I lost my patience and went on without him. For about two hours, I think, I advanced without once looking behind me. I then paused, and cast my eyes back to the western horizon.

There was no sign of Dthemetri, nor of any other living creature. This I expected, for I knew that I must have far outdistanced all my followers. I had ridden away from my party merely by way of humoring my impatience, and with the intention of stopping as soon as I felt tired, until I was overtaken. I now observed, however (this I had not been able to do whilst advancing so rapidly) that the track which I had been following was seemingly the track of only one or two camels. I did not fear that I had diverged very largely from the true route, but still I could not feel any reasonable certainty that my party would follow any line of march within sight of me.

I had to consider, therefore, whether I should remain where I was upon the chance of seeing my people come up, or whether I should push on alone, and find my own way to Suez. I had now learned that I could not rely upon the continued guidance of any track, but I knew that (if maps were right) the point for which I was bound bore just due east of Cairo, and I thought that although I might miss the line leading most directly to Suez, I could not well fail to find my way, sooner or later, to the Red Sea. The worst of it was that I had no provision of food or water with me, and already I was beginning to feel thirst. I deliberated for a minute, and then determined that I would abandon all hope of seeing my party again in the desert, and would push forward as rapidly as possible towards Suez.

It was not without a sensation of awe that I swept with my sight the vacant round of the horizon, and remembered that I was all alone and unprovisioned in the midst of the arid waste; but this very awe gave tone and zest to the exultation with which I felt myself launched. Hitherto in all my wanderings I had been under the care of other people—sailors, Tatars, guides, and dragomen had watched over my welfare; but now, at last, I was here in this African desert, and I *myself, and no other, had charge of my life*. I liked the office well. I had the greatest part of the day before me, a very fair dromedary, a fur pelisse, and a brace of pistols, but no bread, and, worst of all, no water; for that I must ride—and ride I did.

For several hours I urged forward my beast at a rapid though steady pace, but at length the pangs of thirst began to torment me. I did not relax my pace, however, and I had not suffered long when a moving object appeared in the distance before me. The intervening space was soon traversed, and I found myself approaching a Bedouin Arab, mounted on a camel, attended by another Bedouin on foot. They stopped. I saw that there hung from the pack-saddle of the camel one of the large skin water-flasks commonly carried in the desert, and it seemed to be well filled. I steered my dromedary close up alongside of the mounted Bedouin, caused my beast to kneel down, then alighted, and keeping the end of the halter in my hand, went up to the mounted Bedouin without speaking, took hold of his water-flask, opened it, and drank long and deep from its leathern lips. Both of the Bedouins stood fast in amazement and mute horror; and really, if they had never happened to see an European before, the apparition was enough to startle them. To see for the first time a coat and a waistcoat with the semblance of a white human face at the top, and for this ghastly figure to come swiftly out of the horizon upon a fleet dromedary, approach them silently and with a demoniacal smile, and drink a deep draught from their water-flask— this was enough to make the Bedouins stare a little; they, in fact, stared a great deal—not as Europeans stare, with a restless and puzzled expression of countenance, but with features all fixed and rigid, and with still, glassy eyes. Before they had time to get decomposed from their state of petrifaction, I had remounted my dromedary and was darting away towards the east.

Without pause or remission of pace, I continued to press forward; but after a while I found, to my confusion, that the slight track which had hitherto guided me now failed altogether. I began to fear that I must have been all along following the course of some wandering Bedouins, and I felt that if this were the case my fate was a little uncertain.

I had no compass with me, but I determined upon the eastern point of the horizon as accurately as I could by reference to the sun, and so laid down for myself a way over the pathless sands.

But now my poor dromedary, by whose life and strength I held my own, she began to show signs of distress; a thick, clammy, and glutinous kind of foam gathered about her lips, and piteous sobs burst from her bosom in the tones of human misery. I doubted for a moment whether I would give her a little rest or relaxation of pace, but I decided that I would not, and continued to push forward as steadily as before.

The character of the country became changed; I had ridden away from the level tracts, and before me now, and on either side, there were vast hills of sand and calcined rocks that interrupted my progress and baffled my doubtful road; but I did my best. With rapid steps I swept round the base of the hills, threaded the winding hollows, and at last, as I rose in my swift course to the crest of a lofty ridge, thalatta! thalatta! the sea—the sea was before me!

It has been given me to know the true pith and to feel the power of ancient pagan creeds, and so (distinctly from all mere admiration of the beauty belonging to nature's works) I acknowledge a sense of mystical reverence when first I approached some illustrious feature of the globe—some coast-line of ocean, some mighty river or dreary mountain-range, the ancient barrier of kingdoms. But the Red Sea! It might well claim my earnest gaze by force of the great Jewish migration which connects it with the history of our own religion. From this very ridge, it is likely enough, the panting Israelites first saw that shining inlet of the sea. Aye, aye! but moreover, and best of all, that beckoning sea assured my eyes, and proved how well I had marked out the east for my path, and gave me good promise that sooner or later the time would come for me to drink of water cool and plenteous, and then lie down and rest. It was distant, the sea, but I felt my own strength, and I had heard of the strength of dromedaries. I pushed forward as eagerly as though I had spoiled the Egyptians and were flying from Pharaoh's police.

I had not yet been able to see any mark of distant Suez, but after a while I descried far away in the east a large, blank, isolated building. I made towards this, and in time got down to it. The building was a fort, and had been built there for the protection of a well contained within its precincts. A cluster of small huts adhered to the fort, and in a short time I was receiving the hospitality of the inhabitants, a score or so of people who sat grouped upon the sands near their hamlet. To quench the fires of my throat with about a gallon of muddy water, and to swallow a little of the food placed before me, was the work of a few minutes; and before the astonishment of my hosts had even begun to subside, I was pursuing my onward journey. Suez, I found, was still three hours distant, and the sun going down in the west warned me that I must find some other guide to keep me straight. This guide I found in the most fickle and uncertain of the elements. For some hours the wind had been freshening, and it now blew a violent gale; it blew, not fitfully and in squalls, but with such steadiness that I felt convinced it would blow from the same quarter for several hours; so when the sun set, I carefully looked for the point whence the wind came, and found that it blew from the very west—blew exactly in the direction of my route. I had nothing to do, therefore, but to go straight to leeward, and this I found easy enough, for the gale was blowing so hard that, if I diverged at all from my course, I instantly felt the pressure of the blast on the side towards which I had deviated. Very soon after sunset there came on complete darkness, but the strong wind guided me well, and sped me, too, on my way.

I had pushed on for about, I think, a couple of hours after nightfall, when I saw the glimmer of a light in the distance, and this, I ventured to hope, must be Suez. Upon approaching it, however, I found that it was only a solitary fort, and this I passed by without stopping.

On I went, still riding down the wind; but at last an unlucky misfortune befell me—a misfortune so absurd that, if you like, you shall have your laugh against me. I have told you what sort of lodging it is that you have upon the back of a camel. You ride the dromedary in the same fashion: you are perched rather than seated on a bunch of carpets or quilts upon the summit of the hump. It happened that my dromedary veered rather suddenly from her onward course. Meeting the movement, I mechanically turned my left wrist as though I were holding a bridle-rein, for the complete darkness prevented my eyes from reminding me that I had nothing but a halter in my hand. The expected resistance failed, for the halter was hanging upon that side of the dromedary's neck to-wards which I was slightly leaning. I toppled over, head foremost, and then went falling through air till my crown came whang! against the ground; and the ground, too, was perfectly hard (com-pacted sand); but my thickly wadded head-gear (this I wore for protection against the sun) now stood me in good part and saved my life. The notion of my being able to get up again after falling head foremost from such an immense height seemed to me at first too paradoxical to be acted upon, but I soon found that I was not a bit hurt. My dromedary had utterly vanished. I looked round me, and saw the glimmer of a light in the fort which I had lately passed, and I began to work my way back in that direction. The violence of the gale made it hard for me to force my way towards the west, but I succeeded at last in regaining the fort. To this, as to the other fort which I had passed, there was attached a cluster of huts, and I soon found myself surrounded by a group of vil-lainous, gloomy-looking fellows. It was sorry work for me to swagger and look big at a time when I felt so particularly small on account of my tumble and my lost dromedary, but there was not help for it; I had no Dthemetri now to "strike terror" for me. I knew hardly one word of Arabic, but somehow or other I con-trived to announce it as my absolute will and pleasure that these fellows should find me the means of gaining Suez. They acceded; and having a donkey, they saddled it for me, and appointed one of their number to attend me on foot.

I afterwards found that these fellows were not Arabs, but Algerine refugees, and that they bore the character of being sad scoundrels. They justified this imputation to some extent on the following day. They allowed Mysseri, with my baggage and the camels, to pass unmolested; but an Arab lad belonging to the party happened to lag a little way in the rear, and him (if they were not maligned) these rascals stripped and robbed. Low indeed is the state of bandit morality when men will allow the sleek traveler with well laden camels to pass in quiet, reserving their spirit of enterprise for the tattered turban of a miserable boy.

I reached Suez at last. The British agent, though roused from his midnight sleep, received me in his home with the utmost kindness and hospitality. Heaven! how delightful it was to lie on fair sheets, and to dally with sleep, and to wake, and to sleep, and to wake once more, for the sake of sleeping again!

CHAPTER
XXII

Suez.

I WAS hospitably entertained by the British consul, or agent, as he is there styled; he is the employee of the East India Company, and not of the home government. Napoleon, during his stay of five days at Suez, had been the guest of the consul's father; and I was told that the divan in my apartment had been the bed of the great commander.

There are two opinions as to the point where the Israelites passed the Red Sea. One is that they traversed only the very small creek at the northern extremity of the inlet, and that they entered the bed of the water at the spot on which Suez now stands; the other, that they crossed the sea from a point eighteen miles down the coast. The Oxford theologians who, with Milman, their professor,* believe that Jehovah conducted his chosen people without disturbing the order of nature, adopt the first view, and suppose that the Israelites passed during an ebb-tide aided by a violent wind. One among many objections to this supposition is that the time of a single ebb would not have been sufficient for the passage of that vast multitude of men and beasts, or even for a small fraction of it. Moreover, the creek to the north of this point can be compassed in an hour, and in two hours you can make the circuit of the salt-marsh over which the sea may have extended in former times. If, therefore, the Israelites crossed so high up as Suez, the Egyptians, unless infatuated by divine interference, might easily have recovered their stolen goods from the encumbered fugitives by making a slight detour. The opinion which fixes the point of passage at eighteen miles' distance, and from thence right across the ocean depths to the eastern side of the sea, is supported by the

---

* See Milman's "History of the Jews," first edition, Family Library.

unanimous tradition of the people, whether Christians or Mussulmans, and is consistent with Holy Writ: "The waters were a wall unto them on their right hand, *and on their left.*" The Cambridge mathematicians seem to think that the Israelites were enabled to pass over dry land by adopting a route not usually subjected to the influx of the sea. This notion is plausible in a mere hydrostatical point of view, but it is difficult to reconcile it with the account given in Exodus, unless we can suppose that the words "sea" and "waters" are there used in a sense implying dry land.

Napoleon, when at Suez, made an attempt to follow the supposed steps of Moses by passing the creek at this point; but it seems, according to the testimony of the people of Suez, that he and his horsemen managed the matter in a way more resembling the failure of the Egyptians than the success of the Israelites. According to the French account, Napoleon got out of the difficulty by that warriorlike presence of mind which served him so well when the fate of nations depended on the decision of a moment: he commanded his horsemen to disperse in all directions, in order to multiply the chances of finding shallow water, and was thus enabled to discover a line by which he and his people were extricated. The story told by the people of Suez is very different: they declare that Napoleon parted from his horse, got water-logged and nearly drowned, and was only fished out by the aid of the people on shore.

I bathed twice at the point assigned to the passage of the Israelites, and the second time that I did so, I chose the time of low water and tried to walk across; but I soon found myself out of my depths, or at least in water so deep that I could only advance by swimming.

The dromedary which had bolted in the desert was brought into Suez the day of my arrival; but the treasures attached to the saddle, including my pelisse and my dearest pistols, had disappeared. These things were of great importance to me at that time, and I moved the Governor of the town to make all possible exertions for their recovery. He acceded to my wishes as well as he could, and very obligingly imprisoned the first seven poor fellows he could lay his hands on.

At first the Governor acted in the matter from no other motive than that of courtesy to an English traveler; but afterwards, and when he saw the value I set upon the lost property, he pushed his measures with a degree of alacrity and heat which seemed to show that he felt a personal interest in the matter. It was supposed either that he expected a large present in the event of succeeding, or that he was striving by all means to trace the property in order that he might lay his hands on it after my departure.

I went out sailing for some hours, and when I returned I was horrified to find that two men had been bastinadoed by order of the Governor, with a view to force them to a confession of their theft. It appeared, however, that there really was good ground for supposing them guilty, since one of the holsters was actually found in their possession. It was said, too (but I could hardly believe it), that whilst one of the men was undergoing the bastinado, his comrade was overheard encouraging him to bear the torment without peaching. Both men, if they had the secret, were resolute in keeping it, and were sent back to their dungeon. I of course took care that there should be no repetition of the torture, at least so long as I remained at Suez.

The Governor was a thorough Oriental, and until a comparatively recent period had shared in the old Mohammedan feeling of contempt for Europeans. It happened, however, one day, that an English gun-brig had appeared off Suez, and sent her boats ashore to take in fresh water. Now fresh water at Suez is a somewhat scarce and precious commodity; it is kept in tanks, and the largest of these is at some distance from the place. Under these circumstances, the request for fresh water was refused, or at all events was not complied with. The captain of the brig was a simple-minded man with a strongish will, and he at once declared that if his casks were not filled in three hours he would destroy the whole place. "A great people indeed!" said the Governor. "A wonderful people, the English!" He instantly caused every cask to be filled to the brim from his own tank, and ever afterwards entertained for our countrymen a high degree of affection and respect.

The day after the abortive attempt to extract a confession from the prisoners, the Governor, the consul, and I sat in council, I know not how long, with a view of prosecuting the search for the stolen goods. The sitting, considered in the light of a criminal investigation, was characteristic of the East. The proceedings began, as a matter of course, by the prosecutor's smoking a pipe and drinking coffee with the judge, jury, and sheriff—that is, with the Governor, for in this one personage were vested almost all the functions connected with the administration of injustice. I got on very well with my host (this was not my first interview), and he gave me the pipe from his lips in testimony of his friendship. I recollect, however, that my prime adviser, thinking me, I suppose, a great deal too shy and retiring in my manner, entreated me to put up my boots and to soil the Governor's divan, in order to inspire respect and strike terror. I thought it would be as well for me to retain the right of respecting myself, and that it was not quite necessary for a well-received guest to strike any terror at all.

Our deliberations were assisted by the numerous attendants who lined the three sides of the room not occupied by the divan. Any one of these who took it into his head to offer a suggestion would stand forward and humble himself before the Governor, and then state his views; every man thus giving counsel was listened to with some attention.

After a great deal of fruitless planning, the Governor directed that the prisoners should be brought in. I was shocked when they entered, for I was not prepared to see them come *carried* into the room upon the shoulders of others. It had not occurred to me that their battered feet would be too sore to bear the contact of the floor. They persisted in asserting their innocence. The Governor wanted to recur to the torture, but that I prevented, and the men were lifted back to their dungeon.

One of the attendants now suggested a scheme—a scheme which seemed to me most childishly absurd, but nevertheless it was tried. A man went down to the dungeon with instructions to make the prisoners believe that he had gained permission to see them upon some invented pretext; and when the spy had thus won a little of their confidence, he was to attempt a sham treaty with them for

[198]

the purchase of the stolen goods. This shallow expedient failed.

The Governor himself had not nominally the power of life and death over the people in his district, but he could, if he chose, send them to Cairo, and have them hanged there. I proposed that the prisoners should be *threatened* with this fate. The answer of the Governor made me feel rather ashamed of my effeminate suggestion. He said that if I wished it he would willingly threaten them with death; but he also declared that if he threatened, *he surely would make his words good.*

Thinking at last that nothing was to be gained by keeping the prisoners any longer in confinement, I requested that they might be set free. To this the Governor assented, though only, as he said, out of favor to me, for he had a strong impression that the men were guilty. I went down to see the prisoners let out with my own eyes. They were very grateful, and fell down to the earth, kissing my boots. I gave them a present to console them for their wounds, and they seemed to be highly delighted.

Although the matter ended in a manner so satisfactory to the principal sufferers, there were symptoms of some angry excitement in the place: it was said that public opinion was much shocked at the fact that Mohammedans had been beaten on account of a loss sustained by a Christian. My journey was to recommence the next day, and it was hinted that if I persevered in my intention of going forward into the desert the people would have an easy and profitable opportunity of wreaking their vengeance on me. If ever they formed any scheme of the kind, they at all events refrained from any attempt to carry it into effect.

One of the evenings during my stay at Suez was enlivened by a triple wedding. There was a long and slow procession. Some carried torches, and others were thumping drums and firing pistols. The bridegrooms came last, all walking abreast. My only reason for mentioning the ceremony is that I scarcely ever in all my life saw any phenomena so ridiculous as the meekness and gravity of those three young men whilst being "led to the altar."

CHAPTER
XXIII

Suez to Gaza.

THE route over the desert from Suez to Gaza is not frequented by merchants, and is seldom passed by a traveler. This part of the country is less uniformly barren than the tracts of shifting sand that lie on the El Arish route. The shrubs yielding food for the camel are more frequent, and in many spots the sand is mingled with so much of productive soil as to admit the growth of corn. The Bedouins are driven out of this district during the summer by the want of water; but before the time for their forced departure arrives, they succeed in raising little crops of barley from these comparatively fertile patches of ground. They bury the fruit of their labors, and take care so to mark the spot chosen that when they return they can easily find their hidden treasures. The warm, dry sand stands them for a safe granary. The country, at the time I passed it (in the month of April), was pretty thickly sprinkled with Bedouins expecting their harvest; several times my tent was pitched alongside of their encampments; but I have already told you all I wanted to tell about the domestic—or rather the castral—life of the Arabs.

I saw several creatures of the antelope kind in this part of the desert; and one day my Arabs surprised in her sleep a young gazelle (for so I called her), and took the darling prisoner. I carried her before me on my camel for the rest of the day, and kept her in my tent all night. I did all I could to gain her affections, but the trembling beauty refused to touch food, and would not be comforted; whenever she had a seeming opportunity of escaping, she struggled with a violence so painfully disproportioned to her fine, delicate limbs that I could not go on with the cruel attempt to make her my own. In the morning, therefore, I set her loose, anticipating some pleasure from the joyous bound with which, as

I thought, she would return to her native freedom. She had been so stupefied, however, by the exciting events of the preceding day and night, and was so puzzled as to the road she should take, that she went off very deliberately, and with an uncertain step. She was quite sound in limb, but she looked so idiotic that I fancied her intellect might have been really upset. Never, in all likelihood, had she seen the form of a human being until the dreadful moment when she woke from her sleep and found herself in the gripe of an Arab. Then her pitching and tossing journey on the back of a camel, and, lastly, a soirée with me by candle-light! I should have been glad to know, if I could, that her heart was not broken.

My Arabs were somewhat excited, one day, by discovering the fresh print of a foot—the foot, as they said, of a lion. I had no conception that the lord of the forest (better known as a crest) ever stalked away from his jungles to make inglorious war in these smooth plains against antelopes and gazelles. I supposed that there must have been some error of interpretation, and that the Arabs meant to speak of a tiger. It appeared, however, that this was not the case; either the Arabs were mistaken, or the noble brute, uncooped and unchained, had but lately crossed my path.

The camels with which I traversed this part of the desert were very different in their ways and habits from those that you hire on a frequented route. They were never led. There was not the slightest sign of a track in this part of the desert, but the camels never failed to choose the right line. By the direction taken at starting, they knew the point (some encampment, I suppose) for which they were to make. There is always a leading camel (generally, I believe, the eldest), who marches foremost and determines the path for the whole party. When it happens that no one of the camels has been accustomed to lead the others, there is very great difficulty in making a start; if you force your beast forward for a moment, he will contrive to wheel and draw back, at the same time looking at one of the other camels with an expression and gesture exactly equivalent to *après vous*. The responsibility of finding the way is evidently assumed very unwillingly. After some time, however, it becomes understood that one of the beasts has reluctantly consented to take the lead, and he accordingly advances for that purpose. For a minute or two he marches with great indecision, taking first one line and then another; but soon, by the aid of some mysterious sense, he discovers the true direction, and thenceforward keeps to it steadily, going on from morning to night. When once the leadership is established, you cannot by any persuasion, and scarcely even by blows, induce a junior camel to walk one single step in advance of the chosen guide.

On the fifth day I came to an oasis, called the Wady el Arish, a ravine, or rather a gully. Through this during the greater part of the year there runs a stream of water. On the sides of the gully there were a number of those graceful trees which the Arabs call *tarfa*. The channel of the stream was quite dry in the part at which we arrived; but at about half a mile off some water was found, and this, though very muddy, was tolerably sweet. Here was indeed a happy discovery, for all the water we had brought from the neighborhood of Suez was rapidly putrefying.

The want of foresight is an anomalous part of the Bedouin's character, for it does not result either from recklessness or stupidity. I know of no human being whose body is so thoroughly the slave of mind as the Arab. His mental anxieties seem to be forever torturing every nerve and fiber of his body; and yet, with all this exquisite sensitiveness to the suggestions of the mind, he is grossly improvident. I recollect, for instance, that when setting out upon this passage of the desert, my Arabs (in order to lighten the burden of their camels) were most anxious that we should take with us no more than two days' supply of water. They said that by the time that supply was exhausted we should arrive at a spring which would furnish us for the rest of the journey. My servants very wisely, and with much pertinacity, resisted the adoption of this plan, and took care to have both the large skins well filled. We went on, and found no water at all, either at the expected spring or for many days afterwards, so that nothing but the precaution of my own people saved us from the very severe suffering which we should have endured if we had entered upon the desert with only a two days' supply. The Arabs themselves, being on foot, would have suffered much more than I from the consequences of their improvidence.

This want of foresight prevents the Bedouin from appreciating at a distance of eight of ten days the amount of the misery which he entails upon himself at the end of the period. His dread of a city is one of the most painful mental affections that I have ever observed, and yet, when the whole breadth of the desert lies between him and the town you are going to, he will freely enter into an agreement to *land* you in the city for which you are bound. When, however, after many a day of toil, the distant minarets at length appear, the poor Bedouin relaxes the vigor of his pace; his steps become faltering and undecided; every moment his uneasiness increases; and at length he fairly sobs aloud, and, embracing your knees, implores, with the most piteous cries and gestures, that you will dispense with him and his camels, and find some other means of entering the city. This, of course, one can't agree to, and the consequence is that one is obliged to witness and resist the most moving expressions of grief and fond entreaty. I had to go through a most painful scene of this kind when I entered Cairo, and now the horror which these wilder Arabs felt at the notion of entering Gaza led to consequences still more distressing. The dread of cities results partly from a kind of wild instinct which has always characterized the descendants of Ishmael, but partly, too, from a well founded apprehension of ill-treatment. So often it befalls the poor Bedouin (when once entrapped between walls) to be seized by the Government authorities for the sake of his camels that his innate horror of cities becomes really justified by results.

The Bedouins with whom I performed this journey were wild fellows of the desert, quite unaccustomed to let out themselves or their beasts for hire; and when they found that by the natural ascendancy of Europeans they were gradually brought down to a state of subserviency to me, or rather to my attendants, they bitterly repented, I believe, of having placed themselves under our control. They were rather difficult fellows to manage, and gave Dthemetri a good deal of trouble, but I liked them all the better for that.

Selim, the chief of the party, and the man to whom all our camels belonged, was a fine, savage, stately fellow. There were, I think, five other Arabs of the party; but when we approached the end of the journey, they, one by one, began to make off towards the neighboring encampments, and by the time that the minarets of Gaza were in sight, Selim, the owner of the camels, was the only one who remained. He, poor fellow, as we neared the town, began to discover the same terrors that my Arabs had shown when I entered Cairo. I could not possibly accede to his entreaties, and consent to let my baggage be laid down on the bare sands, without any means of having it brought on into the city. So at length, when poor Selim had exhausted all his rhetoric of voice and action and tears, he fixed his despairing eyes for a minute upon the cherished beasts that were his only wealth, and then suddenly and madly dashed away into the farther desert. I continued my course, and reached the city at last, but it was not without immense difficulty that we could constrain the poor camels to pass under the hated shadow of its walls. They were the genuine beasts of the desert, and it was sad and painful to witness the agony they suffered when thus they were forced to encounter the fixed habitations of men. They shrank from the beginning of every high, narrow street as though from the entrance of some horrible cave or bottomless pit; they sighed and wept like women. When at last we got them within the courtyard of the khan, they seemed to be quite broken-hearted, and looked round piteously for their loving master; but no Selim came. I had imagined that he would enter the town secretly by night, in order to carry off those five fine camels, his only wealth in this world, and seemingly the main objects of his affection. But no; his dread of civilization was too strong. During the whole of the three days that I remained at Gaza he failed to show himself, and thus sacrificed, in all probability, not only his camels, but the money which I had stipulated to pay him for the passage of the desert. In order, however, to do all I could towards saving him from this last misfortune, I resorted to a contrivance frequently adopted by the Asiatics. I assembled a group of grave and worthy Mussulmans in the courtyard of the khan, and in their presence paid over the gold to a sheik well known in the place and accustomed to communicate with the Arabs of the desert. Then all present solemnly promised that, if ever Selim should come to claim his rights, they would bear true witness in his favor.

I saw a great deal of my old friend the Governor of Gaza. He had received orders to send back all persons coming from Egypt, and force them to perform quarantine at El Arish. He knew so little of quarantine regulations, however, that his dress was actually in contact with mine whilst he insisted upon the stringency of the orders which he had received. He was induced to make an exception in my favor, and I rewarded him with a musical snuff-box—a toy which I had bought at Smyrna for the purpose of presenting it to any man in authority who might happen to do me an important service. The Governor was delighted with the gift, and in great exultation and glee he carried it off to his harem. Soon, however, poor fellow, he returned with an altered countenance: his wives, he said, had got hold of the box, and had put it quite out of order. So short-lived is human happiness in this frail world!

The Governor fancied that he should incur less risk if I remained at Gaza for two or three days more, and he wanted me to become his guest. I persuaded him, however, that it would be better for him to let me depart at once. He wanted to add to my baggage a roast lamb and a quantity of other cumbrous viands, but I escaped with half a horse-load of leaven-bread; this was very good of its kind, and proved a most useful present. The air with which the Governor's slaves affected to be almost breaking down under the weight of the gifts reminded me of the figures one sees in some of the old pictures.

CHAPTER
XXIV

Gaza to Nablus.

PASSING now once again through Palestine and Syria, I retained the tent which I had used in the desert, and found that it added very much to my comfort in traveling. Instead of turning out a family from some wretched dwelling, and depriving them of rest without gaining rest for myself, I now, when evening came, pitched my tent upon some smiling spot within a few hundred yards of the village to which I looked for my supplies—that is, for milk, for bread (if I had it not with me), and sometimes also for eggs. The worst of it was that the needful viands were not to be obtained by coin, but only by intimidation. I at first tried the usual agent—money. Dthemetri, with one or two of my Arabs, went into the village near which I was encamped, and tried to buy the required provisions, offering liberal payment; but he came back empty-handed. I sent him again, but this time he held different language: he required to see the elders of the place, and, threatening dreadful vengeance, commanded them upon their responsibility to take care that my tent should be immediately and abundantly supplied. He was obeyed at once; and the provisions refused to me as a purchaser soon arrived, trebled or quadrupled, when demanded by way of a forced contribution. I quickly found (I think it required two experiments to convince me) that this peremptory method was the only one which could be adopted with success; it never failed. Of course, however, when the provisions have been actually obtained, you can, if you choose, give money exceeding the value of the provisions to *somebody*; an English—a thoroughbred English traveler will always do this (though it is contrary to the custom of the country) for the quiet (false quiet though it be) of his own conscience: but so to order the matter that the poor fellows who have been forced to contribute should be the persons to receive the value of their supplies is not possible; for a traveler to attempt anything so grossly just as that would be too outrageous. The truth is that the usage of the East in old times required the people of the village at their own cost to supply the wants of travelers; and the ancient custom is now adhered to—not in favor of travelers generally, but in favor of those who are deemed sufficiently powerful to enforce its observance. If the villagers, therefore, find a man waiving this right to oppress them, and offering coin for that which he is entitled to take without payment, they suppose at once that he is actuated by fear (fear of *them*, poor fellows!); and it is so delightful to them to act upon this flattering assumption that they will forego the advantage of a good price for their provisions rather than the rare luxury of refusing for once in their lives to part with their own possessions.

The practice of intimidation thus rendered necessary is utterly hateful to an Englishman. He finds himself forced to conquer his daily bread by the pompous threats of the dragoman—his very subsistence, as well as his dignity and personal safety, being made to depend upon his servant's assuming a tone of authority which does not at all belong to him. Besides, he can scarcely fail to see that, as he passes through the country, he becomes the innocent cause of much extra injustice—many supernumerary wrongs. This he feels to be especially the case when he travels with relays. To be the owner of a horse or a mule within reach of an Asiatic potentate is to lead the life of the hare and the rabbit—hunted down and ferreted out. Too often it happens that the works of the field are stopped in the daytime, that the inmates of the cottage are roused from their midnight sleep, by the sudden coming of a Government officer; and the poor husbandman, driven by threats and rewarded by curses, if he would not lose sight forever of his captured beasts must quit all and follow them. This is done that the Englishman may travel. He would make his way more harmlessly if he could; but horses or mules he *must* have, and these are his ways and means.

The town of Nablus is beautiful. It lies in a valley hemmed in with olive-groves, and its buildings are interspersed with frequent palm-trees. It is said to occupy the site of the ancient Shechem. I know not whether it was there, indeed, that the father of the Jews was accustomed to feed his flocks, but the valley is green and smiling, and is held at this day by a race more brave and beautiful than Jacob's unhappy descendants.

Nablus is the very furnace of Mohammedan bigotry; and I believe that only a few months before the time of my going there it would have been madly rash for a man, unless strongly guarded, to show himself to the people of the town in a Frank costume; but since their insurrection the Mohammedans of the place had been so far subdued by the severity of Ibrahim Pasha that they dared not now offer the slightest insult to an European. It was quite plain, however, that the effort with which the men of the old school refrained from expressing their opinion of a hat or a coat was horribly painful to them. As I walked through the streets and bazaars a dead silence prevailed. Every man suspended his employment, and gazed on me with a fixed glassy look, which seemed to say: "God is good; but how marvelous and inscrutable are his ways, that thus he permits this white-faced dog of a Christian to hunt through the paths of the Faithful!"

The insurrection of these people had been more formidable than any other that Ibrahim Pasha had to contend with; he was only able to crush them at last by the assistance of a fellow renowned for his resources in the way of stratagem and cunning, as well as for his knowledge of the country. This personage was no other than Aboo Goosh ("the father of lies"*). The man had been suddenly taken out of prison and sent into his native hill-country, with orders to procreate a few choice falsehoods and snares for entrapping the rebellious mountaineers; and he performed his function so well that he quickly enabled Ibrahim to hem in and extinguish the insurrection. He was rewarded with the governor-

---

* This is an appellation not implying blame, but merit; the "lies" which it purports to affiliate are feints and cunning stratagems rather than the baser kind of falsehoods. The expression, in short, has nearly the same meaning as the English word "Yorkshireman."

ship of Jerusalem, and this he held when I was there. I recollect, by
the by, that he tried one of his stratagems upon me. I had not gone
to see him (as I ought in courtesy to have done) upon my arrival
at Jerusalem, but I happened to be the owner of a rather handsome amber chibouk-piece; this the Governor heard of, and having also by some means contrived to see it, he sent me a softly
worded message with an offer to buy the pipe at a price immensely
exceeding the sum I had given for it. He did not add my chibouk
to the rest of his trophies.

There was a small number of Greek Christians resident in Nablus, and over these the Mussulmans held a high hand, not even
allowing them to speak to each other in the open streets. But if the
Moslems thus set themselves above the poor Christians of the
place, I, or rather my servants, soon took the ascendant over *them*.
I recollect that just as we were starting from the place, and at a
time when a number of people had gathered together in the main
street to see our preparations, Mysseri, being provoked at some
piece of perverseness on the part of a true believer, coolly thrashed
him with his horsewhip before the assembled crowd of fanatics. I
was much annoyed at the time, for I thought that the people
would probably rise against us. They turned rather pale, but stood
still.

The day of my arrival at Nablus was a fête—the New Year's
Day of the Mussulmans.* Most of the people were amusing themselves in the beautiful lawns and shady groves without the city.
The men were all remotely apart from the other sex. The women
in groups were diverting themselves and their children with
swings. They were so handsome that they could not keep up their
yashmaks; I believed that they had never before looked upon a
man in the European dress, and when they now saw in me that
strange phenomenon, and saw, too, how they could please the
creature by showing him a glimpse of beauty, they seemed to think
it more pleasant to do this than to go on playing with swings. It
was always, however, with a sort of zoölogical expression of coun-

---

* The 29th of April.

tenance that they looked on the horrible monster from Europe; and whenever one of them gave me to see for one sweet instant the blushing of her unveiled face, it was with the same kind of air as that with which a young, timid girl will edge her way up to an elephant, and tremblingly give him a nut from the tips of her rosy fingers.

CHAPTER
XXV

Mariam.

THERE is no spirit of propagandism in the Mussulmans of the Ottoman dominions. True it is that a prisoner of war, or a Christian condemned to death, may on some occasions save his life by adopting the religion of Mohammed, but instances of this kind are now exceedingly rare, and are quite at variance with the general system. Many Europeans, I think, would be surprised to learn that which is nevertheless quite true, namely, that an attempt to disturb the religous repose of the empire by the conversion of a Christian to the Mohammedan faith is positively illegal. The event which now I am going to mention shows plainly enough that the unlawfulness of such interference is distinctly recognized even in one of the most bigoted strongholds of Islam.

During my stay at Nablus I took up my quarters at the house of the Greek "papa," as he is called—that is, the Greek priest. The priest himself had gone to Jerusalem upon the business I am going to tell you of, but his wife remained at Nablus, and did the honors of her home.

Soon after my arrival, a deputation from the Greek Christians of the place came to request my interference in a matter which had occasioned vast excitement.

And now I must tell you how it came to happen, as it did continually, that people thought it worth while to claim the assistance of a mere traveler, who was totally devoid of all just pretensions to authority or influence of even the humblest description; and especially I must explain to you how it was that the power thus attributed did really in some measure belong to me, or rather to my dragoman. Successive political convulsions had at length fairly loosed the people of Syria from their former rules of conduct and from all their old habits of reliance. Mehemet Ali's

success in crushing the insurrection of the Mohammedan population had utterly beaten down the head of Islam, and extinguished, for the time at least, those virtues and vices which spring
from the Mohammedan faith. Success so complete as Mehemet
Ali's, if it had been attained by an ordinary Asiatic potentate,
would have induced a notion of stability. The readily bowing
mind of the Oriental would have bowed low and long under the
feet of a conqueror whom God had thus strengthened. But Syria
was no field for contests strictly Asiatic—Europe was involved;
and though the heavy masses of Egyptian troops, clinging with
strong gripe to the land, might seem to hold it fast, yet every
peasant practically felt and knew that in Vienna, or Petersburg, or
London, there were four or five pale-looking men who could pull
down the star of the Pasha with shreds of paper and ink. The
people of the country knew, too, that Mehemet Ali was strong
with the strength of the Europeans—strong by his French general,
his French tactics, and his English engines. Moreover, they saw
that the person, the property, and even the dignity of the humblest
European was guarded with the most careful solicitude. The consequence of all this was that the people of Syria looked vaguely
but confidently to Europe for fresh changes; many would fix upon
some nation, France or England, and steadfastly regard it as the
arriving sovereign of Syria. Those whose minds remained in doubt
equally contributed to this new state of public opinion—a state of
opinion no longer depending upon religion and ancient habits, but
upon bare hopes and fears. Every man wanted to know, not who
was his neighbor, but who was to be his ruler; whose feet he was
to kiss, and by whom his feet were to be ultimately beaten. Treat
your friend, says the proverb, as though he were one day to become your enemy, and your enemy as though he were one day to
become your friend. The Syrians went further, and seemed inclined to treat every stranger as though he might one day become
their pasha. Such was the state of circumstances and of feeling
which now for the first time had thoroughly opened the mind of
western Asia for the reception of Europeans and European ideas.
The credit of the English especially was so great that a good

Mussulman flying from the conscription or any other persecution would come to seek from the formerly despised hat that protection which the turban could no longer afford; and a man high in authority (as, for instance, the Governor in command of Gaza) would think that he had won a prize, or at all events a valuable lottery-ticket, if he obtained a written approval of his conduct from a simple traveler.

Still, in order than any immediate result should follow from all this unwonted readiness in the Asiatic to succumb to the European, it was necessary that some one should be at hand who could see and would push the advantage. I myself had neither the inclination nor the power to do so; but it happened that Dthemetri, who, as my dragoman, represented me on all occasions, was the very person of all others best fitted to avail himself with success of this yielding tendency in the Oriental mind. If the chance of birth and fortune had made poor Dthemetri a tailor during some part of his life, yet religion and the literature of the church which he served had made him a man, and a brave man, too. The lives of his honored saints were full of heroic actions provoking imitation; and since faith in a creed involves a faith in its ultimate triumph, Dthemetri was bold from a sense of true strength. His education, too, though not very general in its character, had been carried quite far enough to justify him in pluming himself upon a very decided advantage over the great bulk of the Mohammedan population, including the men in authority. With all this consciousness of religious and intellectual superiority, Dthemetri had lived for the most part in countries lying under Mussulman governments, and had witnessed (perhaps, too, had suffered from) their revolting cruelties; the result was that he abhorred and despised the Mohammedan faith and all who clung to it. And this hate was not of the dry, dull, and inactive sort; Dthemetri was in his sphere a true crusader, and whenever there appeared a fair opening in the defenses of Islam, he was ready and eager to make the assault. Such feelings, backed by a consciousness of understanding the people with whom he had to do, made Dthemetri not only firm and resolute in his constant interviews with men in authority, but sometimes also (as you may know already) very violent and even insulting. This tone, which I always disliked, though I was fain to profit by it, invariably succeeded; it swept away all resistance; there was nothing in the then depressed and succumbing mind of the Mussulman that could oppose a zeal so warm and fierce.

As for me, I of course stood aloof from Dthemetri's crusades, and did not even render him any active assistance when he was striving (as he almost always was, poor fellow!) on my behalf; I was only the death's-head and white sheet with which he scared the enemy. I think, however, that I played this spectral part exceedingly well, for I seldom appeared at all in any discussion, and whenever I did, I was sure to be white and calm.

The event which induced the Christians of Nablus to seek for my assistance was this: A beautiful young Christian, between fifteen and sixteen years old, had lately been married to a man of her own creed. About the same time (probably on the occasion of her wedding) she was accidentally seen by a Mussulman sheik of great wealth and local influence. The man instantly became madly enamoured of her. That strict morality so generally prevailing wherever the Mussulmans have complete ascendancy prevented the sheik from entertaining any such sinful hopes as a Christian might have ventured to cherish under the like circumstances, and he saw no chance of gratifying his love except by inducing the girl to embrace his own creed. If he could get her to take this step, her marriage with the Christian would be dissolved, and then there would be nothing to prevent him from making her the last and brightest of his wives. The sheik was a practical man, and quickly began his attack upon the theological opinions of the bride. He did not assail her with the eloquence of any imams or Mussulman saints; he did not press upon her the eternal truths of "the Cow," or the beautiful morality of "the Table"*; he sent her no tracts—not even a copy of the holy Koran. An old woman acted as mis-

---

* "The Cow," "the Table": these are the names given by the Prophet to certain chapters of the Koran.

sionary. She brought with her a whole basketful of arguments—jewels and shawls and scarfs and all kinds of persuasive finery. Poor Mariam! she put on the jewels and took a calm view of the Mohammedan religion in a little hand-mirror—she could not be deaf to such eloquent ear-rings, and the great truths of Islam came home to her young bosom in the delicate folds of the cashmere; she was ready to abandon her faith.

The sheik knew very well that his attempt to convert an infidel was unlawful, and that his proceedings would not bear investigation, so he took care to pay a large sum to the Governor of Nablus in order to gain his connivance.

At length Mariam quitted her home, and placed herself under the protection of the Mohammedan authorities. These men, however, refrained from delivering her into the arms of her lover, and kept her safe in a mosque until the fact of her real conversion (for this had been indignantly denied by her relatives) should be established. For two to three days the mother of the young convert was prevented from communicating with her child by various evasive contrivances, but not, it would seem, by a flat refusal. At length it was announced that the young lady's profession of faith might be heard from her own lips. At an hour appointed the friends of the sheik and relatives of the damsel met in the mosque. The young convert addressed her mother in a loud voice, and said, "God is God, and Mohammed is the Prophet of God; and thou, O my mother, art an infidel feminine dog!"

You would suppose that this declaration, so clearly enounced, and that, too, in a place where Mohammedanism is perhaps more supreme than in any other part of the empire, would have sufficed to confirm the pretensions of the lover. This, however, was not the case. The Greek priest of the place was despatched on a mission to the Governor of Jerusalem (Aboo Goosh), in order to complain against the proceedings of the sheik, and obtain a restitution of the bride. Meanwhile the Mohammedan authorities at Nablus were so conscious of having acted unlawfully in conspiring to disturb the faith of the beautiful infidel that they hesitated to take any further steps, and the girl was still detained in the mosque.

Thus matters stood when the Christians of the place came and sought to obtain my aid.

I felt (with regret) that I had no personal interest in the matter, and I also thought that there was no pretense for my interfering with the conflicting claims of the Christian husband and the Mohammedan lover. I declined to take any step.

My speaking of the husband, by the by, reminds me that he was extremely backward about the great work of recovering his youthful bride. The kinsmen of the girl (they felt themselves personally disgraced by her conduct) were vehement and excited to a high pitch, but the Menelaus of Nablus was exceedingly calm and composed.

The fact that it was no duty of mine to interfere in a matter of this kind was a very sufficient, and yet a very unsatisfactory, reason for my refusal of all assistance. Until you are placed in situations of this kind, you can hardly tell how painful it is to refrain from intermeddling in other people's affairs—to refrain from intermeddling when you feel that you can do so with happy effect, and can remove a load of distress by the use of a few small phrases. Upon this occasion, however, an expression fell from one of the girl's kinsmen which not only determined me to abstain from interference, but made me hope that all attempts to recover the proselyte would fail. This person, speaking with the most savage bitterness, and with the cordial approval of all the other relatives, said that the girl ought to be beaten to death. I could not fail to see that if the poor child were restored to her family she would be treated with the most frightful barbarity; I heartily wished, therefore, that the Mussulmans might be firm, and preserve their young prize from any fate so dreadful as that of a return to her own relations.

The next day the Greek priest returned from his mission to Aboo Goosh; but "the father of lies," it would seem, had been well plied with the gold of the enamoured sheik, and contrived to put off the prayers of the Christians by cunning feints. Now, therefore, a second and more numerous deputation than the first waited upon me, and implored my intervention with the Governor. I informed the assembled Christians that since their last application I had carefully considered the matter. The religious question, I thought, might be put aside at once, for the excessive levity which the girl had displayed proved clearly that, in adopting Mohammedanism, she was not quitting any other faith; her mind must have been thoroughly blank upon religious questions, and she was not, therefore, to be treated as a Christian straying from the flock, but rather as a child without any religion at all—a child incapable of imagining any truer worshipers than those who would deck her with jewels and clothe her in cashmere shawls.

So much for the religious part of the question. Well, then, in a merely temporal sense it appeared to me that (looking merely to the interests of the damsel, for I rather unjustly put poor Menelaus quite out of the question) the advantages were all on the side of the Mohammedan match. The sheik was in a higher station of life than the superseded husband, and had given the best possible proof of his ardent affection by the sacrifices made and the risks incurred for the sake of the beloved object. I therefore stated fairly, to the horror and amazement of all my hearers, that the sheik, in my view, was likely to make a capital husband, and that I entirely "approved of the match."

I left Nablus under the impression that Mariam would soon be delivered to her Mussulman lover. I afterwards found, however, that the result was very different. Dthemetri's religious zeal and hate had been so much excited by the account of these events, and by the grief and mortification of his coreligionists, that when he found me firmly determined to decline all interference in the matter, he secretly appealed to the Governor in my name, and (using, I suppose, many violent threats, and telling no doubt, good store of lies about my station and influence) extorted a promise that the proselyte should be restored to her relatives. I did not understand that the girl had actually given up whilst I remained at Nablus, but Dthemetri certainly did not desist from his instances until he had satisfied himself by some means or other (for mere words amounted to nothing) that the promise would be actually performed. It was not till I had quitted Syria, and when Dthemetri was no longer in my service, that this villainous though well-motived trick of his came to my knowledge. Mysseri, who informed me of the step which had been taken, did not know it himself until some time after we had quitted Nablus, when Dthemetri exultingly confessed his successful enterprise. I know not whether the engagement extorted from the Governor was ever complied with. I shudder to think of the fate which must have befallen poor Mariam if she fell into the hands of the Christians.

CHAPTER
XXVI

The prophet Damoor.

FOR some hours I passed along the shores of the fair Lake of Galilee; then turning a little to the westward, I struck into a mountainous tract, and as I advanced thenceforward, the features of the country kept growing more and more bold. At length I drew near to the city of Safed. It sits proud as a fortress upon the summit of a craggy height; yet, because of its minarets and stately trees, the place looks happy and beautiful. It is one of the holy cities of the Talmud; and, according to this authority, the Messiah will reign there for forty years before he takes possession of Zion. The sanctity and historical importance thus attributed to the city by anticipation render it a favorite place of retirement for Israelites; of these it contains, they say, about four thousand, a number nearly balancing that of the Mohammedan inhabitants. I knew by my experience of Tabariyeh that a "holy city" was sure to have a population of vermin somewhat proportionate to the number of its Israelites, and I therefore caused my tent to be pitched upon a green spot of ground at a respectful distance from the walls of the town.

When it had become quite dark (for there was no moon that night), I was informed that several Jews had secretly come from the city, in the hope of obtaining some help from me in circumstances of imminent danger. I was also informed that they claimed my aid upon the ground that some of their number were British subjects. It was arranged that the two principal men of the party should speak for the rest, and these were accordingly admitted into my tent. One of the two called himself the British vice-counsul, and he had with him his consular cap; but he frankly said that he could not have dared to assume this emblem of his dignity in the daytime, and that nothing but the extreme darkness of the night rendered it safe for him to put it on upon this occassion. The other of the spokesmen was a Jew of Gibraltar, a tolerably well-bred person, who spoke English very fluently.

These men informed me that the Jews of the place, though exceedingly wealthy, had lived peaceably and undisturbed in their retirement until the insurrection of 1834; but about the beginning of that year a highly religious Mussulman, called Mohammed Damoor, went forth into the market-place, crying with a loud voice, and prophesying that on the 15th of the following June the true believers would rise up in just wrath against the Jews, and despoil them of their gold and their silver and their jewels. The earnestness of the prophet produced some impression at the time; but all went on as usual, until at last the 15th of June arrived. When that day dawned, the whole Mussulman population of the place assembled in the streets that they might see the result of the prophecy. Suddenly Mohammed Damoor rushed furious into the crowd, and the fierce shout of the prophet soon insured the fulfilment of his prophecy. Some of the Jews fled and some remained, but they who fled and they who remained alike and unresistingly left their property to the hands of the spoilers. The most odious of all outrages, that of searching the women for the base purpose of discovering such things as gold and silver concealed about their persons, was perpetrated without shame. The poor Jews were so stricken with terror that they submitted to their fate even where resistance would have been easy. In several instances a young Mussulman boy, not more than ten or twelve years of age, walked straight into the house of a Jew, and stripped him of his property before his face, and in the presence of his whole family.* When the insurrection was put down, some of the Mussulmans (most probably those who had got no spoil wherewith they might buy immunity) were punished, but the greater part of them escaped; none of the booty was restored, and the pecuniary redress which the

---

* It was after the interview which I am talking of, and not from the Jews themselves, that I learned this fact.

Pasha had undertaken to enforce for them had been hitherto so carefully delayed that the hope of ever obtaining it had grown very faint. A new Governor had been appointed to the command of the place, with stringent orders to ascertain the real extent of the losses, to discover the spoilers, and to compel immediate restitution. It was found that, notwithstanding the urgency of his instructions, the Governor did not push on the affair with any perceptible vigor; the Jews complained, and either by the protection of the British consul at Damascus, or by some other means, had influence enough to induce the appointment of a special commissioner—they called him "the Modeer"—whose duty it was to watch for and prevent anything like connivance on the part of the Governor, and to push on the investigation with vigor and impartiality.

Such were the instructions with which, some few weeks since, the Modeer came charged; the result was that the investigation had made no practical advance, and that the Modeer, as well as the Governor, was living upon terms of affectionate friendship with Mohammed Damoor and the rest of the principal spoilers.

Thus stood the chance of redress for the past. But the cause of the agonizing excitement under which the Jews of the place now labored was recent and justly alarming: Mohammed Damoor had again gone forth into the market-place, and lifted up his voice, and prophesied a second spoliation of the Israelites. This was a grave matter; the words of such a practical and clear-sighted prophet as Mohammed Damoor were not to be despised. I fear I must have smiled visibly, for I was greatly amused, and even, I think, gratified, at the account of this second prophecy. Nevertheless, my heart warmed towards the poor oppressed Israelites; and I was flattered, too, in the point of my national vanity, at the notion of the far-reaching link by which a Jew in Syria, because he had been born on the rock of Gibraltar, was able to claim me as his fellow-countryman. If I hesitated at all between the "impropriety" of interfering in a matter which was no business of mine, and the "infernal shame" of refusing my aid at such a conjuncture, I soon came to a very ungentlemanly decision—namely, that I would be guilty of the "impropriety," and not of the "infernal shame." It seemed to me that the immediate arrest of Mohammed Damoor was the one thing needful to the safety of the Jews, and I felt sure (for reasons which I have already mentioned in speaking of the Nablus affair) that I should be able to obtain this result by making a formal application to the Governor. I told my applicants that I would take this step on the following morning. They were very grateful, and were for a moment much pleased at the prospect of safety thus seemingly opened to them; but the deliberation of a minute entirely altered their views, and filled them with new terror: they declared that any attempt or pretended attempt on the part of the Governor to arrest Mohammed Damoor would certainly produce an immediate movement of the whole Mussulman population, and a consequent massacre and robbery of the Israelites. My visitors went out, and remained I know not how long consulting with their brethren, but all at last agreed that their present perilous and painful position was better than a certain and immediate attack, and that if Mohammed Damoor was seized their second estate would be worse than their first. I myself did not think that this would be the case, but I could not, of course, force my aid upon the people against their will; and, moreover, the day fixed for the fulfilment of this second prophecy was not very close at hand; a little delay, therefore, in providing against the impending danger would not necessarily be fatal. The men now confessed that although they had come with so much mystery and (as they thought) at so great risk to ask my assistance, they were unable to suggest any mode in which I could aid them, except, indeed, by mentioning their grievances to the consul-general at Damascus. This I promised to do, and this I did.

My visitors were very thankful to me for my readiness to intermeddle in their affairs, and the grateful wives of the principal Jews sent to me many compliments, with choice wines and elaborate sweetmeats.

The course of my travels soon drew me so far from Safed that

I never heard how the dreadful day passed off which had been fixed for the accomplishment of the second prophecy. If the predicted spoliation was prevented, poor Mohammed Damoor must have been forced, I suppose, to say that he had prophesied in a metaphorical sense. This would be a sad falling off from the brilliant and substantial success of the first experiment.

CHAPTER
XXVII

Damascus.

FOR a part of two days I wound under the base of the snow-crowned Djibel el Sheik, and then entered upon a vast and desolate plain rarely pierced at intervals by some sort of withered stem. The earth in its length and its breadth, and all the deep universe of the sky, was steeped in light and heat. On I rode through the fire, but long before evening came there were straining eyes that saw, and joyful voices that announced, the sight of Shaum Shereef—the "Holy," the "Blessed"—Damascus.

But that which at last I reached with my longing eyes was not a speck in the horizon, gradually expanding to a group of roofs and walls, but a long, low line of blackest green, that ran right across in the distance from east to west. And this, as I approached, grew deeper—grew wavy in its outline; soon forest-trees shot up before my eyes, and robed their broad shoulders so freshly that all the throngs of olives, as they rose into view, looked sad in their proper dimness. There were even now no houses to see, but minarets peered out from the midst of shade into the glowing sky, and, kindling, touched the sun. There seemed to be here no mere city, but rather a province, wide and rich, that bounded the torrid waste.

Until about a year or two years before the time of my going there, Damascus had kept up so much of the old bigot zeal against Christians, or rather against Europeans, that no one dressed as a Frank could have dared to show himself in the streets; but the firmness and temper of Mr. Farren, who hoisted his flag in the city as consul-gneral for the district, had soon put an end to all intolerance of Englishmen. Damascus was safer than Oxford.* When

* An enterprising American traveler, Mr. Everett, lately conceived the bold project

I entered the city, in my usual dress, there was but one poor fellow that wagged his tongue, and him, in the open streets, Dthemetri horsewhipped. During my stay I went wherever I chose, and attended the public baths without molestation. Indeed, my relations with the pleasanter portion of the Mohammedan population were upon a much better footing here than at most other places.

In the principal streets of Damascus there is a path for foot-passengers raised a foot or two above the bridle-road. Until the arrival of the British consul-general none but a Mussulman had been allowed to walk upon the upper way; Mr. Farren would not, of course, suffer that the humiliation of any such exclusion should be submitted to by an Englishman, and I always walked upon the raised path as free and unmolested as if I had been in Pall Mall. The old usage was, however, maintained with as much strictness as ever against the Christian Rayas and Jews: not one of these could have set his foot upon the privileged path without endangering his life.

I was walking one day, I remember, along the raised path, "the path of the Faithful," when a Christian Raya from the bridle-road below saluted me with such earnestness and craved so anxiously to speak and be spoken to, that he soon brought me to a halt. He had nothing to tell, except only the glory and exultation with which he saw a fellow-Christian stand level with the imperious Mussulmans. Perhaps he had been absent from the place for some time, for otherwise I hardly know how it could have happened that my exaltation was the first instance he had seen. His joy was great; so strong and strenuous was England (Lord Palmerston reigned in those days) that it was a pride and delight for a Syrian Christian to look up and say that the Englishman's faith was his,

---

of penetrating to the University of Oxford, and this notwithstanding that he had been in his infancy (they being very young, those Americans) a Unitarian preacher. Having a notion, it seems, that the ambassadorial character would protect him from insult, he adopted the stratagem of procuring credentials from his Government as minister plenipotentiary at the court of her Britannic Majesty; he also wore the exact costume of a Trinitarian. But all his contrivances were vain: his infantine sermons were strictly remembered against him; the enterprise failed.

too. If I was vexed at all that I could not give the man a lift and shake hands with him on level ground, there was no alloy in *his* pleasure. He followed me on, not looking to his own path, but keeping his eyes on me; he saw, as he thought and said (for he came with me on to my quarters), the period of the Mohammedan's absolute ascendancy—the beginning of the Christian's. He had so closely associated the insulting privilege of the path with actual dominion that seeing it now in one instance abandoned he looked for the quick coming of European troops. His lips only whispered, and that tremulously, but his flashing eyes spoke out their triumph more fiercely: "I, too, am a Christian. My foes are the foes of the English. We are all one people, and Christ is our King."

If I poorly deserved, yet I liked this claim of brotherhood. Not all the warnings I heard against their rascality could hinder me from feeling kindly towards my fellow-Christians in the East. English travelers (from a habit perhaps of depreciating sectarians in their own country) are apt to look down upon the Oriental Christians as being "dissenters" from the established religion of a Mohammedan empire. I never did thus. By a natural perversity of disposition which nursemaids call contra*iri*ness, I felt the more strongly for my creed when I saw it despised among them. I quite tolerated the Christianity of Mohammedan countries, notwithstanding its humble aspect, and the damaged character of its followers. I went further, and extended some sympathy towards those who, with all the claims of superior intellect, learning, and industry, were kept down under the heel of the Mussulmans by reason of their having *our* faith. I heard, as I fancied, the faint echo of an old crusader's conscience, that whispered and said, "Common cause!" The impulse was, as you may suppose, much too feeble to bring me into trouble; it merely influenced my actions in a way thoroughly characteristic of this sluggish century—that is, by making me speak almost as civilly to the followers of Christ as I did to their Mohammedan foes.

This "holy" Damascus, this "earthly Paradise" of the Prophet, so fair to the eyes that he dared not trust himself to tarry in her blissful shades, she is a city of hidden palaces, of copses, and gardens, and fountains, and bubbling streams. The juice of her life is the gushing and ice-cold torrent that tumbles from the snowy sides of Anti-Lebanon. Close along on the river's edge, through seven sweet miles of rustling boughs and deepest shade, the city spreads out her whole length. As a man falls flat, face forward on the brook, that he may drink, and drink again, so Damascus, thirsting forever, lies down with her lips to the stream, and clings to its rushing waters.

The chief places of public amusement, or rather of public relaxation, are the baths and the great café. This last is frequented at night by most of the wealthy men of the city, and by many of the humbler sort. It consists of a number of sheds, very simply framed and built in a labyrinth of running streams—streams so broken and headlong in their course that they foam and roar on every side. The place is lit up in the simplest manner by numbers of small pale lamps, strung upon loose cords, and so suspended from branch to branch that the light, though it looks so quiet amongst the darkening foliage, yet leaps and brightly flashes, as it falls upon the troubled waters. All around, and chiefly upon the very edge of the torrents, groups of people are tranquilly seated. They drink coffee, and inhale the cold fumes of the narghile; they talk rather gently the one to the other, or else are silent. A father will sometimes have two or three of his boys around him, but the joyousness of an Oriental child is all of the sober sort, and never disturbs the reigning calm of the land.

It has been generally understood, I believe, that the houses of Damascus are more sumptuous than those of any other city in the East. Some of these—said to be the most magnificent in the place—I had an opportunity of seeing.

Every rich man's house stands detached from its neighbors, at the side of a garden, and it is from this cause, no doubt, that the city (severely menaced by prophecy) has hitherto escaped destruction. You know some parts of Spain, but you have never, I think, been in Andalusia; if you had, I could easily show you the interior of a Damascene house by referring you to the Alhambra or Alcazar of Seville. The lofty rooms are adorned with a rich inlaying of many colors and illuminated writing on the walls. The floors are of marble. One side of any room intended for noonday retirement is generally laid open to a quadrangle, and in the center of this is the dancing jet of a fountain. There is no furniture that can interfere with the cool, palace-like emptiness of the apartments. A divan (that is, a low and doubly broad sofa) runs round the three walled sides of the room; a few Persian carpets (they ought to be called Persian rugs, for that is the word which indicates their shape and dimension) are sometimes thrown about near the divan; they are placed without order, the one partly lapping over the other—and thus disposed, they give to the room an appearance of uncaring luxury. Except these, there is nothing to obstruct the welcome air; and the whole of the marble floor, from one divan to the other, and from the head of the chamber across to the murmuring fountain, is thoroughly open and free.

So simple as this is Asiatic luxury! The Oriental is not a contriving animal—there is nothing intricate in his magnificence. The impossibility of handing down property from father to son for any long period consecutively seems to prevent the existence of those traditions by which, with us, the refined modes of applying wealth are made known to its inheritors. We know that in England a newly made rich man cannot, by taking thought and spending money, obtain even the same-looking furniture as a gentleman. The complicated character of an English establishment allows room for subtle distinctions between that which is *comme il faut* and that which is not. All such refinements are unknown in the East; the Pasha and the peasant have the same tastes. The broad cold marble floor, the simple couch, the air freshly waving through a shady chamber, a verse of the Koran emblazoned on the wall, the sight and sound of falling water, the cold, fragrant smoke of the narghile, and a small collection of wives and children in the inner apartments—all these, the utmost enjoyments of the grandee, are yet such as to be appreciable by the humblest Mussulman in the empire.

But its gardens are the delight—the delight and the pride—of

Damascus. They are not the formal parterres which you might expect from the Oriental taste; rather, they bring back to your mind the memory of some dark old shrubbery in our northern isle that has been charmingly *un*-"kept up" for many and many a day. When you see a rich wilderness of wood in decent England, it is like enough that you see it with some soft regrets. The puzzled old woman at the lodge can give small account of "the family." She thinks it is "Italy" that has made the whole circle of her world so gloomy and sad. You avoid the house in lively dread of a lone housekeeper; but you make your way on by the stables. You remember that gable, with all its neatly nailed trophies of fitches and hawks and owls now slowly falling to pieces; you remember that stable, and that: but the doors are all fastened that used to be standing ajar; the paint of things painted is blistered and cracked; grass grows in the yard. Just there, in October mornings, the keeper would wait with the dogs and the guns: no keeper now. You hurry away, and gain the small wicket that used to open to the touch of a lightsome hand; it is fastened with a padlock (the only new-looking thing), and is stained with thick green damp; you climb it, and bury yourself in the deep shade, and strive but lazily with the tangling briers, and stop for long minutes to judge and determine whether you will creep beneath the long boughs and make them your archway, or whether perhaps you will lift your heel and tread them down underfoot. Long doubt, and scarcely to be ended, till you wake from the memory of those days when the path was clear, and chase that phantom of a muslin sleeve that once weighed warm upon your arm.

Wild as that, the nighest woodland of a deserted home in England, but without its sweet sadness, is the sumptuous garden of Damascus. Forest-trees, tall and stately enough, if you could see their lofty crests, yet lead a tussling life of it below, with their branches struggling against strong numbers of bushes and wilful shrubs. The shade upon the earth is black as night. High, high above your head, and on every side all down to the ground, the thicket is hemmed in and choked up by the interlacing boughs that droop with the weight of roses, and load the slow air with their damask breath.* There are no other flowers. Here and there, there are patches of ground made clear from the cover, and these are either carelessly planted with some common and useful vegetable, or else are left free to the wayward ways of nature, and bear rank weeds, moist-looking and cool to your eyes, and freshening the sense with their earthy and bitter fragrance. There is a lane opened through the thicket, so broad in some places that you can pass along side by side, in some so narrow (the shrubs are forever encroaching) that you ought, if you can, to go on the first, and hold back the bough of the rose-tree. And through the sweet wilderness a loud rushing stream flows tumbling along, till it is halted at last in the lowest corner of the garden, and there tossed up in a fountain by the side of the simple alcove. This is all.

Never for an instant will the people of Damascus attempt to separate the idea of bliss from these wild gardens and rushing waters. Even where your best affections are concerned, and you—wise preachers abstain and turn aside when they come near the mysteries of the happy state, and we (wise preachers, too), we will hush our voices, and never reveal to finite beings the joys of the "earthly Paradise."

---

* The rose-trees which I saw were all of the kind we call "damask"; they grow to an immense height and size.

CHAPTER
XXVIII

Pass of the Lebanon.

"THE ruins of Baalbec!" Shall I scatter the vague solemn thoughts and all the airy fantasies which gather together when once those words are spoken, that I may give you, instead, tall columns, and measurements true, and phrases built with ink? No, no; the glorious sounds shall still float on as of yore, and still hold fast upon your brain with their own dim and infinite meaning.

The pass by which I crossed the Lebanon is like, I think, in its features, to that of the Furka in the Bernese Oberland. For a great part of the way I toiled rather painfully through the dazzling snow, but the labor of ascending added to the excitement with which I looked for the summit of the pass. The time came. There was a minute, and I saw nothing but the steep white shoulder of the mountain; there was another minute, and that the next, which showed me a nether heaven of fleecy clouds,—clouds floating along far down in the air beneath me,—and showed me, beyond, the breadth of all Syria west of the Lebanon. But chiefly I clung with my eyes to the dim, steadfast line of the sea which closed my utmost view. I had grown well used, of late, to the people and the scenes of forlorn Asia—well used to tombs and ruins, to silent cities and deserted plains, to tranquil men, and women sadly veiled; and now that I saw the even plain of the sea, I leaped with an easy leap to its yonder shores, and saw all the kingdoms of the West in that fair path that could lead me from out of this silent land straight on into shrill Marseilles, or round by the pillars of Hercules, to the crash and roar of London. My place upon this dividing barrier was as a man's puzzling station in eternity, between the birthless past and the future that has no end. Behind me I left an old and decrepit world—religions dead and dying, calm tyrannies expiring in silence, women hushed and swathed and turned into waxen dolls, love flown, and in its stead mere royal and "Paradise" pleasures. Before me there waited glad bustle and strife—love itself an emulous game, religion a cause and a controversy, well smitten and well defended, men governed by reasons and suasion of speech, wheels going, steam buzzing, a mortal race, and a slashing pace, and the devil taking the hindmost—taking *me*, by Jove! (for that was my inner care) if I lingered too long upon the difficult pass that leads from thought to action.

I descended, and went towards the West.

The group of cedars remaining on this part of the Lebanon is held sacred by the Greek Church, on account of a prevailing notion that the trees were standing at the time when the Temple of Jerusalem was built. They occupy three or four acres on the mountain's side, and many of them are gnarled in a way that implies great age; but, except these signs, I saw nothing in their appearance or conduct that tended to prove them contemporaries of the cedars employed in Solomon's Temple. The final cause to which these aged survivors owed their preservation was explained to me in the evening by a glorious old fellow (a Christian chief) who made me welcome in the valley of Eden. In ancient times the whole range of the Lebanon had been covered with cedars; and as the fertile plains beneath became more and more infested by Government officers and tyrants of high and low estate, the people by degrees abandoned them, and flocked to the rugged mountains for protection, well knowing that the trouble of a walk uphill would seriously obstruct their weak and lazy oppressors. The cedar forests gradually shrank under the ax of the encroaching multitudes, and seemed at last to be on the point of disappearing entirely, when an aged chief who ruled in this district, and who had witnessed the great change effected even in his own lifetime, chose to say that some sign or memorial should be left of the vast woods with which the mountains had formerly been clad, and commanded accordingly that this group of trees (a group probably situated at the highest point to which the forest had reached) should remain untouched. The chief, it seems, was not moved by the notion I have mentioned as prevailing in the Greek Church, but rather by some sentiment of veneration for a great natural feature—a sentiment akin, perhaps, to that old and earth-born religion which made men bow down to creation before they had yet learned to know and worship the Creator.

The chief of the valley in which I passed the night was a man of large possessions, and he entertained me very sumptuously. He was highly intelligent, and had had the sagacity to foresee that Europe would intervene authoritatively in the affairs of Syria. Bearing this idea in mind, and with a view to give his son an advantageous start in the ambitious career for which he was destined, he had hired for him a teacher of Italian, the only accessible European tongue. The tutor, however (a native of Syria), either did not know, or did not choose to teach, the European form of address, but contented himself with instructing his pupil in the mere language of Italy. This circumstance gave me an opportunity (the only one I ever had, or was likely to have*) of hearing Oriental courtesies expressed in a European tongue. The boy was about twelve or thirteen years old, and having the power of speaking to me without the aid of an interpreter, he took a prominent part in the hospitable duties of the day. He did the honors of the house with untiring assiduity, and with a kind of gracefulness which by mere description can scarcely be made intelligible to those who are unacquainted with the manners of the Asiatics. The boy's address resembled a little that of a highly polished and insinuating Roman Catholic priest, but had more of girlish gentleness. It was strange to hear him gravely and slowly enunciating the common and extravagant compliments of the East in good Italian, and in soft, persuasive tones. I recollect that I was particularly amused at the gracious obstinacy with which he maintained that the house and the surrounding estates belonged, not to his father, but to me. To say this once was only to use the common form of speech, signifying no more than our sweet word "welcome"; but the amusing part of the matter was that whenever, in

---

* A dragoman never interprets in terms the courteous language of the East.

the course of conversation, I happened to speak of his father's mansion or the surrounding domain, the boy invariably interfered to correct my pretended mistake, and to assure me once again, with a gentle decisiveness of manner, that the whole property was really and exclusively mine, and that his father had not the most distant pretensions to its ownership.

I received from my host some good information respecting the people of the mountains, and their power of resisting Mehemet Ali. The chief gave me very plainly to understand that the mountaineers, being dependent upon others for bread and gunpowder (the two great necessaries of martial life), could not long hold out against a power occupying the plains and commanding the sea; but he also assured me, and that very significantly, that if this source of weakness were provided against, *the mountaineers were to be depended upon.* He told me that in ten or fifteen days the chiefs could bring together some fifty thousand fighting men.

CHAPTER
XXIX

Surprise of Satalieh.

WHILST I was remaining upon the coast of Syria I had the good fortune to become acquainted with the Russian Sataliefsky,* a general officer who in his youth had fought and bled at Borodino, but was now better known among diplomats by the important trust committed to him at a period highly critical for the affairs of eastern Europe. I must not tell you his family name; my mention of his title can do him no harm, for it is I, and I only, who have conferred it, in consideration of the military and diplomatic services performed under my own eyes.

The general, as well as I, was bound for Smyrna, and we agreed to sail together in an Ionian brigantine. We did not charter the vessel, but we made our arrangement with the captain upon such terms that we could be put ashore upon any part of the coast that we might choose. We sailed, and day after day the vessel lay dawdling on the sea, with calms and feeble breezes for her portion. I myself was well repaid for the painful restlessness occasioned by slow weather, because I gained from my companion a little of that vast fund of interesting knowledge with which he was stored—knowledge a thousand times the more highly to be prized, since it was not of the sort that is to be gathered from books, but only from the lips of those who haved acted a part in the world.

When, after nine days of sailing, or trying to sail, we found ourselves still hanging by the mainland to the north of the Isle of Cyprus, we determined to disembark at Satalieh, and to go on thence by land. A light breeze favored our purpose, and it was with great delight that we neared the fragrant land, and saw our

---

* A title signifying Transcender or Conqueror of Satalieh.

anchor go down in the bay of Satalieh within two of three hundred yards of the shore.

The town of Satalieh* is the chief place of the pashalic in which it is situate, and its citadel is the residence of the Pasha. We had scarcely dropped our anchor when a boat from the shore came alongside with officers on board. These men announced that strict orders had been received for maintaining a quarantine of three weeks against all vessels coming from Syria, and they directed, accordingly, that no one from the vessel should disembark. In reply we sent a message to the Pasha, setting forth the rank and titles of the general, and requiring permission to go ashore. After a while the boat came again alongside, and the officers, declaring that the orders received from Constantinople were imperative and unexceptional, formally enjoined us, in the name of the Pasha, to abstain from any attempt to land.

I had been hitherto much less impatient of our slow voyage than my gallant friend; but this opposition made the slow sea seem to me like a prison from which I must and would break out. I had an unbounded faith in the feebleness of Asiatic potentates, and I proposed that we should set the Pasha at defiance. The general had been worked up to a state of most painful agitation by the idea of being driven from the shore which smiled so pleasantly before his eyes, and he adopted my suggestion with rapture.

We determined to land.

To approach the sweet shore after a tedious voyage, and then to be suddenly and unexpectedly prohibited from landing, this is so maddening to the temper that no one who had ever experienced the trial would say that even the most violent impatience of such restraint is wholly inexcusable. I am not going to pretend, however, that the course we chose to adopt on the occasion can be perfectly justified. The impropriety of a traveler's setting at naught the regulations of a foreign state is clear enough, and the bad taste of compassing such a purpose by mere gasconading is still more glaringly plain. I knew perfectly well that if the Pasha understood

---

* Spelled "Attalia" and sometimes "Adalia" in English books and maps.

his duty, and had energy enough to perform it, he would order out a file of soldiers the moment we landed, and cause us both to be shot upon the beach, without allowing more contact than might be absolutely necessary for the purpose of making us stand fire; but I also firmly believed that the Pasha would not see the befitting line of conduct nearly so well as I did, and that even if he did know his duty, he would hardly succeed in finding resolution enough to perform it.

We ordered the boat to be got in readiness, and the officers on shore, seeing these preparations, gathered together a number of guards. These assembled upon the sands; we saw that great excitement prevailed, and that messengers were continually going to and fro between the shore and the citadel.

Our captain, out of compliment to his Excellency, had provided the vessel with a Russian war flag, and during our voyage he had been in the habit of hoisting it alternately with the Union Jack. We agreed that we would attempt our disembarkation under this the Russian standard. I was glad to have it so resolved, for I should have been sorry to engage the honored flag of England in an affair like this. The Russian ensign was therefore committed to one of the sailors, and the man honored with this charge took his station at the stern of the boat. We gave particular instructions to the captain of the brigantine, and when all was ready, the general and I, with our respective servants, got into the boat, and were slowly rowed towards the shore. The guards gathered together at the point for which we were making, but when they saw that our boat went on without altering her course, *they ceased to stand very still.* None of them ran away, or even shrank back, but looked as if *the pack were being shuffled*, every man seeming desirous to change places with his neighbor. They were still at their post, however, when our oars went in and the bow of our boat ran up—well up upon the beach.

The general was lame by an honorable wound received at Borodino, and could not, without some help, get out of the boat; I, therefore, landed the first. My instructions to the captain were attended to with the most perfect accuracy, for scarcely had my

foot indented the sand when the four six-pounders of the brigantine quite gravely rolled out their brute thunder. Precisely as I had
expected, the guards, and all the people who had gathered about
them, gave way under the shock produced by the mere sound of
guns, and we were all allowed to disembark without the least
molestation.

We immediately formed a little column, or rather, as I should
have called it, a procession, for we had no fighting aptitude in us,
and were only trying, as it were, how far we could go in frightening full-grown children. First marched the sailor with the Russian flag of war bravely flying in the breeze; then came the general
and I; then our servants; and lastly, if I rightly recollect, two more
of the brigantine's crew. Our flag-bearer so exulted in his honorable office, and bore the colors aloft with so much of pomp and
dignity, that I found it exceedingly hard to keep a grave countenance. We advanced towards the castle, but the people had now
had time to recover from the effect of the six-pounders (only, of
course, loaded with powder), and they could not help seeing, not
only the numerical weakness of our party, but the very slight
amount of wealth and resource which it seemed to imply. They
began to hang round us more closely; and just as this reaction was
beginning, the general (he was perfectly unacquainted with the
Asiatic character) thoughtlessly turned round in order to speak to
one of the servants. The effect of this slight move was magical: the
people thought we were going to give way, and instantly closed
round us. In two words, and with one touch, I showed my comrade the danger he was running, and in the next instant we were
both advancing more pompously than ever. Some minutes afterwards there was a second appearance of reaction, followed again
by wavering and indecision on the part of the Pasha's people; but
at length it seemed to be understood that we should go unmolested into the audience-hall.

Constant communication had been going on between the receding crowd and the Pasha, and so, when we reached the gates of
the citadel, we saw that preparations were made for giving us an
awe-striking reception. Parting at once from the sailors and our

servants, the general and I were conducted into the audience-hall; and there, at least, I suppose the Pasha hoped that he would confound us by his greatness. The hall was nothing more than a large whitewashed room. Oriental potentates have a pride in that sort of simplicity when they can contrast it with the exhibition of power; and this the Pasha was able to do, for the lower end of the hall was filled with his officers. These men (in number, as I thought, about fifty or sixty) were all handsomely, though plainly, dressed in the military frock-coats of Europe; they stood in mass, and so as to present a hollow, semicircular front towards the end of the hall at which the Pasha sat. They opened a narrow lane for us when we entered, and as soon as we had passed they again closed up their ranks. An attempt was made to induce us to remain at a respectful distance from his Mightiness. To have yielded in this point would have been fatal to our success—perhaps to our lives; but the general and I had already determined upon the place which we should take, and we rudely pushed on towards the upper end of the hall.

Upon the divan, and close up against the right-hand corner of the room, there sat the Pasha—his limbs gathered in, the whole creature coiled up like an adder. His cheeks were deadly pale, and his lips perhaps had turned white, for without moving a muscle the man impressed me with an immense idea of the wrath within him. He kept his eyes inexorably fixed as if upon vacancy, and with the look of a man accustomed to refuse the prayers of those who sue for life. We soon discomposed him, however, from this studied fixity of feature, for we marched straight up to the divan, and sat down, the Russian close to the Pasha, and I by the side of the Russian. This act astonished the attendants, and plainly disconcerted the Pasha; he could no longer maintain the glassy stillness of his eyes, and evidently became much agitated. At the feet of the satrap there stood a trembling Italian; this man was a sort of medico in the potentate's service, and now, in the absence of our attendants, he was to act as an interpreter. The Pasha caused him to tell us that we had openly defied his authority, and had forced our way on shore in the teeth of his officers.

[243]

Up to this time I had been the planner of the enterprise, but now that the moment had come when all would depend upon able and earnest speechifying, I felt at once the immense superiority of my gallant friend, and gladly left to him the whole conduct of this discussion. Indeed, he had vast advantages over me, not only by his superior command of language, and his far more spirited style of address, but also in his consciousness of a good cause; for, whilst I felt myself completely in the wrong, his Excellency had really worked himself up to believe that the Pasha's refusal to permit our landing was a gross outrage and insult. Therefore, without deigning to defend our conduct, he at once commenced a spirited attack upon the Pasha. The poor Italian doctor translated one or two sentences to the Pasha, but he evidently mitigated their import. The Russian, growing warm, insisted upon his attack with redoubled energy and spirit; but the medico, instead of translating, began to shake violently with terror, and at last he came out with his *non ardisco*, and fairly confessed that he dared not interpret fierce words to his master.

Now, then, at a time when everything seemed to depend upon the effect of speech, we were left without an interpreter.

But this very circumstance, though at first it appeared so unfavorable, turned out to be advantageous. The general, finding that he could not have his words translated, ceased to speak in Italian, and recurred to his accustomed French; he became eloquent. No one present, except myself, understood one syllable of what he was saying; but he had drawn forth his passport, and the energy and violence with which, as he spoke, he pointed to the graven Eagle of all the Russias, began to make an impression. The Pasha saw at his side a man, not only free from every the least pang of fear, but raging, as it seemed, with just indignation, and thenceforward he plainly began to think that, in some way or other (he could not tell how), he must certainly have been in the wrong. In a little time he was so much shaken that the Italian ventured to resume his interpretation, and my comrade had again the opportunity of pressing his attack upon the Pasha. His argument, if I rightly recollect its import, was to this effect: "If the vilest Jews

[244]

were to come into the harbor, you would but forbid them to land, and force them to perform quarantine; yet this is the very course, O Pasha, which your rash officers dare to think of adopting with *us!* Those mad and reckless men would have actually dealt towards a Russian general officer and an English gentleman as if they had been wretched Israelites! Never, never will we submit to such an indignity. His Imperial Majesty knows how to protect his nobles from insult, and would never endure that a general of his army should be treated in a matter of quarantine as though he were a mere Eastern Jew!" This argument told with great effect; the Pasha fairly admitted that he felt its weight, and he now only struggled to obtain such a compromise as might partly save his dignity: he wanted us to perform a quarantine of one day for form's sake, and in order to show his people that he was not utterly defied; but finding that we were inexorable, he not only abandoned his attempt, but promised to supply us with horses.

When the discussion had arrived at this happy conclusion, chibouks and coffee were brought, and we passed, I think, nearly an hour in friendly conversation. The Pasha, it now appeared, had once been a prisoner of war in Russia: during his captivity he could not have failed to learn the greatness of the Czar's power, and it was this piece of knowledge perhaps which made him more alive than an untraveled Turk might have been to the force of my comrade's eloquence.

The Pasha now gave us a generous feast. Our promised horses were brought without much delay. I gained my loved saddle once more, and when the moon got up and touched the heights of Taurus, we were joyfully winding our way through the first of his rugged defiles.